Where are you on the autism spectrum?

An alternative understanding of the autism spectrum
and a multisensory Live – Love – Learn approach.

HELENA EASTWOOD

authorHOUSE

AuthorHouse™ UK
1663 Liberty Drive
Bloomington, IN 47403 USA
www.authorhouse.co.uk
Phone: UK TFN: 0800 0148641 (Toll Free inside the UK)
*   UK Local: (02) 0369 56322 (+44 20 3695 6322 from outside the UK)*

Published by AuthorHouse 09/26/2024

ISBN: 978-1-7283-5185-8 (sc)
ISBN: 978-1-7283-5188-9 (e)

Print information available on the last page.

Any people depicted in stock imagery provided by Getty Images are models, and such images are being used for illustrative purposes only. Certain stock imagery © Getty Images.

This book is printed on acid-free paper.

Contents

PART ONE

UNDERSTANDING AUTISM

Contents

Introduction

The author Helena Eastwood has been working with positive insights into possible causes and ways of working successfully with autistic people since she began teaching in a special school after completing her Mainstream Education. Her book 'WHERE ARE YOU – on the Autism Spectrum' briefly presents her present understanding of autism and how it may be relevant to us all. If we can gain an understanding of the autism spectrum we may be able to scaffold the areas of interactive development that support wellbeing, positive behaviour and holistic development.

The industrial revolution brought mass production of identical items and now society seems to have replicated this into a manufacturing of predictable responses for mass-produced toys and associated repetitive and predictable human behaviour. This can be seen alongside an ever more dominant life style of socially conforming *media entertainment* and an ever growing academic style of *education*. Our passive western lifestyle appears to develop alongside of an ever growing amount of 'compulsive repetitive behaviour!' Thus our human potential of genuine creative and social interaction has been squashed into predetermined moulds structured by industrial activity, media entertainment and mass media communication systems.

> There can be few more numbing experiences than having to work on an assembly line in a car factory, keeping pace with a moving belt, condemned to repeat the same operation over and over again..........My back ached; my legs grew tired; my brain died! I have never known time pass so slowly.....Manufacturing was revolutionised, factory workers dehumanised.'
> (Quoted from 'Nothing else to Fear' by David W. Ellis; Monarch Books 2003)

Intellectual development has been predominantly related to abstract intellectual skills. Thus the creativity of left and right brain interaction has become marginalised for those considered normal (i.e. useful to the materialistic society); and minimised for those considered abnormal (i.e. not useful to our present materialistic society based on monetary wealth, competitive businesses and financial working incentives.)

The industrial revolution seems to have also supported the development of drugs described as *medication*. The drug companies appear to control even greater financial power and domination than industrial reproduction. The free childcare offered by state education allows both adults to feed their children and encourages industrialised material growth. In order to keep working and thereby earning, parents over-ride natural healing by choosing quick fix medication for themselves and their children. Similarly a natural healthy diet is too time-consuming and the working population relies on convenience and comfort foods.

> [Philip Day in his book 'Health Wars' - a comprehensive and informative information on many of today's health issues that may be considered relevant to the amount of autism diagnosed in today's western world.]

An Alternative Perspective

<u>Glossary of terms:</u>

Environment: External sensory stimulus.

Self-direct: The application of personal *'will'* onto the environment, expressed through thought, action and creative endeavour.

Stimulus-response: unconsciously organised responses to the environmental stimulus.

Reaction: an immediate uncontrollable reaction to an environmental stimulus/ situation.

Interaction: a consciously directed response to an external stimulus/situation.

Primitive/primal: a biological (animalistic) level of survival/fear based behaviour.

Entertainment: passive forms of occupation directed by an external environmental stimulus.

Addiction: an obsessional desire for an *internal response* to a specific *external* (environmental) sensory stimulus.

Self-directed mental activity relates our 'will' to the environmental geography and our 'moment by moment interaction' with a personal perspective on reality. In contrast, abstract mental activity is directed by primal survival strategies and abstract thoughts and feelings that may not be directly related to a present reality. These contrasting types of mental activity can instigate opposing behaviours. For example:-

- Willed meditation and natural periods of sleep are both designed to quieten the mind and create a period of rest for the brain whereby activity is minimised to that essential to basic issues of wellbeing.
- An un-natural dominance of abstract mind activity may also influence the body biology which should ideally be just a little alkaline. The modern day diet of processed convenience foods, excessive drinking of coffee and alcohol can also cause unhealthy levels of acidity in the body. Added to this an abnormal abstract mental dominance can cause stress and anxiety both of which are also associated with higher acidity levels in the body.

This could suggest that a balance of abstract (fantasy based) and constructive (reality based) brain activity may help the body to stay alkaline and thus help the body to stay calm and healthy. Good quality sleep and a calm peaceful disposition may help the body and mind to establish a balance that helps establish healthy neutral or slightly alkaline PH level in the body's biological condition. An abnormal abstract mental dominance can cause stress and anxiety both of which are associated with higher acidity levels in the body. This could suggest that a balance of abstract (fantasy based) and constructive (reality based) brain activity may help the body to stay alkaline and thus help the body to stay both <u>calm and healthy</u>.

When self-directed and consciously organised mental activity is weak, our mental activity is organised on the simplest level of primal survival based reactions. Therefore, reactions are generally responses that are directly related to our physical and emotional needs. Reactions are primal responses that are not consciously evaluated and directed by predetermined conscious thought.

Human consciousness is directed by our own individual 'will'. The will directs what motives us to engage with self-directed behaviour, and how we perceive and accommodate others. Our consciousness directs the style of behaviour by choosing from the following areas of human brain activity:-

<u>Prioritize,</u> how and what sensory experience gains our attention;
<u>Imitate,</u> meaningfully copying what we have experienced form an external source;
<u>Repeat,</u> repeating something we have done before;
<u>Choose,</u> choosing from a range of possibilities;
<u>Oppose,</u> an opposite or opposing response to an external experience;
<u>Invent,</u> creating a personal and unique response;
<u>Accept or Reject,</u> an inner manifestation of <u>Attitude;</u> embracing actions and emotions either from a positive inner disposition of accommodation and co-operation or a negative disposition of reaction and defence.

The author defines *'abstract'* brain activity as that which is directed by our human capacity for imaginative and fanciful thought. In contrast to this abstract thinking our capacity to assess and consciously accommodate our sensory reality is defined as 'concrete' thinking. Concrete thinking gives us the human capacity to think logically, interpret sensory information and direct the environment from thoughtful levels of intelligent understanding.

It is the nature of the human mind to be active and alert <u>at all times</u> day and night. If our mind could be switched off *completely* our survival and wellbeing would be seriously compromised. Even simple dangers may go undetected or ignored. For example if the mind was completely shut down during sleep we would not be able to:-

Maintain a comfortable and safe body position.
Our sleeping body position may cause an area of restricted blood flow.
We may fall out of bed.

We may not awake when we need the toilet.
We may not awake when in a dangerous situation such as a fire or intruder.
We may awake startled by sounds associated with unimportant sensory information i.e. weather changes, the washing machine or fridge noises, a family member talking or moving around.......

Therefore even when we are asleep essential subconscious 'abstract' brain activity is directed from a basic primal survival perspective. While sleeping the mind has a primal alert system and keeps itself active with comforting movements and imaginative dreaming. It is thought that dreaming when asleep at night and day-dreaming during the day can provide useful opportunity to actively process stressful experiences, fears and aspirations. The biologist Jeremy Griffith describes the human condition as one of biological instincts ('abstract' brain activity) and consciousness. Biological instincts are directed by abstract brain activity whereas consciousness is associated with our free-will thinking and areas of higher consciousness, intellectual and practical (concrete) interaction with reality.

Jeremy Griffith presents that adverse human behaviour is caused by <u>conflicting areas of thought</u> which separate the biological instincts from our human consciousness - our capacity for thoughtful consideration. Thus our biological blue-print and our free will thinking fail to co-ordinate. Inner conflicts then cause external reactions and mental conflicts and dysfunctions. These inner conflicts disturb our sense of;-love and compassion, harmony and inner peace, adaptability and intelligence.

An additional area of consideration is that, even a small undiagnosed area of biological brain dysfunction may disturb the natural biological instincts and associated abstract brain activity. This may explain why those with specific learning difficulties and disabilities are commonly seen to have associated sleep problems. For example falling out of bed could be related to a proprioceptive disorder or restlessness due to hyperactivity. Sudden awakening and night-time fears could be caused by unexpected noises setting off an over-sensitive, retained pre-birth startle reflex; troublesome nightmares during the dream period may be caused by a dominant and overactive amount of abstract brain activity during the day and/or during the night due to anxiety and stress.

During the daytime an 'awake' state of mind may be over stimulated by the sensory environment, or dominated by a specific strong area of sensory perception. These types of sensory over-load can cause stressful confusion, fanciful chaos and areas of unmanageable fear based brain activity.

The young child's brain activity may be largely unconsciously directed and thereby separated from their moment by moment reality and knowledge of cause and effect. Consciously premeditated responses may not necessarily bring the best outcome. Here the incentive is motivated by personal wants and needs and thereby presented as controlling behaviours and aggressive primal responses. However, consciously premeditated responses do at least give an opportunity to witness the results and thereby learn from consequential experience.

Consciously directed activity can also relate to future situations with a greater assessment of possibility and probability. However, in some situations young children may lack personal experience and therefore be vulnerable to the risk of misinterpreting unreal digital media presentations as part of their own reality. For example: one young sensible and sensitive child was found hitting ants with a hammer. His mother was quite shocked to see this behaviour because he was normally an exceptionally caring child toward all animals. She asked him why he was killing the ants and he confidently replied that it was alright "Just watch mummy they will get up again in a minute". Together they patiently watched and as the seconds collected into minutes the young boy's eyes filled with tears that overflowed in a cascade down his cheeks. Needless to say this child was imitating what he had seen on a cartoon film. His previous knowledge and experience of hitting nails into a piece of wood had no way of telling him that real ants would be killed. This misconception was corrected when the ants failed to come back to life. The little boy had no personal experience of anyone hitting him with a hammer and the cartoon did not give him any opportunity to explore any of the real perspectives and subsequent learning.

This example illustrates that the young child's brain activity is very susceptible to external examples of behaviour presented by digitally generated media based fictional entertainment and reality based (non-fiction) information.

The author equates this example to her theory that the present day predominance of media entertainment has some serious repercussions within society today. The growth of 'in school' violence and serious violent crimes in the community could be directly attributed to the growth in time spent engaging in abstract forms of entertainment and dramatic violence viewed on video games, TV, DVDs and Horror Films.

The author considers the following as the predominant attributing factors:-

1. When abstract aspects of brain activity are over stimulated they dominate over natural opportunities to directly experience learning through personal endeavour and practical experience.
2. Abstract mind dominance can cause separation from reality and logical perspectives such as natural issues of cause and effect become distorted and bizarre. A dominance of abstract thinking may distort a person's intellectual understanding and exaggerate unrealistic and imagined fears and anxieties. Abstract thinking processes obscure ones perception of cause and effect and 'natural consequences' are experienced from a personal survival perspective. Adversities thereby stimulate domination using defensive and aggressive reactions. Dramatic reactive responses also obscure a person's development of logical and concrete thinking skills.
3. Repeated exposure to media violence is presented as a means of successfully gaining further levels entertainment and future rewards. Thus dominant abstract mind activity leads to obsessional behaviours and subsequent addictions. Addiction is here defined as a need for something as comfort or entertainment that compensates for a lack of self-directed activity and constructive thinking. Any type of addiction will ultimately limit one's active relationship with reality.
4. The lifestyles of today can be hectic and intense; even a young child may be experiencing many different transitions from one sensory environment into another during a single day;

e.g. from one room to another; into a buggy or car; from one building into another building; from one carer to another; from one social situation into another etc. Routines may be constantly disrupted by outside influences i.e. mobile phones, siblings, parents working from home.......<u>E</u><u>xternal disturbance</u>, <u>disruptive sensory experiences</u> and <u>transitions</u> from one type of experience into a different environment inevitably disturb one's flow of self-directed activity. Transitional experience instigates a new range of sensory experience and one's sensory assessment is primal to inner adjustments and thereby inhibitive to self-directed and personal interaction. Transitional periods moving from one environment into a contrasting environments and a different or new environmental experience demand that one's present sensory perceptual experience is given priority over specified consciously organised and self-directed interactive activity....Only a good quality experience for a suitable period of time in a familiar sensory environment can support self-directed interaction through play and constructive co-operative activity.

5. In Britain 2019 fatal knife crimes rose to 17 before the end of March. Few children and young people of today have any personal experience of human death through accident or violence. Our libertarian freedoms and highly stimulating ever changing environments of today do not encourage responsibility for our actions or reality based awareness of consequences and disciplines or real awareness of a consequential prison confinement. Many young girls of today do not have any association with pregnancy or responsibility for an infant until they themselves become pregnant. Also boys of today have little real experience of the consequences for those convicted of a violent crime or the victim's traumatic experience.

> In the past extended family life brought children and youth closer to responsibility and consequences through their personal experience of extended family affairs and responsibility for their own actions at home and in the wider community.

Few jobs of today can be attained through apprentiship. Learning through experience is no longer an option for most careers, academic qualifications are essential. Sadly academic studies are generally focused on abstract academic performance which has little or no relevance to practical hands on work experience and constructive use of consciously organised thinking. Also, many jobs are now predominantly in a computerised format that prevents contact with real people, places and practical skills. Practical skills now hold little value and are generally bypassed as insignificant in our computerised world of programmed machines, mass production and robot based services.

The present day presents the narcissistic approach to life as a growing trend and one may consider that excessive 'selfie' picture posing, Facebook and other cell-phone communication systems may have attributed to the present recognition of this unnatural anti-social disposition, due to a genuine lack of interpersonal understanding.

The world of today is one of media entertainment, instant gratification, convenience foods, externally directed learning and financial benefit systems designed to prop up our lack of personal responsibility and self-directed endeavours required for general daily care and provisions. For example food is not grown it is bought, clothes are bought rather than made, entertainment is a push button system of instant rewards and fitness is attained by those who go to the gym. Our personal development is no-longer a unique process of interactive and co-operative experience, but rather one of mainstream and cult influences and 'media initiated' imitated behaviours. Our endeavour towards self-directed activity and consciousness may be critically important if we are to retain a sense of individual authenticity out-side of media induced beliefs and behaviours.

The author presents that genuine creativity is achieved when abstract and concrete thinking activity is successfully integrated within a self-directed use of environmental resources and imaginative application of practical skills and divergent thinking. Thus knowledge of how to balance <u>passive</u> abstract media entertainment with *interactive* concrete self-directed activity' is essential if the present human race is to embrace conscientious care of ourselves others and our environment. Our future understanding of the autism spectrum may include an understanding of how dominant abstract brain activity inhibits positive interaction with people places and things. Indeed abstract brain dominance may influence social interactions, daily life styles and diets based upon convenience foods which subsequently encourage a passive uncaring disposition, and associated mental conditions such as, addictive, obsessional and compulsive behaviours; poor memory skills, and later areas of deterioration in the biological performance of the brain seen asAlzheimer's and Dementia.

Practical use of interactive memory skills is dependent upon active interaction motivated by self-directed purpose and endeavour. Outstanding automated (rote) memory skills are classically seen as an autistic trait. Lack of everyday memory skills may be rightly associated with a lack of personal motivation and focus on a specific self-directed activity. This may be attributed to a lack of reality based responsibility for oneself, and/or others combined with abstract thoughts, daydreams and imaginary fears and a general lack of personal incentive.

Self-directed mental activity relates our will to the environmental geography and our moment by moment interaction with a personal perspective of reality. In contrast, abstract mental activity is directed by primal survival strategies and abstract thoughts and feelings that may not be directly related to our present reality. These contrasting types of mental activity can instigate opposing behaviours. For example:-

Self-directed interaction and structured activity - <u>versus</u> primal survival strategies using dominating, intimidating, defensive and competitive interaction.

Personal self-interests and self-protection - *versus* Compassionate understanding

Obsessional intellectual activity - *versus*. Sharing, caring and actively supporting humanitarian projects.

Intellect could be related to the person's capacity to apply brain activity to a reality perspective of calculation and understanding. An alternative perspective on intelligence could be seen as how well a person can consciously evaluate and regulate hemispheric integration and manage conflicting abstract and concrete thinking; such that divergent thinking is maximised and the limitations of dominant abstract thinking are monitored and directed appropriately.

Both Steiner and Montessori approaches appear to appreciate the need to balance abstract fantasy based learning with practical reality based learning through the acquisition of knowledge and understanding. The development of logical thinking can be founded upon a balance of logical and imaginative thinking. This balance is shown within a project/topic curriculum of:- science and crafts, maths and drama, gardening and interactive sports, imaginative fictional stories and factual knowledge.

Steiner did not want the young child's imagination to be suppressed by formal learning before the age of seven. Steiner proposed that it is only after the age of seven that a child is old enough to take responsibility for formal learning. Intellectual development demands that the learner surpasses fantasy and imaginative abstract thinking in favour of self-directed discovery based learning and logical thinking skills. Steiner schools today discourage parents from giving young children access to media/screen entertainment and unsupervised access to screen technology.

Montessori encouraged self-direct learning with the support of didactic materials that scaffold discovery learning, self-correction and self-discipline through free play, repetition, regular practice and positive guidance.

Consequences experienced by a young child would normally be presented within the context of normal family life. Parents, siblings and extended family members are all likely to express boundaries and disciplines within their understanding of each individual situation the child's unique personality, strength and weaknesses and other extenuating circumstances related to emotional and physical disposition. This level of flexibility and understanding can ensure that consequences are appropriate and avoid excessive confrontation and stress. If however, family life style chaos not help a child to develop positive social skills then sooner or later the large community is likely to express consequences enforce boundaries and controls. For example the school institution is designed to enforce corrective behaviour using deterrents and undesired consequences. By this stage consequences are not necessarily addressing the individual's needs and best interests and consequences can be felt as dictator and controlling measures that create resentments and counteractive defensive behaviours. For teenagers the outside community and peers take on a role in consequences and for adults it is the judicial system. Thus as we get older our experience of consequences for our actions can become distorted by inappropriate levels of leniency and lack of compassion and unfair severity. Without suitable consequential experiences the concrete thinking and self-directed incentives and self-discipline gets overwhelmed by the abstract survival systems of brain activity and associated reactive behaviours. Montessori presented that all adverse behaviour in children is due to their not getting suitable learning experience. The author proposes that antisocial behaviour is also caused by an unnatural dominance of abstract thinking. Abstract thought separates us from self-directed activity and conscious thinking skills associated with a broad personal awareness and application of will through positive interaction with the environment – people places and things.

Helena Eastwood

During the daytime an 'awake' state of mind may be over stimulated by the sensory environment, or dominated by a specific strong area of sensory perception. These types of sensory over-load can cause stressful confusion, fanciful mental chaos, distorted understanding and other areas of unconsciously managed brain productivity.

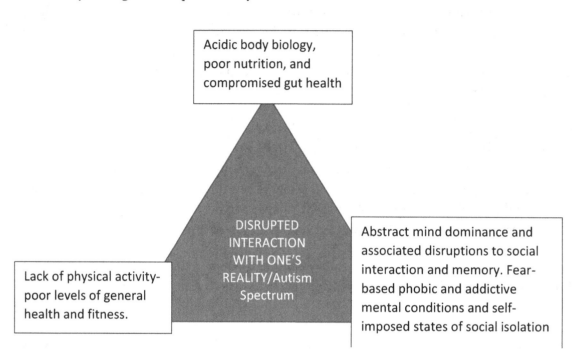

Acidic body biology, poor nutrition, and compromised gut health

DISRUPTED INTERACTION WITH ONE'S REALITY/Autism Spectrum

Lack of physical activity-poor levels of general health and fitness.

Abstract mind dominance and associated disruptions to social interaction and memory. Fear-based phobic and addictive mental conditions and self-imposed states of social isolation

An Alternative View on Autism

The autistic child may not appear to have specific problems with sensory reception and subsequent stimulus-response interaction. When motivated to do something they illustrate very good and sometimes exceptional sensory perception and quick accurate responses to stimulus within the context of automated responses and reactions.

However, a common feature of all aspects of the autism spectrum is that of attempting to shut out sensory reception either by a withdrawal into an inner world or physically separation from environmental stimulation.

Although autistic children often seem shut off from sensory stimulation they can also appear to be overwhelmed and distressed by everyday levels of sensory experience. We know that they can also have the ability to receive and accurately recall reception of sensory information, e.g. echolalia, balancing, climbing, singing and drawing. Similarly some of those on the autism spectrum can demonstrate exceptional motor coordination and manipulative skills of dexterity while others can have disabilities associated with dyspraxia, dysphasia, and proprioceptive disorders.

In general, our daily life offers a kaleidoscope of environmental stimuli that is fundamental to our personal perspective of 'reality'.

If autistic children are able to accurately receive and coordinate sensory information, why do they withdraw physically and/or mentally from the sensory stimulation that is around them?

As individuals we have a choice to either:-

*respond to an external environmental stimulus or
*explore any inner desire to specifically direct external interaction or
*engage with any potential to influence the external environment.

When an autistic child is drawn into relating with the environment s/he does appear to be subject to abnormally high levels of distraction and sensory overload. If the autism spectrum involves a heightened receptivity to environmental sensory stimuli? Then interaction and integration of relatively normal environmental sensory experience may feel overwhelming, intense, exhausting and difficult to manage. Thus, opportunities for self-directed interaction are dominated by overwhelming environmental stimulation and a personal need to find a 'quieter' sensory environment for recovery and relaxation. The questions to ask in relation to this may be:

Are they not able to <u>isolate</u> the sensory input they want to attend to?

Are they unable to <u>adjust</u> the levels of sensory perception?

Are they unable to <u>regulate</u> their stimulus-response reactions?

> The author proposes that autism is a learning difficulty caused by a notable deficit within these three processes; i.e. one's capacity to <u>isolate</u>, <u>adjust</u> and <u>regulate</u> external stimulus according to one's conscious will.

This lack of 'willed' organisation of sensory experience may create an unnatural imbalance in the development and integration of:-

Investigation through exploration and experimentation.
Abstract (imaginative) and concrete (logical) thinking.
Self-directed learning and conceptual understanding.
'Discovery learning' and self-correction.
Creative activity.

When anyone experiences a situation in which s/he is unable to regulate their reception of sensory stimulation, compensatory behaviours fill the gap! Natural compensatory behaviours are based upon basic (primal-survival) stimulus-response reactions.

Classic primal survival actions include:

- <u>Copied Behaviour</u> This tendency can be anti-social, when the copied behaviour is presented in other situations where it is received as inappropriate or a copy of a previous extreme response to a challenging situation. When under stress an adult carer or partner may present adverse levels of emotional and physical behaviour which when copied, escalates into adverse levels of anti-social interaction within an already challenging situation. Copied behaviour lacks authenticity and originality from a personal perspective.
- <u>Defensive Reactions</u> that reject any external opportunity for constructive interaction and help. These responses will carry either a passive or an active negative energy. If a person insists on an interactive relationship, the autistic person may resort to a defensive reaction of physical and verbal abuse.
- <u>Withdrawal</u> from their present situation i.e. people, places, things, social interaction and responsibility for one's own actions and present reality. This may result in lack of co-operation and lack of basic personal care. A withdrawn person is unable to address their own best interests and thereby certain to fail to accommodate anyone else's needs and perspective.

> Any state of withdrawal, defence or copied behaviour blocks out any potential for consciously organised self-directed interaction with the present environment.

When the autistic person opens his sensory reception s/he may not be able to control the incoming sensory information? The sensory input may then induce high levels of distraction that disturb any natural development of:-

Focus and attention (due to sensory overwhelm)
Specified adjustment to levels of sensory reception.
Personalised prioritisation and integration of sensory information.
Self-directed interactive behaviour.
Creative perspectives and authentic responses.

We are all influenced and to a certain degree governed by a kaleidoscope of environmental stimulus. The strongest stimulus presented at any one time, may take precedence over how, what and why we respond in any specific situation.

If an autistic person has no sensory '*volume control*' or '*means of focused selection*' then they would be over stimulated by normal levels of environmental stimulation.

The ability to select (focus) on a specific stimulus and at the same time turn down superfluous environmental stimulation, is surely essential to any successful interaction with one's present environment. Without these skills a person experience an uncomfortable and stressful existence within our world of complex, continuous and often intense environmental stimulation much of which *may not* have any reference to one's personal reality and daily survival issues.

This may explain why autistic children appear most comfortable in a natural or very unstimulating environment and distressed/anxious in unnatural, exciting and highly stimulating situations?

The ability to consciously regulate sensory input must be fundamental to the development of consciously organised learning as opposed to subconscious learning, i.e. that of intuitive and direct stimulus-response behaviour.

The ability to consciously regulate sensory input - fundamental to the development of consciously organised learning

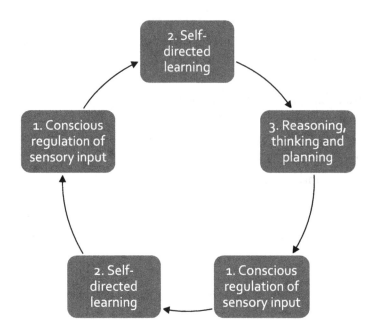

This can look like the 'chicken and egg syndrome' where by no egg means no chicken and no chicken means no egg ....The diagram above illustrates a similar impasse in that – conscious regulation of sensory input is required for self-directed learning and self-directed learning motivates conscious regulation of incoming sensory experiences. The above diagram presents a classic self-promoting loop where by child development is locked into a progressive loop of self-empowerment which when disrupted becomes a source of disempowerment.

Any deficit in one's ability to regulate sensory reception of stimulus thereby inhibits the development of consciously organised thinking and subsequent self-directed learning experience! Without self-directed learning discovery learning is diminished and with it a sense of consequences and this prevents self-correction and self-correction forms the foundation to reasoning, thinking and planning.

If the autistic child/person is unable to learn through trial and error (exploration and experimentation) s/he will fail to gain the rewards of instigating cause and effect in his/her environment. Presenting stimulus that can cause an environmental response is fundamental to the development of consciously controlled learning and intellectual thinking

If autistic children <u>are able</u> to receive and recall environmental stimulus, but are <u>not able,</u> to consciously organise their influence on the environment, their learning difficulties will be based on a lack of self-directed interaction with people, places and things. This lack of social interaction can disrupt their sense of authentic personal responsibility for their own actions. The author considers autism as a collection of compensatory behaviour patterns designed to safely accommodate subtle and unseen disruptions within the normal development of perception, accommodation and assimilation of external sensory stimulus. Examples of unseen perceptual disabilities experienced as profound areas of specific learning difficulty have been diagnosed as 'proprioceptive disorders', 'dyspraxia', 'dysphasia', 'auditory integration problems' etc.

Severe learning difficulties which are predominantly related to sensory perceptual dysfunction such as being blind or deaf or physically disabled are related to the perceptual aspects of impaired sensory <u>reception</u>. However, autism could be a natural way of accommodating an <u>inability to regulate</u> the reception of environmental stimulation which disrupts normal development of self-directed learning and social interaction. This may be the cause of several autistic behaviours that appear to be associated with exclusion from environmental stimulus such as:-

Hiding in small or confined spaces e.g. cupboards and curtains.
Avoiding physical touch and other social and loving forms of social contact.
Using the hands to cover over the ears
Repetitive rocking movements and other strong and repetitive tactile experiences.
The production of abnormal and characteristically autistic sounds.

One may also concede that this lack of self-directed activity also has a profound influence upon social development simply because social development is based upon personal interaction with others. Other people, animals and unknown environments present everyone with 'sensory reception' and 'sensory regulating' challenges beyond those experienced in a controlled and familiar physical environment.

The sensory perception of <u>external movement</u>, <u>touch</u> and <u>mother's voice</u> are automatically dominant and stronger than all other forms of sensory experience. This heightened sensory receptivity initially supports the infant's survival, protection and comfort. However, if the child is overwhelmed by these early sensory experiences the infant may be unable to develop self-directed learning experiences. Every infant is thought to have a strong affinity and an alert association to the mother's voice. However, if this causes intense levels of sensory overwhelm it may disrupt the child's ability to regulate their own intellectual relationship with other areas of environmental stimulation.

A heightened dominance of primal sensory perception i.e. <u>external movement</u>, <u>touch</u> and <u>mother's voice</u> may also explain why autistic children reject physical communications of love and care? If the infant fails to develop a capacity to <u>isolate</u>, <u>adjust</u> and <u>regulate</u> these heightened areas of sensory receptivity these important survival issues may adversely disrupt the infant's development of sensory regulation and self-directed learning. Without self-directed learning there is little motivation for the conscious development of one's capacity to <u>isolate</u>, <u>adjust</u> and <u>regulate</u> external stimulus according to one's conscious will.

It is the infant's development of conscious 'will' that facilitates and motivates their capacity to separate from instinctive baby responses and primitive reflexes in order to take on a personal journey of growing independence and empowerment.

If the autistic child is unable to regulate and accommodate incoming sensory information, it would be understandable that intimate social interaction would include high levels of incoming sensory information and associated sensory overload. This overload in itself may cause an autistic person to feel unsafe and unable to self-direct authentic social responses. This disposition of guarded unnatural social interactions then disrupts social development, interactive learning and one's sense of personal empowerment and safety within any given environment either with people or in isolation.

Any social sense of <u>isolation</u> can bring up adverse survival issues related to <u>separation</u> and <u>exclusion</u>. The social emotional issues associated with separation and exclusion can create survival programmes that cause the person to reject a source of comfort and block the communication of feelings and emotions. These issues of social withdrawal increase issues of exclusion which in themselves may cause <u>exclusive</u> compensatory behaviours and anti-social perspectives.

<u>Exclusive</u> compensatory behaviours can create anti-social behaviours based upon abstract fears and fantasies initiated from abstract mental activity and primal survival responses to one's everyday environment. As a child develops a lifestyle of <u>exclusive</u> compensatory behaviours, dispositions of guilt, blame and abnormal control issues can direct unprovoked anti-social behaviour founded upon abstract fears and fantasies.

Abstract & Concrete Thinking

The following diagram has been designed by the author to illustrate her own understanding of the relationship between the development of abstract and concrete thinking skills. It is important that everyone (especially children) are encouraged to integrate functions in the brain in a balanced way that promotes more complex areas of learning and appropriate intellectual responses.

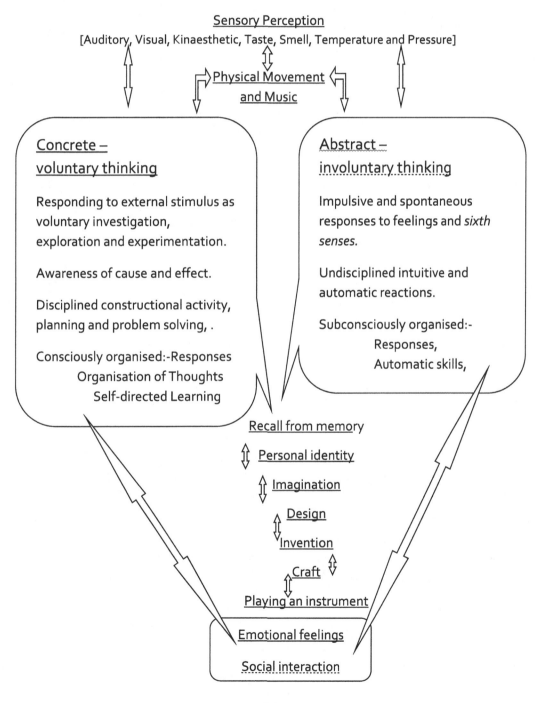

Helena Eastwood

The following graphs A to-D illustrate the commensurate relationship between abstract and concrete thinking. e.g Graph [B] Illustrates that if <u>concrete thinking</u> fails to develop normally, <u>abstract thinking</u> develops an abnormal compensatory dominance.

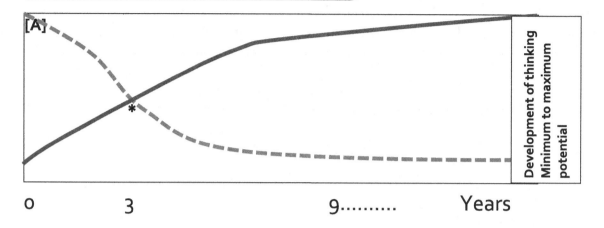

*Concrete Thinking dominates over Abstract thinking

- - - - -   Decline of abstract subconscious thinking and related primal survival behaviour.

━━━━━━   Progressive development of 'concrete thinking skills' and related intellectual understanding and constructive interaction with ones external reality (people, places and things).

<u>Concrete thinking skills</u> relate to a logical consideration of <u>cause and effect</u> and related <u>strategic thinking, cognitive and conceptual understanding</u>.

> The above graph A illustrates that around the age of three years children normally develop a level of <u>Concrete thinking</u> that can successfully dominate over <u>abstract thinking</u> activity. This facilitates the development of skills related to the <u>reception, adjustment, focus,</u> and regulation of sensory input.

<u>Conscious thinking</u> skills are also essential to the development and management of one's <u>ability to present information into memory and retrieve appropriately from memory.</u>

> Memory skills are essential to observation of cause and effect and knowledge related to consequences and intellectual understanding.
> A knowledge of consequences is essential to the development of strategic thinking skills.

Thus, conscious thinking regulates how, when and where in the brain we organise and integrate our perception of external stimulus. Subsequent intellectual development is directed within the context of one's ability to consciously organise how information is stored and retrieved from memory.

In Graph [B] both abstract and concrete thinking have failed to develop normally. Graph [B] illustrates what may happen when Concrete thinking skills fail to dominate over <u>Abstract thinking</u> presented on graph [A].

In graph [B] the progressive lack of concrete thinking skills disturbs the development of a growing capacity to <u>isolate</u>, <u>adjust</u> and <u>regulate</u> external stimulus Graph[A] When *<u>Concrete Thinking</u> dominates over <u>Abstract thinking</u> the reception of environmental stimulus can be consciously

- monitored,
- regulated,
- and adjusted.

These skills facilitate the persons ability to focus on environmental stimulus according to personal choice and motivated 'willed' endevour.

according to one's conscious will. The dominant abstract mental activity inhibits one's sense of reality and subsequent development of intellectual understanding.

> The excessive and dominating development of abstract thinking, and associated compensatory behaviours, can be released if external stimulus is directly related to personal perspectives; i.e. a relatively simple and natural environment and possitive one to one social interaction.

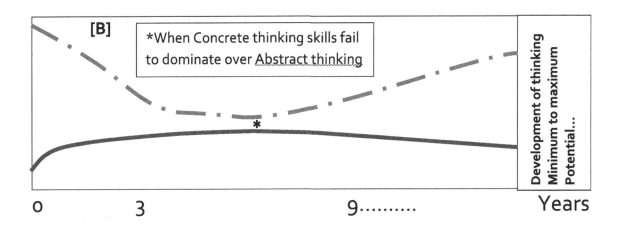

Graph [B] –presents a possible scenario if <u>concrete thinking</u> fails to dominate over <u>abstract thinking;</u> such that normal development of concrete thinking is compromised and the concrete thinking skills fail to develop as presented above (Graph A). Graph B presents that a<u>bstract thinking skills</u> may then become progressively more dominant as an attempt to compensate for lack of concrete thinking. The development of abstract thinking skills now establish and maintain survival within the context of everyday needs and physical growth. Thus, to compensate for a deficit in concrete thinking, the abstract primal thinking activity in the mind increases! because abstract mental thinking develops progressively as a way of establishing adequate compensatory survival behaviour.

These compensatory behaviours may include;

i. Abnormal mother child attachment, usually expressed as disruptions to independent sleep, abnormal responses to the weaning process, and lack of independent play.
ii. Withdrawal as a way of managing excessive complex sensory experience.
iii. Exclusive automated skills.
iv. Obsessional occupational behaviours (OCD).
v. Copied and echolalia responses.
vi. Food and other unhealthy forms of addiction.

Without a structured analysis of one's reality, <u>external sensory information is likely to dominate</u> over ones ability to focus and concentrate. This unregulated reception of external stimulus causes perception and understanding to develop within an abstract unreal prespective. This abstract perspective may then create an un-natural dominance of survival fears and fantasy based thoughts and desires for dramatic forms of entertainment. Without a structured perception of one's reality, abstract thinking skills may thereby take on a dominant role. As a means of nutralising the abstract dominance the subconscious mind may organise compensatory behaviours based on primal survival instincts. Whereby, dominant survival instincts, command automated responses to external stimulus such as eating and drinking, vocalised expressive sounds, 'fight and flight' reactions and actions of defense and related issues of control.

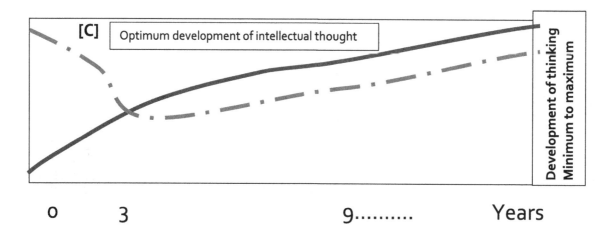

Diagram [c] represents the optimum development of human conscious thought and the application of structured interaction with the daily environment. Intellectual integration of sensory perceptual information within cognitive and conceptual understanding enables a person to direct and organise constructive activity. This <u>consciously organised mental development</u> is essential to personal empowerment and wellbeing, progressive learning and responsibility for the wellbeing of the environment and other people.

Diagram [C] presents that optimum intellectual development occurs when the concrete thinking maintains a dominance over the abstract thinking while accommodating that the abstract thinking skills continue to develop at a similar rate.

[Helena Eastwood originally presented the above chapter as a paper titled 'An Alternative View on Autism' at the conference Biological Perspectives in Autism April 5th-7th 1993 organised by Autism Research Unit at the University of Sunderland.]

Abstract and Concrete Activity

Abstract mental processes and Survival Issues

The author considers that abstract mental processes create a dominance of *survival issues*. This dominance can disrupt learning and relationships and subsequently

- block a person's ability to engage in a positive and useful lifestyle
- and inhibits development of human consciousness.

An unnatural dominance of 'Abstract Brain Activity' (ABA) is described by the author as one of the visible results of the learning differences caused by autism. The severely autistic child is unable to develop self-directed interaction with their material and social environment. Late onset of infant autism is noted as an unexpected and unexplainable disruption of normal childhood development. This type of autism is seen by the author as a failure to develop the natural dominance of self-directed behaviour during the two and a half to three year period of development. This period would normally establish that the child successfully learns to suppress their subconscious stimulus-response reactions in order to favour the organisation of consciously self-directed activity using the will.

> Self-directed activity involves an integration of sensory information, environmental awareness and understanding within the self-directed areas of thinking and subsequent co-ordination of activity.

It is a notable concern that the autistic child may have suffered brain damage that inhibits normal development of:- co-ordination of movement, social integration, auditory integration skills, language development, or a general sensory integration deficit.

The brain's plasticity and outstanding lifelong ability to adapt and learn can in theory, over-come any and all of these areas of difficulty. However, the primal survival systems may, especially at a young age, direct a strong compensatory development of subconsciously organised Abstract Brain Activity and thus effectively over-ride normal consciously organised self-directed activities. The author considers some adverse experiences may strongly motivate an abnormally dominant use of Abstract Brain Activity due to related subconscious survival issues. Some examples of this may include:-

- Early childhood trauma, (e.g., physical injury, debilitating illnesses, long-term and extreme forms of physical confinement, medical forms of drug induced sedation, Unpredictable abuse from trusted loved ones, life threatening experiences such as natural disasters and war.)

- A long term loss of floor mobility during the first/early years,
- Severe or prolonged experiences of isolation and associated issues of separation and exclusion.
- Breathing difficulties and shallow breathing habits caused by lack of exercise and movements that require general fitness and stamina.
- Anti-biotic, medical and recreational drugs and vaccines that damage the gut flora and thereby compromise the body's absorption of nutrition.

Dominance of Abstract Brain Activity

> The development and maintenance of the brain and the nervous system requires a consistent and notable level of oxygen and nutritional intake to ensure essential neurological health, development and ongoing progress. Therefore, any notable adversities are likely to induce an unnatural form of brain development and a subsequent abnormal dependence upon automated and <u>Abstract Brain Activity</u>. Abstract brain activity uses minimal intercellular brain activity and negligible brain development as a way of maintaining optimum primal survival strategies.

Abstract mental processes may create a dominance of *survival issues*. This dominance can disrupt learning and relationships and then block a person's ability to engage in a positive and useful lifestyle and thus, inhibits development of human consciousness.

Abstract mental responses based on primitive fears and related survival processes have minimal influence over our development of movement and sensory integration. If fantasy and imagination are given priority over every day living and learning, then occupational abstract thinking may dominate the person's activities and wellbeing. Abstract thinking gives priority to survival related mental and physical activity. This survival mode of behaviour, may block the development and potential influence of conscious thinking upon behaviour and learning:- e.g.

 I. One's ability to integrate sensory information with conscious brain functions

 II. One's awareness of possible choices within any given situation

 III. One's awareness of physical consequences

 IV. One's ability to predict the results of a specific action

 V. One's ability to integrate abstract and concrete thinking and thereby engage in creative endeavour

 VI. One's ability to engage in self-directed learning

 VII. One's ability to communicate with body language, facial expressions and lauguaged thought.

 VIII. One's ability to engage in *positive/co-operative* social activities, (as opposed to negative anti-social behaviour and excessive levels of control/defense).

 IX. One's ability to express compassion and empathy within a sharing/caring context.

 X. One's development of a social and moral conscience.

The author considers dominance of Abstract Mental activity is caused by an unnatural disruption within either or both of the following <u>two specific areas of human social development</u>. These areas of social development (a and b) would normally be established through consciously organised thinking and self-directed learning.

A. <u>The first</u> is established usually around the age of nine. At this age a child would normally develop the ability to imagine what it is like if they were to be in a different situation i.e. awareness of <u>personal consequences</u>. For example they know that they need gloves if they want to play in the snow outside without getting freezing cold hands.

B. <u>The second</u> level of self-directed consciously organised thinking normally develops around the age of eleven years. This stage of social development allows the child to <u>imagine someone else's</u> situation. This is the ability to assess how a certain action may adversely affect another person, from an understanding of the other person's unique perspective. For example – 'if I do not return home when I am expected, my parent/partner may be worried that I have had an accident and set out to find me.'

Sadly the intellectual version of autism previously diagnosed as Asperger's presented in adults may also incorporate mental conditions related to addiction and mental disorders:- such as Obsessional Compulsive Behaviour (O.C.D.), phobias, psychosis, Tourettes and panic attacks. The author considers that all these adult conditions may also be considered as a state of over whelming Dominant Abstract Mind activity and associated aspects of primal survival.

Dominant Abstract Mind Activity may disturb an adult's ability to

- organise self-directed activity,
- integrate consciously organised thinking skills
- witness and modify compensatory behaviours.

This disability and associated learning differences may also inhibit the person's ability to integrate and assess moral and social considerations as part of a premeditated choice of <u>genuine</u>, as opposed to, <u>copied</u> sharing and caring interaction.

Activities that Encourage and Maintain Dominance of Abstract Brain Activity

The following list of popular activities for both adults and children illustrates the type of activity that may encourage and maintain Dominant Abstract Brain Activity in adults &children.

- ➤ <u>Cartoon films</u>
- ➤ <u>Battery operated toys</u>. (Inevitably these toys encourage repetitive and thereby quickly automated stimulus-response styles of interaction.
- ➤ <u>Fantasy and fiction films</u> (including science fiction)
- ➤ <u>Small Lego</u> (this is because the uniform shape of each brick encourages automated building skills through a repetition of set movements and interactive activity). Even advanced small logo building activity is largely based on the use of a visual picture or visual diagrammatic instructions. These predisposed activities can become automated building activity, and require no personal imagination or personal interpretation. Thus the activity becomes a robotic style of automated activity.

29

> ➤ <u>Computer games</u>. These games require a repetitive and thereby quick, automated, stimulus-response styles of interaction.
> ➤ <u>Competitive games</u>; particularly those based on skills of speed and repetition. (These activities draw on abstract survival techniques, often seen as the competitive aspect of winning in order to get the best and superior survival results.

Activities that Encourage and Maintain Self-Directed Thinking and Learning

This type of activity can encourage <u>constructive behaviour</u> and maintain a dominance of Self-Directed interaction with people, places and things.

Self-directed thinking and learning activity is predominantly based on the integration of both left and right hemispheric brain activity. This type of brain activity relates to the reality of our world and the physical principles of interaction, cause and effect, imagination and social awareness. Indeed all forms of sensory integration and associated learning are based on complex skills that are self-directed from a self-motivated personal perspective.

The following list describes activities that the author presents as conducive to the development of self-directed behaviour; where by dominant abstract thinking and obsessional and addictive behaviours can be moderated so as to weaken the adversities of dominant abstract and fantasy based thinking.

<u>Art and design</u> these activities also integrate self-directed thought and accommodating action from both left and right brain hemispheres.

<u>Sculptural and traditional crafts</u> e.g. learning to knit. Although knitting is traditionally an automated skill, the use of both hands and the responsibility for the tension, pattern and sustained accuracy, bring knitting activity into a self-directed area of learning and responsibility; beyond that of automated abstract mind occupational repetition.

<u>Music</u> Composing one's own music is the best form of self-directed brain activity integrating both hemispheres. Playing a musical instrument by ear or from a music score is also very good. Live music is the best for quietening any dominance of abstract mind activity. Listening to gentle music and natural musical sounds can also integrate both hemispheric thinking. Even digital music can sooth and encourage a self-directed approach to thinking and doing. (classical music and Hand drum music is notably calming and therefore some music can release a person from abstract mind dominance. However, if the music is challenging, the individual can feel unsafe or over-stimulated into biological adrenalin responses. These responses will encourage the abstract survival responses associated with dominant abstract mind and subconsciously organised survival behaviour.

<u>Outdoor pursuits</u> Especially the activities that accommodate an unpredictable natural element that requires application of practical survival skills such as canoeing, sailing, hiking, climbing, horse riding, gardening, cross country running, mountain biking etc.

Helena Eastwood

Dance
Ice-skating
Circus skills

Acrobatics (Acrobatic activities also have the potential to help a person gain greater control over known and unknown areas of fear. The author also considers that acrobatic physical activity can help to release pre-birth reflexes and encourage adult reflexes which are related to the physical environment rather than the womb and birth environment.

Creative writing and poetry
Community Projects.

Social sharing and caring Eg Looking after children, co-operative games, caring for animals and wildlife.

Creating a home environment organisation of a supportive home environment from a concrete and constructive perspective. E.g. Cooking, mending, decorating, and collecting wood building a shed etc.

Abstract Mental Activity

Sadly our world of today also presents a strong focus on intellectual development as superior to that of practical, creative and construction skills.

The Abstract mind is used by the author to describe any area of brain activity that specifically deals with abstract thinking. The abstract mind also deals with abstract thinking which is organised subconsciously from primal directives.

> Abstract brain activity is NOT related to structural reality, logic, consequences, compassion, moral consideration or self-directed logical and creative activity.

Abstract mental activity can include:-

- Primitive reflexes,
- Fantasy,
- Imagination,
- Language reception,
- Primal survival instinct and associated aggressive defensive actions,
- Compensatory behaviour patterns,
- Automated skills,
- Unconsciously organised reactions.

Autism could be seen as personal learning differences dominated by:-

- abstract thinking skills
- heightened sensory perception,
- automatic responses (including balance, fear, fight and flight, and high adrenaline),
- fixed programmes of repetitive stimulation,
- occupational stimulation
- sensory entertainment.

The above lists present an assortment of *strategies for sensory assimilation* that are directly related to *basic survival issues* such as movement, sensory reception, and brain activity.

Abstract Mind Dominance

Abstract mind dominance limits the individual's ability to accommodate a personal view at any given moment of their environmental reality and therefore may inhibit their own willed choices and genuine personal responses.

Helena Eastwood

Those on the autism spectrum illustrate a notable dominance of imitation, repetition and defensive behaviours and thereby emphasise an ongoing development of abstract mind dominance. This in turn inhibits the development and utilisation of *consciously organised self-directed activity* – Thus abstract mind dominance can successfully over-ride an individual's consciously *willed* and *premeditated* interactions. The normal development of exploration, experimentation, practise of skills and socially acceptable interaction may become consistently suppressed by the dominating abstract mental activity and lack of hemispheric interaction and sensory integration.

The author's understanding of the autism spectrum relates to a developmental deficit that disrupts the person's ability to interact with life as a 'Live, Love, Learn' journey based on meaningful intellectual growth through:-

- *Integrated* multi-sensory experience,
- *Adventures of* interactive activity,
- *Authentic* social development,
- *Creative* endeavour.

What does 'Autistic' mean in everyday terms?

- A restricted Live – Love – Learn prospective during childhood and the Early years.
- A lack of self-directed learning through play, creative activity and personal endeavour.
- Heightened survival responses.
- Exceptional sensory perceptual skills
- Disrupted reality and consequences
- Avoidance of social interaction
- Exclusive repetitive activities
- Language and communication disorders
- Lack of social conscience and moral understanding

> The autism spectrum is defined by the author as a developmental difference seen as a failure in development of self-directed interaction with the physical environment and positive social interaction with those who are providing companionship, care and support.

In the early years the young child learns how to regulate their impulsive interactions in favour of self-directed actions. Self-directed activity and interaction is organised by the 'will' and motivated within play and learn activity. Thus the young child develops the ability to supress impulsive reactions, in order to actively engage in comprehensive considerations and choices supported by intellectual understanding and self-directed endeavour. Self-directed activity can transform thinking into imaginative ideas and sensory experience of construction within ones concrete reality.

> A young child development is defined by the way we learn to direct what we do from our own inner personal incentives. This disposition directs the conscious learning directed by the 'will' to *take inter-active responsibility for* how, and with what and whom, we interact on a moment by moment basis.

Self-directed interactions project our own inner perspective of personal care, needs and empowerment. The author describes this as a 'Live - Love – Learn' approach that motivates and activates 'interactive activity' which is the foundation of all successful learning and personal empowerment.

Basic Survival Responses

If self-directed activity fails to develop normally, external actions and events stimulate impulsive survival based responses. These survival responses generally exclude a sense of social awareness and consideration of another person's perspective and wellbeing.

> The fact that autistic children all over the world manifest similar patterns of behaviour, suggests that lack of self-direct may create a specified repertoire of compensatory behaviours that are not necessarily influenced by different environmental and social experiences.

Adults who have undergone long periods of solitary or severe confinement have been seen to present autistic behaviours. Even when placed in the very best levels of care these adults may retain their autistic behaviours. These observations suggest that self-directed behaviour grows and develops when our daily lifestyle is experienced within a positive social environment. Inversely the development of self-directed behaviour may be lost if not actively practiced. A positive social environment can successfully scaffold 'self-directed' interaction organised from a conscious disposition, over and above issues of primal survival. Primal survival skills are often present and enhanced in autistic children. Autistic children can illustrate outstanding performances related to: balance and movement, heightened sensory perception, imitative responses and memory skills.

[Examples of this known to the author include: one child who lived in London, could run across five lanes of moving traffic, dodging the oncoming cars; a child could climb large trees and high fences at great speed with impeccable co-ordination and balance;.a child could repeat word for word with perfect accent and intonation the whole of the sound track to his favourite film; a child who could draw a detailed picture of pattern he had seen. These examples illustrate the human capacity to co-ordinate outstanding levels of physical ability from a subconsciously organised use of the brain and sensory perception.

> *When self-directed activity is inhibited* for whatever reason, we are driven to instinctively look for external directions, thus the strongest stimulus takes precedence and commands that imitation and other types of survival and compensatory behaviour are used to over-ride unwanted levels of sensory reception.

Some adults in extremely dangerous and life threatening situations have accomplished unique - *superhuman* actions that were beyond their everyday levels of ability. We know and appreciate that the blind person can attain auditory perceptual skills well beyond the norm. Similarly, it would appear that the lack of (consciously organised) self-directed and creative activity present in autism can be associated with extreme levels of sensory perception and abnormally high levels of subconsciously organised *responses*.

[The author has worked successfully with the elderly using the same techniques for empowerment and self-directed activity used with children and adults on the autism spectrum.]

Is Autism simply a specified collection of compensatory behaviours? Behaviours designed to counteract the vulnerability presented by:-

- Lack of learner directed learning.
- Specific learning differences and associated learning difficulties.
- Learning difficulties caused by specified areas of brain damage/dysfunction

Changes in the environment

Changes in the environment are generally monitored from the following three areas of personal reality and personal safety:-

- Where am I?! (The environmental geography)
- Who am I with?! (The person and people around me)
- What is happening?! (The incoming sensory stimulus from movements, actions and activities going on around me.)

Those on the Autism spectrum often develop complex and intense controlling behaviours in order to avoid changes and retain what has become routine, comfortable and/or familiar. Alternatively, any high sensitivity to external stimulus may be over-ridden by systems of self-stimulation such as rocking, spinning, screeching, or self-harm.

Sadly those on the Asperger's end of the spectrum can turn to addictions as a way of avoiding unpredictable external stimulus and controlling unexpected and unwanted environmental sensory encounters.

Sadly lack of self-direct can create an excessive need for external direction. However, external sensory directives may ultimately inhibit self-directed learning processes and disrupt development of personal discernment and personal choices. A subsequent disempowered disposition may create a resentful attitude towards external activity because the external environment is perceived suppressive to the person's own development of *self-directed* interaction, *personal* expression and discovery *learning*. This resentment and suppression of personal empowerment may lead to counter responses that motivate excessive control over other people, places and things. This excessive need for control may then create <u>unreasonable fears and anxieties about changes</u> and <u>periods of transition</u> seen throughout the autism spectrum.

> The human disposition is related to a kaleidoscope of personal choice whereby we
> either   direct what we do from our own inner incentives i.e. personal choice
>   Or
>   *what we do* is directed by the actions and events occurring in our physical
> environment and presented to us from the needs and actions of others.

The growing development and maturity of the young child would normally enhance the ability to self-direct one's actions independently from the directions of others. When environmental experiences disrupt one's ability to manage and accommodate unwanted and overwhelming levels of environmental stimulus, then a personally tailored system of self-directed learning, may become difficult or even impossible.

The development of consciously organised thinking is essential to our development of:-

- Self-directed activity
- concrete thinking,
- self-correction
- sensory selection
- focus and concentration
- differentiate between fantasy and reality
- moderation of abstract fears
- development of a compassionate consideration of others
- conscious development
- self-worth and personal identity as a unique individual
- social conscience

<u>Abstract mental activity</u> does not generally support self-directed interaction with the present environment. However, abstract mental activity can embrace:- *imagination, *language reception, *primal survival instincts, *primitive reflexes, *compensatory behaviour patterns, *survival instincts and *automated skills.

Autism is described by the author as an overwhelming dominance of unconsciously organised abstract skills and automatic responses, such as balance, fear directed reactions, fixed programmes of stimulus-response, and assimilation strategies that are directly related to basic survival issues.

Some of those on the autism spectrum illustrate a notable absence of consciously organised self-directed activity. Thus, abstract mind dominance inhibits the individual's ability to accommodate a personal view of their environmental reality at any given moment. Abstract mind dominance may successfully inhibit self-directed, consciously willed and premeditated interaction and suppress exploration, experimentation, inspiration and socially acceptable interaction.

If one fails to develop or to maintain the ability to interact as a unique individual then one may also fail to establish and maintain a capacity to express oneself in an authentic manner. When one's personal options and self-directed activity is limited daily activity may be simply that of a copied and/or repetitive behaviour based on what others have presented previously. This disposition seeds a potential to blame others for every adverse situation, event and consequence, along with a notable inability to relate to consequences and external boundaries.

Self-directed activity is almost exclusively formulated as a result of conscious application of choice within the geographical reality of any given situation. If, however, one's inner personal directives are weak, personal choices are not necessarily considered and the behaviour and actions of others are taken on as important external directives.

> ### Personal Directives and Choices
>
> When personal directives and choices fail to secure purpose and personal choices then we naturally seek external directives and external boundaries of control. However, this need for external directives may ultimately lead to resentment that others are taking control of our life for their own benefit. This resentment can then motivate an abnormal need to exercise control over the people, places and things around us.

This negative disposition, created by a lack of normal self-directed activity, is fuelled by our survival instincts seated in the subconscious mind which eliminates self-directed personal and creative interactions.

A notable lack of self-directed behaviour is often seen in Children and the Elderly. Young children are learning how to command their thinking in order to regulate their reception and responses to external sensory stimulus presented by their environment. The elderly can lose their ability to command their thinking and successfully regulate their reception and responses to external sensory stimulus. The loss of self-directed activity for elderly people can be due to memory loss and mental confusion and other degenerative health issues e.g *lack of mobility; *loss of memory; *medication; *social isolation. Indeed it may be that this regressive loss of authentic interaction, for whatever reason, that sets up a subsequent elderly decline; seen as states of confusion, Alzheimer's and dementia. The author proposes that retaining and motivating a self-directed, active and independent lifestyle is the best way forward for both the elderly and autistic children.

> Our fast, intensive modern day life-styles, may direct us away from 'Basic Human Needs' and thereby limit personal motivation and self-directed activity.

Natural Order of Priority for Maintaining our Human Potential

Sleep - a comfortable, safe, quiet environment for the required length of time.

Food – adequate amounts of food, free from stimulants and artificial additives, containing the required nutrition.

Movement – a safe and suitable quality and size of space.

Free play – uninterrupted activity within a suitable free play environment.

Creative activity – self-confidence, enthusiasm, imagination.

Authentic social interaction

Intimacy

Devotional service to *Highest Good*.

[Similar to Maslow's Hierarchy of Needs}

Basic Human Needs

Natural Order of Priority for Maintaining our Human Potential.

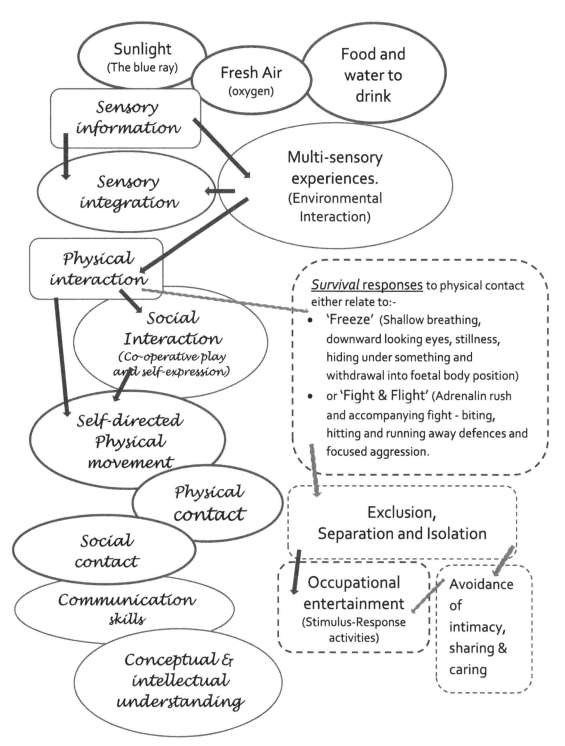

Sunlight
(The blue ray)

Fresh Air
(oxygen)

Food and
water to
drink

Sensory
information

Sensory
integration

Multi-sensory
experiences.
(Environmental
Interaction)

Physical
interaction

Social
Interaction
(Co-operative play
and self-expression)

Survival <u>responses</u> to physical contact
either relate to:-
- 'Freeze' (Shallow breathing,
  downward looking eyes, stillness,
  hiding under something and
  withdrawal into foetal body position)
- or 'Fight & Flight' (Adrenalin rush
  and accompanying fight - biting,
  hitting and running away defences and
  focused aggression.

Self-directed
Physical
movement

Physical
contact

Exclusion,
Separation and Isolation

Social
contact

Communication
skills

Occupational
entertainment
(Stimulus-Response
activities)

Avoidance
of
intimacy,
sharing &
caring

Conceptual &
intellectual
understanding

The following chart describes possible consequences for anyone without the ability to 'self-direct'.

Area of difference	Consequential Symptoms	Limiting Disposition
Lack of sensory regulation	Sensory overwhelm	Hypersensitivity
Impaired sensory integration	One Specific area of sensory dominance	Attachment to specific and repetitive sensory experience.
Poor use and organisation of the working memory	Failure to recall appropriate information from the working memory to suit practical requirements.	Memory skills are erratic, unsuitable and unstable within real life appropriated practical contexts.
Self-directed activity limited to personal issues of survival - food, warmth, safety, sensual/sexual gratification.	Lack of original play	Lack of constructive activity
Unable to organise one's physical environment to suit one's personal needs and desires.	Either very untidy and disorganised or obsessional about keeping their surroundings exactly the same at all times.	Failure to establish a working relationship of organisational interaction with one's environment:- people places and things.
Lack of creative interaction	Limited forms of verbal communication	Limited authentic social interaction
Limited sense of exploration	Limited application of experimentation	Lack of personal incentive
Lack of enthusiasm	Lack of motivation	General lack of inspiration
Lack of individuality	Serotyped behaviours	Lack of authentic expression
Dominant abstract thinking	Desire for external entertainment	Obsessional compulsive behavioural disorders (O.C.D.)
Specified intellectual field of interest and subsequently narrow fields of communication	Exclusive hobbies that dominate free-time activity and social connections	Obsessional projects that dominate over ones social opportunities and general wellbeing
Primitive pre-occupational dominance of survival issues	Lack of self-control	Addictions and mental instability
No awareness of self-created consequences	Predominance of copied and repetitive activity	Dependence upon external directives – i.e. rules, laws, governing and authoritative systems of regulation.
Projecting one's personal responsibilities onto others	Unreasonable projections of blame onto others	Jealousy and competitive forms of domination.
Abusive styles of social interaction	Aggressive anti-social behaviour	Revengeful thinking and active forms of retaliation
Isolation and depression	Exclusion and paranoia	Separation from ones reality psychosis
Lethargy and limited levels of physical activity	Melancholia	Habitual presentation of negative responses

Helena Eastwood

<u>Four Consecutive Stages of Learning</u>: established during childhood development:-

1. <u>Sensory Perception and Assimilation</u> This first stage is dominated by <u>*Sensory stimulus*</u> and the subsequent assimilation of sensory information presented by the environment to the physical sensory systems. This initial stage is facilitated and enhanced by the person's level of physical mobility. <u>Mobility</u> actively supports one's ability to:- explore; assess, and test the environment in order to establish a geographical knowledge of the environmental and establish an awareness of boundaries from a safety perspective

2. <u>Gross Motor Interaction</u> Concrete integration *of sensory information - p*hysical and multi-sensory enrichment. Experiential experiences, constructional sensory-motor activity. Increasing the sensory experiences by physical efforts that initiate recall of *sensory information* from memory. Physical multi-sensory enrichment is acquired through child directed exploration and experimentation as the '*director*' of experiential experiences through constructional sensory-motor activity. Personal motivation directs a '*Willed*' – recall from memory and previous sensory experiences are now upgraded to a maximum. Excitement and enthusiasm, over enthusiastic attention seeking and challenging behaviour seeking and engineering stronger sensory stimulus, a strong sense of action and reaction. feelings as an awareness of energy, moods, disposition, attitude, desires. Intuitive exploration and environmental and social aspects of control and testing boundaries

3. *Abstract* <u>thinking</u> - imagination and conceptual understanding;
   <u>Creativity</u> as the '*director*'- *Now* the *integration of a, b, and c (sensory, concrete, and abstract) is guided by* inner incentives and external objectives. *When this integration is genuinely* authentic, unique aspects of personal individuality blend with the *heart* and soul connections that nurture dreams, morals and beliefs. This can initiate *Spiritual experiences* of reverence, compassion, gratitude and appreciation

4. <u>Multi-sensory integration</u> Recapping and remembering, constructive expression of creative ideas. Integration of new information with past and present personal experiences. Embracing recall as a personal meditation, a *spiritual experiences* of reverence, compassion, gratitude and appreciation divergent thinking

Environmental stimulus

a. <u>Constructive</u> movement and physical interaction with the environment.
b. *Abstract* - thinking - conceptual understanding; <u>feeling</u> - energy, moods, disposition, attitude, will, memory and - desires,.
c. *Creative*- imaginative *integration of a, b, and c (sensory, concrete, and abstract) with* authentic and unique aspects of personal individuality. The *heart* and soul connections that initiate *Spiritual experiences* of reverence, nurture dreams, morals and belief, compassion, gratitude and appreciation.
d. *Uniquely personal and spiritual actively engaging with* ones unique and authentic relationship with one's own individual 'live, love, learn' journey

42

An example of the above theory of the above four consecutive stages of learning is described as a four day experience of play and learning on a natural beach environment.

Day one (a) Mobility - sensory exploration, assessment of environment, testing and establishing physical boundaries and acquiring a basic knowledge of the environmental geography.

Day two (b)
Gross motor interaction Increasing the sensory experiences by physical efforts that initiate excitement and enthusiasm. This may be explored through a strong sense of action and reaction and include attention seeking /challenging behaviour directed by a desire to seek or engineer stronger sources of sensory stimulus as a form of exciting entertainment. Sensory experiences upgraded to a maximum, exploring environmental and social aspects of control and testing boundaries. For example running away from the waves; splashing, diving, sitting in the shallow waves; throwing sand, digging a hole, covering parts of yourself or someone else in the sand; playing chase games on the sand, or in the water, stamping on shells and collecting seaweed or driftwood for a fire, collecting other items from shore line old rope containers etc.

Day three (c)
Relating to the environment through creative activity.
Sand structures; designing, building and decorating a sandcastle, waterways and other three dimensional structures; playing catch on the beach and or in the sea constructing a sun shade tent or winter break from sticks and stones and hotel building is and village designing; surfing a waves with or without the help of a surf board; learning to swim.

Day four (d) A day of relaxation; a heart-felt accommodation of the previous three days experience, recapping and remembering, recall and meditation.

> Today's highly stimulating environments mean that much of a child's day is occupied by acclimatisation i.e. getting familiar with the ever changing environmental surroundings. Children thereby gain a large amount of sensory input, but may have little opportunity to integrate the context of their different sensory experiences and exercise their own level of understanding and willed organisation of their intellectual application to a given situation.

Much of children's play activity today is occupational rather than educational aspect of 'living and learning'. Occupational activities are focussed on, and dominated by, the reception of sensory stimulus described above as 1. Sensory Assimilation. The child's physical activity is either minimal or directly related to the repetition or the prolonging of a specific structure of sensory experience. Dominating adult schedules, speeds of activity and verbal communication, can present a sensory overload that subsequently prevents the child's own interactive responses, appropriate behaviour and intellectual understanding.

Children, by nature need to be physically active; when their own ability to self-direct is weak, they establish a repertoire of occupational responses. This style of interaction provides opportunity to physically respond when overwhelmed by prolonged or strong sensory stimulation. For example the young child watching TV may suck a blanket or manipulate a cuddly toy, older children play on computer games that require fast repetitive button pushing movements as directed on the computer screen. The author describes these predominantly receptive sensory occupations as entertainment. Entertainment here describes situations that hold our focus in the first level of learning: sensory stimulus. (1)

Entertaining activities support:-

> ➢ passive behaviour;
> ➢ an externally specified repertoire of action;
> ➢ automated reactions;
> ➢ primitive responses to environmental stimulus.

Screen entertainment provides a constant provision of visual stimulus that has no physical connection with the viewer's personal and present reality. The earliest responses to visual information are acknowledged unconsciously and the young child either ignores them or reacts as if the visual information is presenting a potentially unsafe or even dangerous circumstance. A child who is overwhelmed by a specific sensory perceptual experience may become stressed and therefor present a primal adrenaline based response of defensive/aggressive reaction. Therefore, some screen entertainment may also trigger primal adrenalin responses associated with self-protection and personal safety. Prolonged periods of static viewing may neutralise this primal response and thereby disrupt the young child's ability to develop a realistic interpretation of visual information.

The strong visual stimulus may also trigger the child's primal visual alert system. This starts as a visual perception of light and shadows which provides the young infant an awareness of movements and actions as they happen around them. The infant's undeveloped visual perceptual skills and limited understanding of visual information can leave them feeling vulnerable and potentially unsafe. When feeling unsafe we automatically relate to all areas of incoming stimulus from a disposition of high alert and an associated passive inactive disposition. This high alert state of arousal may be so dominant that natural play and learning are suppressed in favour of safety and personal protection.

The strong auditory stimulus that normally accompanies screen entertainment may similarly trigger defensive and personal safety issues as priority and thereby inhibit normal development of auditory perceptual skills and understanding of auditory sensory information received within the context of one's personal reality.

Styles of Entertainment Seen Today:-

- ○ Television, back ground TV, music or radio programmes.
- ○ Repetitively reactive man-made toys and uniform building blocks which minimises the creative potential due to structural formality and pictures of predetermined designs.

- ○ Food stimulants found in junk food (artificial colourings flavourings and preservatives, sugary sweets, chocolate, coffee and peppermint, alcohol.
- ○ Over stimulating new and exciting environments that create abnormally high adrenalin levels for abnormally long periods and disrupt normal healthy sleep patterns.
- ○ Libertarianism, *I* can do anything *I* want, and *you* can do anything *you* want.
- ○ Rigid routines, mechanical or theatrical styles of response that exclude authenticity.
- ○ When the adult replaces a 'don't know' response with a 'yes', or the 'I am sorry I can't let you do that' response with 'it's OK I'll pretend it isn't happening.'
- ○ When verbal communication is overwhelming the child's free expression and movements and/or physical punishment is so intense it dominates over the child's self-directed play responses.
- ○ Adult initiated/motivated/enforced apprenticeship into clubs and classes, e.g. ballet or boxing. [Only when attendance is genuinely child motivated and appropriate to the child's ability, personality, age and development, will the child develop the genuine engagement, empathy and interest related to meaningful learning.]
- ○ Adult entertainment: adult social events, cinema, theatre, dining out etc.

Addiction: an obsessional desire for an *internal response* to a specific *external* (environmental) sensory stimulus.

Types of Addiction Chart

Internal and the external conditions commonly related to specific types of addiction.

External sensory stimulus	Internal response
Cane sugar and glucose	Desire to feel a sweet taste, like mother's milk, and the accompanying 'sugar high'
Alcohol	Carefree lack of responsibility for one's self and a desire to give up on life. Life isn't worth living too much pain and not enough joy.
Pornography	Desire to feel the exhilaration of sexual arousal.
Excessive and dangerous levels of excitement and recreational behaviour.	Desire to feel the exhilaration and extra physical strength caused by high adrenaline levels in the blood.
Recreational drugs	A desire to escape from reality and personal responsibility for one's own survival out in the world working for basic survival. Lack of faith and trust in one's ability to do well as an independent free adult.
Smoking	Initially this is motivated by a desire to feel the sucking mouth movements similar to those of the baby receiving milk from a bottle or the breast. Later the smoking may become an antidote to the suckling reflex. As an addictive compensatory behaviour smoking can become required to relieve the body of nervous stress by supplementing a quick nicotine fix for the nerve cells.

Fearful experiences during the years of growing independence and conscious maturity can disrupt our development of confidence and well-being. From birth to adulthood traumatic emotional disturbance related to issues of safety, separation, isolation or exclusion can disturb the way we meet our development of consciousness. The development through each stage of consciousness is dependent upon the quality of success in the previous stages. Thus emotional disruptions and anti-social behaviours that have adversely influenced one level of development will disrupt subsequent levels of development. Within the context of our dependence upon others for care and safety the development of consciousness becomes vulnerable to stress and emotional disturbance. Without a predominance of trust, love and care survival issues can override our potential development of consciousness. Natural and sweetly spiritual environments, as well as association with mature adults who have established higher consciousness, may aid and repair a person's development of consciousness.

Every individual has a unique perception of the environment and potential dangers are met from the person's personal perspective and worldly understanding. The diagram below illustrates a natural progression of responses to seen or unseen levels of danger.

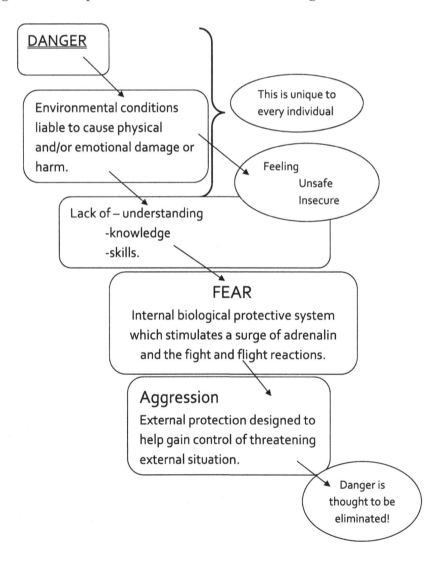

Those who do not develop beyond the primal survival state of stimulus-response remain predominantly influenced by a primitive survival perspective. From this disposition the environment is received as either

a comforting pleasure
or a disturbing threat of discomfort or danger.

At its best this primal disposition develops as a growing desire to obtain environmental sensory pleasures alongside a growing dependence upon repetitive behaviour and rigid routines. This style of ritualistic and predictable behaviour wants a <u>simplistic and controllable interaction</u> with the environment. We see this type of development supported today by the man-made toy industry, media entertainment and technological communication.

A disposition focused upon primal survival responses can encourage development of different forms of hypersensitivity, learning difficulty, addiction, imaginary fears and phobias, illogical thinking and abstract perspectives of reality. When abstract thought processes dominate over a sense of consequence and compassion, anti-social behaviour may develop into lying, stealing and abusive behaviour. When interactive behaviour is directed by the abstract imaginative aspects of thinking there are little or no boundaries of practical logic or social conscience. Later in life, survival responses can establish: victim mentalities, suppression of free will through extreme forms of indoctrination and oppression, psychotic behaviour, and an ever escalating desire to control others, and ultimately destruction of life.

When inner feelings related to survival passions and fears motivate interaction with the environment, <u>all</u> incoming stimuli is perceived as important. All incoming sensory information is received from a survival perspective of needs and safety. A sense of wellbeing is essential if some of the incoming environmental stimulus is to be turned down or even ignored. Thus informal and spontaneous play remains undeveloped; because play and associated social interaction are not related to immediate issues of survival. Indeed play and intimate social interaction is dependent upon relaxed and feelings of safety and wellbeing. Indiscriminate multi-sensory levels of alertness are key to the baby's and young child's daily survival.

> *Love, freedom and safety,*
>
> The foundations for movement.
>
> Movement - The Foundations for Play,
>
> Play - Foundations for Learning.
>
> Learning - Foundations for Intelligence
>
> Intelligence - Foundations for Personal Empowerment
>
> Empowerment - Foundations for Heart-full Living
>
> Heart-full Living - Foundations for the Engagement of the soul.
>
> Engagement of the Soul – Revival of Higher Consciousness
>
> Higher Consciousness - Foundations for Communion with God
>
> Communion with God – The Supreme source of Love and Light
>
> Love and Light – Living the Dream of Heaven on Earth
>
> (From *The Tides of Time* by Helena Eastwood)

Human Development Beyond the **Responder** into the **Director**.

Throughout childhood the young child would normally develop a growing ability to move from 'being the *responder*' into action as 'the *director*'. As self-directed behaviour is established, the child gains the ability to influence the environment according to his own needs and wishes. His *willed* responses thereby become motivated by his own inner directives and the influence of external sensory stimulus becomes attuned to the individual's consciously organised expression of choice.

Choices can be helpful because:-

a. They can direct the child into a voluntary activity of conscious thinking.
b. They can give control to the adults who are organizing the choices and conditions the child must accept with each respective choice
   E.g. 'You can choose to play something that does not disturb the other children or you can play your boisterous game in the garden'.
c. Every set of choices can be tailored to suit individual circumstances and situations accommodating different dispositions, changing circumstances and a wide variety of practicalities.
d. Choices give children a positive alternative to inciting their own changes through disruptive/anti-social behaviour.
e. Choices encourage children to be flexible.

  f. Choices encourage children to organize activities that will support their own inner motivations and purpose.

  g. Choices simplify situations and help children find their way through complex circumstances that may be too hard for them to intellectually accommodate.

Through play the young child explores and learns skills. This *willed manipulation* of the environment supports learning to integrate a *'creative'* application into living and learning.

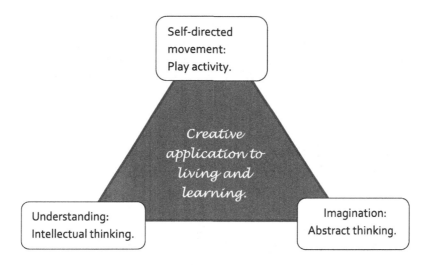

As the child develops, the three aspects A), B), and C), unite and empower the development of voluntary thinking and self-directed exploration through play. Play is naturally prerequisite to the development of a creative application to living and learning

Those children on the autism spectrum will illustrate a notable emphasis on repetitive and copied behaviour, along with a notable absence of self-directed play and creative endeavour. Play embodies personalised directorship over aspects of the environment. For the autistic child, play may be predisposed by their focus upon survival orientated behaviour. Even when the level of physical care is excellent, the autistic child may habitually remain the respondent, searching all sensory information for environmental aspects related to personal survival and safety.

Development of Intellectual Thinking

The development of intellectual thinking is based on structural or concrete understanding, logical assessment and interactive behaviour. This intellectual development moves the child from <u>respondent</u> into a <u>director</u> role over his environmental experiences. Thus the child's initial desire for <u>survival related sensory comforts and entertainments</u> are gradually superseded by his individual <u>desire to organise, structure and influence</u> his external environment. He expresses his unique nature through exploration, experimentation and an enthusiasm for creative expression.

Thus instead of the environmental energies stimulating the child (A) the child influences the environment (B) as shown in the diagrams below.

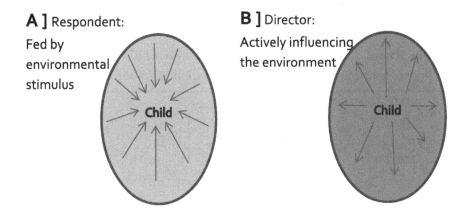

A] Respondent: Fed by environmental stimulus

B] Director: Actively influencing the environment

Normally a child's initial (**A**) dependence upon the sensory environment reverses as the child develops consciously organised interaction through movement and play. Movement and self-directed learning promote the child's ability to energetically influence the environment according to his own endeavour and will; whereby living and learning help the child to direct his own influence upon the surrounding environment (**B**).

Our natural desire to reverse this energy flow from that of (**A**) to that of (**B**), is what gives our human life form superiority over other forms of life. This reversal of energy flow enables us to consciously organise a command over the worldly environment. This ability to influence the environment is initially seen as interactive play, and later develops into creative expression and finally manifests as inventive manipulation using social interaction and/or structural mechanisms. Inventive manipulation is seen in the positive as sharing, caring, parenting, and humanitarian service, and at its best God consciousness. A consciously mature human is able to integrate both an inward flowing energy sensory stimulus (A) and actively influence the environment (B) in accordance with Highest Good – incorporating his own best interest with others, and that of the earth planet and all life that dwells upon it.

When a person remains predominantly under the influence of primitive stimulus-response behaviour, personal survival modes may be expressed through negative perspectives of fear and control. This may ultimately be seen as greed, jealousy, bullying, aggression, rivalry, indoctrination and oppression, dictatorship, military wars and other forms of *worldly* destruction.

Those who do not notably develop beyond the primal survival state of stimulus-response (A) remain predominantly influenced by environmental stimulus from a purely personal and self-motivated perspective. The young and consciously immature person is predominantly influenced by their external environment (A) and understanding is limited to their own experience. This is seen as a growing development of dependence upon others, lack of empathy, hypersensitivity, sensory pleasure seeking, repetitive and ritualistic behaviour and entertainment seeking life styles. This perspective in the longer term can be seen as one of primitive fears, abstract illogical fear-based thinking, victim mentalities, phobias and psychosis. Any fear based disposition escalates into a desire to control others and indeed anything seen as unpredictable/uncontrollable. Thus the person who has not developed their own self-direct, ultimately works to supress the freedom of others which in turn destroys the quality of life for both themselves and those they manage to intimidate.

Autism is present when the reversal of energy flow from that of (A) to (B) is supressed or disrupted. This inhibiting influence may cause the young child, adolescent or adult to remain predominantly and unpredictably under the influence of environmental stimulus and responses related to personal issues of survival.

Autism prevents the development of consciously organised responses (B) and creative play due to a restricted relationship with reality and environmental experiences (A). The absence of an outgoing energy flow (B) adversely affects the development of concrete thinking with the brain.

Structural interaction with our environment is directly related to the person's <u>sense of safety</u> and subsequent development of play and social interaction. When the normal aspects of living and learning are inhibited the more the brain compensates with an emphasis on abstract thinking. The abstract thinking capacity of the brain is influenced by the imagination and 'dream' qualities of unconsciously organised mental activity. The abstract mind does not relate directly to reality or environmental experience beyond that of everyday aspects of survival.

In contrast to this, our concrete thinking skills are directly associated with our conscious view of reality and our personal development of conceptual understanding and social conscience. When our concrete thinking is compromised, our abstract thinking inevitably grows more dominant. In this way the ever active mind fills in the spaces of time. Just as we dream when the body is resting and the mind is awake, we are also inclined to engage in abstract thinking activity when the body is not engaged in activity associated with positive living and constructive learning. For example for most people watching TV stimulates abstract thinking while the body remains passively resting and free from any conscious responsibility. Computer games occupy the mind and body in predominantly unconsciously organised 'stimulus-response' activity which encourages primal brain activity, and imaginative thinking. This releases the player from self-directed living and learning.

Most typically autistic behaviour, especially that seen in young children, imitates the safety of womb-like experiences: i.e. gentle rocking, hands over ears to muffle reception of environmental sounds, repetitive banging imitating the sound of the mother's heartbeat, and obsessional desires for ongoing repetition of certain sounds or experiences in order to acquire feelings of comfort and safety.

We can question whether a womb like association with safety, is recreated as a comforting experience within an autistic person's repetitive behaviours. This association with safety may be present as some form of subconscious comforter. For example one boy was obsessed with coaches, if he saw a coach he would do anything he could to sit on the coach and would refuse to get off even when the coach was stationary. For him the coach may represent travelling in safety within a set internal environment and accompanying comfort of womb like engine noises. Similarly some babies are comforted by a ride in the car or push chair.

Autism may be a survival mechanism designed to establish a self-restricted low level of brain activity essentially designed as a management strategy for everyday living in an over stimulating environment.

Every individual has different strengths and weaknesses. Those with learning difficulties and associated brain damage will inevitably find it harder to experience a safe environment that encourages positive living and learning experiences. The author has found that when a child moves beyond their normal autistic behaviour the child often illustrates specific learning difficulties, such as auditory integration disorder, dysphasia, dyspraxia, visual perceptual disorders, and proprioceptive disorders. Lack of safety can be related to either:-inner stress e.g. overwhelmingly sensory experiences, sensory perceptual disability and specific learning difficulties; or external stress e.g. physical confinement– buggies, car seats, indoor lifestyles, classrooms, etc.

The birth process itself may include traumatic survival issues. Some children may experience their 'normal' birth as a survival challenge. Those who have experienced any form of traumatic potentially life threatening experience, may be triggered by 'normal' experiences into fear based abnormal and defensive behaviour. For example, the child who hides in the curtains when visitors arrive or the girl who spent her school day under the teachers desk acting like a dog or the child that bites the hand that is extended in kindness or the child that loudly screeches and screams without any obvious reason or provocation.

Sensory Focus

It is generally helpful to develop an ability to tune into chosen stimulus while at the same time turning down or even turning off the reception of unwanted stimulus that would otherwise disrupt one's chosen focus. Those described with sensory overwhelm, often associated with the Autistic spectrum, appear to use physical withdrawal, repetitive actions, specialised movements and specific vocal sounds to appease their experiences of sensory overload. It is thought that the autistic person puts his hands over his ears, or hides in a small enclosed space, or eats only one type of food at a time, as an attempt to cut down stimulus receptivity. Does autism represent a person who cannot select one sensory input over others and/or consciously organise the brains ability to integrate different modes of sensory information? Certainly these two difficulties can be experienced by everyone when we encounter a particularly challenging environment. Also, the autistic person may be challenged by hypersensitivity, such that ordinary levels of sensory stimulus are received as overwhelmingly strong and intense levels of sensory input. The difference between hypersensitivity and an inability to integrate a multi-sensory experience, may be key issues for those on the autism spectrum. It has been suggested that diet can adversely affect our ability to successfully manage stress associated with heightened sensitivity, hyperactivity and overwhelming levels of stimulus.

Common Causes Related to Emotional and Physical Over-whelm:-

1. Unable to shut out unwanted stimulus.
2. Too much unfamiliar or overbearing social interaction.
   E.g. Being in close proximity with people I don't know or feel uncomfortable with.
3. Transition:-
   - Unable to meet the change/s in circumstances.
   - Loss of supporting companionship- mother, father, sibling, teacher, friend, familiar companions (child, adult or pet!) and/or environment.
   - Unable to accommodate invading stimulus. For example:-
   - Adult commentary, "Oh what a wonderful castle do you see how that drawbridge is going up?"
   - Unwanted companionship, "Johnny is coming to paint with you."
   - Being told to do something different, "It is time to tidy up for lunch now."
   - Postponement, "No you can't have a piece of this cake until Aunty comes to tea tomorrow."
4. Unable to keep appropriate body temperature, i.e. too hot or too cold or too changeable.
5. Boredom (lack of self-direct): -
   - Unable to motivate engagement in activity.
   - Unable to respond naturally.
   - Unable to relate to the environment in a way that feels right or is requested of me.

The Autism spectrum could be considered a predominance of a reflective relationship with the environment. The dominance of copied repetitive forms of behaviour excludes the person from successful development of self-directed interaction and personal independence.

The empowering aspects of the creative life force are subject to an appropriate balance and interaction between the two principles of life

   - that of yielding - like the flow of water
   - and controlling - like a mountain that blocks the way ahead.

Abstract Imagination & **CONCRETE WILL** These two principles could be described as the alpha and omega of life itself. In the diagram below they are defined as *abstract* imagination and **CONCRETE** will, and associated with different aspects of our everyday thinking and living.

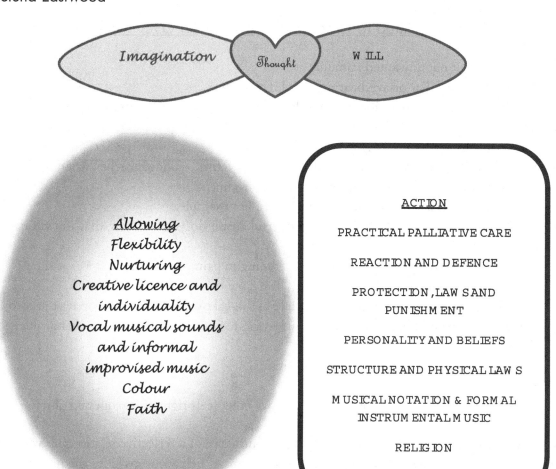

Bach Flower Remedies

Each Bach flower remedy is noted for the negative aspects that it can transform into a positive disposition. For example: Chestnut is noted as a remedy for failure to learn from past mistakes and when taken it is noted for bringing about a positive ability to gain knowledge and positive learning experience. [Dictionary of the Bach Flower Remedies –Positive and negative aspects by T.W.Hyne Jones]

If everyone had Dr Bach's understanding we all may accept our faults without judgement, in the knowledge that they are only the prickly outer casing that over protectively withholds our best qualities. As confidence is gained a safer place is found in which we can flourish and find our true potential.

The author perceives autism as a symptom of unseen learning difficulties and /or emotional trauma. Autism is the way by which the children attempt to *survive*, as opposed to *thrive* in an environment that fails to provide them with the quality of safely and encouragement they need. However, this shutting down mechanism inhibits natural play and learning activities and triggers primitive survival instincts that may stimulate adverse behaviour; for example one young child hide under the kitchen table when in a house fire; or a scared child may scream and run and wave their arms defensively when a strange dog comes too near.

> Therefore unsafe environmental experience can trigger behaviour related to either withdrawal or fight and flight. Autism gives the child the time and space to separate themselves from potentially stressful environmental experience. Thus autism could be an important safety system that relieves the child from extreme reactions of either withdrawal and shut down, or fight and flight behaviour. Neither of these forms of behaviour provides an opportunity to pause and thereby organise an intelligent choice of behaviour. Indeed the fight and flight response is almost always the subconscious motivator of all 'Disruptive and Anti-social behaviour'

Disruptions to our original loving nature are based on 'fear of not being loved, nurtured and cared for' and these fears are expressed as either Mistrust *passive withdrawal* or Control *assertive action/reaction*:-

Mistrust	Control
Reservation	Domination
Unnatural limitations within	Possessiveness and jealousy
social interaction, intimate sharing	Excessive independence
and caring exchanges.	Fixed on doing things their own way.
Indifference to others feelings.	Intolerance
Fear based attitude and a	Desire to chastise, punish,
pessimistic outlook.	discipline, and/or retaliate.
Disrespect	Demands for physical affection,
Avoidance of physical intimacy	and use of emotional blackmail.
Criticism and grief	Blame and anger

It has been recorded that some communities do not have any experience of autism. These communities usually live in remote areas of the world where they live a notably peaceful and natural life-style. Their gentle and loving style of community is one of working together to meet the daily needs. Each individual is compassionately appreciated according to their own individual personality, interests and abilities. Social and creative expression is shared through working together, dance, play, story and music. The children are brought up within the community lifestyle and they are not sent to school but educated through their living and learning as an individual that is loved and cared for as an important member of the community.

One of the positive aspects found in these simple stress free community life styles could be described as a naturally safe environment; where sharing and caring has a strong affinity with the therapeutic qualities presented in the work of the Option Institute USA and the 'Special

Time' play therapy as taught by the late Rachael Pinney. These two alternative approaches to overcoming autism and other forms of disrupted social development are based on <u>The philosophy of *Special Time:-*</u>

- o   Moments of heart-full soul spirit sharing
- o   Trusting and appreciating the other persons chosen actions and interactions.
- o   Gentle moment by moment responses of genuine care and authenticity.
- o   Taking time out to *explore, feel, reflect and listen* without any judgement and free from any preconceived agenda.
- o   Nurturing our emotional disposition rather than goals or levels of achievement.
- o   Resting our physical body from worldly demands and practical work.
     (These and other recommendations are described in detail in the section titled 'What to do?'

The Amish communities in the USA noted that recently autism has appeared in their children. They tried to identify what changed could have caused them to now experience this condition which they had not had in their communities before. The only change that they could identify was that childhood vaccination had now been brought into their communities due to pressure from the State authorities. This example illustrates the depth of complexity that, present-day, parents are faced with when trying to create a safe environment for their children. Philip Day in his book Health Wars lists the concoction of additional 'substances' presented within the vaccine serums as well as the know side effects. Alternatively, for some children the physical stress and pain of receiving a vaccine injection may in itself trigger survival fears that undermine their trust in their parents and their daily environment as 'safe'.

Present day data suggests that the number of children diagnosed with autism is notably increasing. It may also be that adults diagnosed with mental illness and psychosis may be on the autism spectrum.

The escalating presence of autism in our world today may be due to different biological and environmental factors such as:-

- o   Medical drugs administered to mothers and babies during and after birth.
- o   Enforced regimes of vaccination.
- o   Adult addiction especially when it adversely affects the performance of parents and childcare workers.
- o   Auditory noise pollution and visual over-stimulation.
- o   Stressful, unnatural and restrictive environments. For example baby buggies and car seats, indoor life-styles, (confinement to a room in the home or classroom or shops, cafés etc.)

The following chart describes the three choices presented within our human levels of consciousness. It was originally put together to help adult carers recognise that avoiding negative survival responses could be achieved in two stages;

❖ Firstly cancelling the primitive survival responses by moving into a neutral management response,

❖ then positive responses both inner and outer can come forward as a chosen endeavour and positive acknowledgement of responsibility.

Success	Management	Survival
POSITIVE	Neutral	~~NEGATIVE~~
Amusing, inspiring, motivational.	Experiential, entertaining	Unstimulating, boring, Ineffective
Passionate, engaging	Pause and stillness; reflective witnessing.	Disconnected, rejected, isolated.
Personal Expression	Repetition	Echolalia
Original	Imitative	Copy, reproduction
Receptivity	Awareness	Denial
Discerning	Perceiving	Ignoring

Baby Business

Even before birth, the developing baby may show a response to external stimulus. Babies in the womb have been shown to be responsive to music and to suck their own thumb or foot. These responses are stimulated by their surrounding environment; even if it is their own thumb co-incidentally touching their cheek or mouth to stimulate the pre-birth suckling reflex. Thus the baby in the womb is *responding* to an external stimulus.

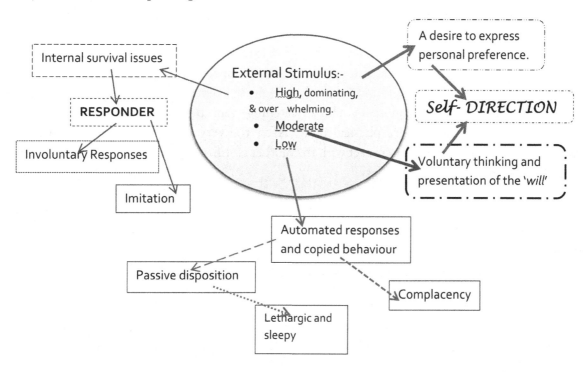

After birth the child has the opportunity to respond to an ever growing external environment that offers an ever expanding complexity of external stimulus. The early responses to environmental stimulus fall into two categories:

A) Withdrawal – the child shuts down, withdrawing into a curled foetal like position [For example a mother knows of the withdrawal response when she is trying to feed or dress a stressful child.]

B) Unpremeditated automatic or instinctive responses, e.g. the child may suck or chew, kick or bite, gurgle, cry or scream. [For example a mother experiences the baby kicking in the womb and later the suckling response to her breast.]

Thus, in accordance with the experiences that providence provides, the baby's earliest subconsciously organised reactions, such as the suckling and grasp reaction, motivate the development of consciously organised responses. Now the baby's inner desires to gain environmental pleasures such as food, warmth and entertainment, motivate the baby to develop consciously directed responses to external stimuli. [For example even very young babies will grasp a soft toy or a blanket as a comforter, or grasp a rattle and wave the arm about in order to make sounds. Bottle fed babies can quickly learn to take hold of the bottle and bring it to their mouth for the milk.]

The ability to express a personal influence upon the external environment, is initially developed through *interactive play*; which supports the development of social interaction and creative expression. Finally as adults we express our influence as inventive manipulation. This may evolve, from a positive perspective, into sharing, caring and parenting, humanitarian service and God consciousness. However, when an adult remains adversely, under the influence of the environment this inventive manipulation may develop as fear based, negative disposition, expressed as aggression, bulling, military domination, wars and other worldly issues of destruction.

In the womb, the maternal mother gives the baby a constant supply of oxygen, food and warmth. The baby experiences his/her life through a constant connection with the mother's physical body i.e. her external movement and internal biological structure and processes. Within any pregnancy separation from the mother is a life threatening event. Being born is the first experience of separation from the mother's physical body. After the very first experience of separation experienced at birth, direct body contact with the mother is still associated with the life sustaining issues of nutrition, warmth and safety.

After the baby is born, the mother instinctively replicates the previous womb connection by carrying the baby on her body. Carrying the baby resolves issues related to the physical separation of birth as well as issues of warmth and safety. The baby's ability to suckle and cry, address the need for life sustaining nutritional provision.

Fortunately, babies need to sleep a lot and sleeping during the day eventually initiates an experience of sleeping during the day in a space separate from the mother's body. This can help the baby to dissolve the survival instincts for warmth and safety from the physical mother-baby connection.

Some parents try to perpetuate this mother baby connection with artificial compensatory comforters such as:-

- Walking about whilst rocking the baby to sleep.
- Offering breast milk to induce sleep. Sadly this easy and highly effective option will only induce a shallow sleep pattern and the baby is unlikely to sleep for long. This is because initially the new born baby needs to breast feed at least every three hours in order to maintain good health and growth. If breast feeding *could* successfully induce a deeper sleep pattern, new born babies would be at risk of missing important feeds required to establish good healthy growth.
- In the past, cradles and prams and rocking chairs were made specifically to produce an imitation of the sensory womb experience when the baby is separate from the mothers physical body. Today's parents may rock and/or walk a baby in a buggy or drive them out in a car seat in order to persuade the baby to sleep.

Sadly these artificial props can fail to support a naturally beneficial relationship with sleep related issues. Rather than risk sleep deprivation, some mothers sleep with their child until the child falls asleep and all night if that avoids being woken in the night. Help from father and extended family members can help the baby to establish an acceptance of sleeping away from the mother's body.

Some families use fictional 'screen entertainment' to provide passive childcare for babies and young children. However, this does not help the child to attain the levels of activity required for healthy levels of tiredness and subsequent sleep. Screen entertainment may be a major factor for children with sleep problems; associated lack of quality sleep, interactive body movement and physical activity are all factors that can adversely affect the child's development of self-directed learning. The author believes that lack of self-directed learning is key to the autism spectrum and sleep problems, and thereby presents that screen entertainment is obviously adverse to any child's natural ability to gain required amounts of sleep and growing confidence in themselves and their environment.

Healthy levels of interactive daily activity help every child to fall asleep. Young children may need to sleep during the day. This establishes an ability to sleep in a place without ongoing physical contact with another person. This is the first developmental marker of growing up as an individual person with a unique life journey.

Once going to sleep for the night without mother's or another person's body contact has been accepted, further developmental stages can be established successfully. For example, successful weaning and independent play are unlikely to go well if an acceptance of independent sleeping has not been established successfully.

> Children and adults can have their personal potential adversely limited by the retention of one or more infant pre-birth reflexes. Every parent is going to be challenged by the developmental limitations caused by a child with retained infant reflexes.

Helena Eastwood

The caring adult responses of many parents of today may fail to support the releasing of a retained infant reflex or indeed the adult caring responses may perpetuate and reinforce the early infant reflexes. For example when a child drops their dummy/baby bottle/comforter the parent quickly picks it up.... Their reasons are both caring and practical:-

> To resolve stress caused by the loss of the comfort item.
> To prevent the item from being lost or accidentally left behind.
> To prevent later periods of unresolved distress when it is needed as a comforter but cannot be found.
> To prevent it getting dirty and harbouring germs.
> To get it washed and free from unhealthy germs. [In terms of hygiene the safest place for the dummy is in the child's mouth and parents may resort to a habitual response that ensures that is where it stays.]

Thus the parent is reinforcing the child's suckling reflex by ensuring the comforter is constantly in use or at least easily available. The parent's ardent responses prevent the child from experiencing situations that would naturally prevent continual stimulation and offer an opportunity to release from the pre-birth suckling reflex. Indeed the adults' quick and efficient responses ensure that the child him/herself has no experience of inadvertently releasing the suckling reflex because the comfort object has been dropped out of reach or lost.

The wise parent will not necessarily return the dropped dummy. On some occasions the dropped dummy may be safely placed out of reach in a place of safe keeping i.e. a handbag or cupboard.

Another situation very similar to the dummy scenario is seen in relation to helping children sleep. A mother may sleep with the child until the child falls asleep because the child goes to sleep quicker and she also can get a rest. However, in order to gain the confidence to fall asleep on their own a child needs to experience the confidence and pleasure associated with trusting a safe loving environment and surrendering into a natural and healthy sleep.

Normally a baby's maternal mother has facilitated the creation and sustenance required after conception through to the weaning stage. Therefore, every baby is dependent upon either the natural mother for breast feeding or a substitute mother such as a wet nurse or person/persons who organises an alternative bottle feeding routine. The pre-birth suckling reflex would normally facilitate feeding until the weaning process has been successfully established and eating of solid foods inevitably replaces the 'baby' suckling activity.

Occasionally a baby has successfully survived alone in a wild natural environment because a wild animal has provided the basic needs of milk, warmth and safety and the wild child has weaned itself.

The three main areas that illustrate successful development from babyhood into an independent individual

Natural development takes us from babyhood into a lifestyle that can survive without a dependence on the maternal mother's care.

The author presents that the rise in autism may be the result of over stimulating environments and over-protective parenting focused around three essential stages of independence normally acquired during babyhood. The author describes these fundamental issues of personal independence as 'Baby Business'. All three initial stages of personal independence are normally established prior to self-directed learning.

There are three main issues that illustrate three essential developmental stages that establish our unique relationship with self-directed play and learning:-

1. **Separation from direct contact with the mother's physical body while awake.**
   The new born baby's greatest need from the mother is 'warmth'. Separating from the mother's physical body encourages the development of movement and mobility both of which are essential to the development of self-regulated temperature.

2. **Separation from direct contact with the mother's physical body, before, during and after sleep.**
   Sleep can only occur when the infant has obtained a suitable level of nutrition and a constant optimum body temperature has been established and maintained prior to entering sleep.

3. **Weaning, separation from one's mother's breast (or a bottle) as the only or primary source of nutritional food.**
   Weaning the infant develops their ability to eat solid foods and thereby experience a separation from direct contact with the mother for breast (or bottled milk) as the main source of food and required nutrition.

The main difference from the babies perspective is that breast and bottle feeding is always brought to the child; all the child has to do is respond with the primitive suckling reflex. However, the weaning process moves the child on from being a passive receiver and responder into active self-directed participation. The child explores the choices of where, when, and how, they receive and respond to any potential food and nourishment from their own self-directed activity. The weaning process is thereby the first motivational calling that initiates the child as an individual to direct positive responses in order to attain essential nourishment from food and drink. When working with severely autistic children, food and drink can be essential motivators for the beginning of self-directed activity within a social structure of related boundaries; i.e. we are all going to eat together at the table; and a direct relationship with environmental consequences i.e. the food and the cooker may be too hot, if the food falls on the floor it may get dirty, we need to eat soup with a spoon food may need to be cut into mouth size pieces etc.

Successful <u>acceptance and completion</u> of the above developmental issues (1-2 and 3)-are essential to the infant's ability to release infant reflexes and go on to develop self-directed movement and associated learning experience. The author believes that the releasing of infant reflexes and the development of self-directed activity is encouraged or discouraged by the way parents and the infant relate to these three initial issues of independence.

It is hard to give guidance to parents on how to successfully scaffold these issues of separation, sleeping and weaning from an individual child's empowerment perspective. Every person and situation is unique to each individual family. Before engaging with help from other adults, each family needs to assess their own situation and their own feelings as best they can. However, the developmental order is not negotiable because separation from the mother is an ongoing element of all areas of 'Live, Love, Learn' empowerment and self-directed activity.

> The conditions that are supportive to entering a healthy period of sleep are the same for babies, children and adults. The differences in each person's willingness to surrender into a period of sleep are always linked to the person's personal confidence to trust that they can remain safe and comfortable <u>during</u> sleep and <u>upon waking.</u>

Some adults may still be struggling to find an acceptable way through the primary mother-child separation issues and compensatory behaviours can become very adverse to their wellbeing. In adult life, these compensatory behaviours can include food disorders, addictions, obsessional compulsive behaviours often associated with Asperger's autism. Sadly, the intimate male to female dynamics of physical desire and physical gratification between mother and son can be very highly charged. Adolescent boys, who have not fully accepted one or more of the three early stages of mother-child separation, are likely to look for a female partner who will reinstate a model of mother child co-dependence in relation to food, sleeping together and intimate body contact. Inevitably his female partner will fail to provide the desired level of mother comforts and the man's profound disappointment can be expressed as an adult level of anger and abuse.

When the initial three issues of separation for weaning, sleep and independence remain unresolved/unaccepted by the boy, the man may struggle with ongoing lack of confidence and resentments. He may struggle to overcome 'Going it alone' adult responsibilities throughout his life and feel that for him 'love is not enough.......'

Similarly any adult may have their personal potential severely affected by the retention of pre-birth reflexes which adversely affect self-directed learning and creative expression.

Peter Blythe pioneered a therapy that successfully releases a person from the unnatural retention of pre-birth reflexes. Peter's partner Sally Goddard Blythe has written books to help teachers and parents understand this therapeutic approach presented at The *Institute for Neuro-Physiological Psychology in* Chester. 'The Well Balanced Child' and 'Reflexes, Learning and behaviour'.

[The Eastwood 'Simple Rocking Method' also works as a therapy that helps children and adults to release retained pre-birth reflexes and reinstate the natural potential for neuro-physiological functions associated with self-directed movement during early childhood development.]

Baby Business

The author describes Primary baby developmental as the following 1-2-3

1. **Sleeping**   To initiate independent sleeping - a period of sleep without body contact or 'substitute 'comforter'. without mother's body contact or 'comforter' object such as a specific blanket, soft toy, dummy or baby bottle - and successfully sustain optimum length and depth of sleep required for wellbeing, growth and development.
2. **Feeding**   To wean Breast/bottle feeding the baby off of suckling sources of nutrition and on to establish independent feeding; solid foods and drinking from a beaker.
3. **Independent play**   To establish happily playing alone with mother in close proximity and regular mother baby interaction. Independent, self-directed play and adventuring, exploring and experimental play. i.e. without mother, or a mother substitute, necessarily having to facilitate nearby as an active or passive supporter.

The three issues listed above are primary elements that mark the baby's development from babyhood (baby business) into an individual and personalised journey towards independence. The above developmental markers are presented in their consecutive natural order. Any unnatural separation from the birth mother during early infancy can jeopardise how well a child accepts and progresses within the three baby business issues listed above. Also, unnecessary over-protection and unrealistic long term co-dependence can disturb the child's progress; and make the child lack confidence in his/her own progression through these critical stages of personal development and associated mobility and self-directed activity.

An alternative caring adult can successful substitute for a biological mother and thereby support an infant to accept and accommodate the Baby Business issues from a positive and nurturing 'Live, Love, Learn' perspective.

How well each individual child accepts the Baby Business will be influenced by the child's personality and childhood experiences; For example:-

Sleep: Stage 1 Surrendering into sleep

A required level of relaxation is essential before going to sleep. This level of holistic relaxation can only be attained when a *safe, warm, familiar sleeping place* is established. For example when the immediate environment is suitably quiet

The young child's startle reflex and light reflex is notably more sensitive than that of most adults. When children are asleep, their primal alert systems are automatically turned up to maximum in order to give maximum protection. Therefore what is scary to the child may not be thought of as scary by the adult. Environmental conditions that trigger the child's startle reflex and/or raise their adrenaline levels will prevent the required relaxation before sleep and during a normal sleep pattern. All tired children will ultimately fall asleep but the quality and duration of any sleep will be directed by external environmental stimulus

- when sleep is initiated
- <u>and</u> during the sleeping period.

In the past an ideal aid to infant relaxation was mother singing nursery rhymes, humming and/ or rocking in a chair. These activities reassured the infant that it is a safe time to go to sleep and that mother is close.

Anxiety within the mother can disturb a sleeping infant /young child ......even if the mother's anxiety is directly related to her desire to help the child sleep well.

Ideal conditions may include candle or a night light instead of electric lighting; no unpredictable or unfamiliar electronic noises; no loud bangs, noises or extreme forms of social exchange such as shouting and screaming, swearing and arguing, etc.

Loud unfamiliar sounds can trigger the infants startle reflex and secrete adrenalin into the bloodstream. Electric lighting can trigger the young child's light reflex, even when their eyes are closed.

Sleep: Stage 2. Maintaining an optimum period of sleep

[Optimum sleep and optimum health are known to be directly related one unto the other.]

An optimum quality and duration of sleep can be established when supported by the following conditions:-

The child and adult carer are confident that the environmental is and will remain safe <u>during</u> their sleeping period and <u>upon waking</u>.

The child and adult are confident that they have has access to emergency help if it is required during the more vulnerable sleeping period.

Sounds of the mother's voice remain quiet and gentle

<u>Sleep: Stage 3</u> Awaking from sleep feeling refreshed, relaxed and confident.

All the potential benefits from a good sleep can be undone by circumstances listed below because they <u>undermine the infant's confidence both during and upon waking</u>:-

- <u>Limited mobility</u> which adversely affects the ability to organised comfortable body positions and warmth from bedding and clothing during the sleeping period.
- Limited mobility which inhibits the child's potential to awake and then go off to find the adult carer.
- <u>External physical retrains</u> such as the height of the bed, a cot enclosure, a closed door, baby gate, baggy clothes…which stop the mobile infant from safely finding the adult carer when their company is desired.
- <u>Anxiety</u> related to previous experience that has left the infant without a trusting and caring adult during the sleeping period.
- When upon waking the child has not found the mother or another trusted carer is nearby and available to meet the child's needs; safety, warmth, food and a familiar carer companion.
- Previous unexpected <u>child-mother separation issues</u>.
- When <u>hunger</u> is always or usually the cause of waking and when hunger before, during or upon waking has been exaggerated by abnormal circumstances such as illness, holiday travel, hospital treatment.
- <u>Low body temperature</u> or just a lack of optimum body temperature before, during sleep or upon waking.
- <u>The triggering of the startle reflex</u> before, during or upon waking. This reflex automatically triggers a rush of adrenalin into the bloodstream and associated fight and flight alert levels and responses.
- <u>Primal fears associated with aloneness,</u> when waking without another person within direct physical contact or within close proximity or without a suitably capable and mindful carer. E.g children left in the care of an alcoholic adult or forgetful senior or immature young child or adolescent.
- <u>Physical disturbance</u> caused by another person's physical activity (lights, movements, noise and sounds etc. When we are asleep it is normal to maintain a heightened sensitivity to normal levels of sensory information. It is normal for any person's senses of <u>touch, sound, light, smell</u> to be especially high before during and after sleep. For example music sounds are heard much louder, cooking smells are more disturbing etc. [Thus, the comforts of

sleeping with another person can also be the direct cause of sleep disturbance, before, during and after sleep. Even within a notably loving and caring relationship]

- Awaking in a different environment to the one present upon falling asleep, especially if it is an unknown or adverse environment.

In order to have a good naturally healthy relationship with our requirements for sleep, everyone needs to establish a wealth of positive experience upon awakening e.g. mobility, safety, warmth, access to desired people, places and things.

Further Considerations

Young children need to experience waking up in a safe' comfortable space with mother/main carer nearby and available if there are any problems. This encourages the child to accommodate their own needs according to their own capacity and desires. However, children with environmental confinements, restrictions or mobility difficulties will remain totally dependent on the carer's ability to perceive and respond if they are genuinely feeling an adverse safety issue upon waking. Physical restrictions and mobility issues can hold the carer responsible for the child's relationship with sleep and thereby prevent the child's natural growth of personal confidence and willingness to accept that sleep is related to each individual, rather than an ongoing dependence upon physical contact with the mother/main carer.

Putting a sweetened liquid in a dummy will motivate the retention of the suckling reflex. This can establish an adverse retention of the suckling reflex for an extended period and possibly even into their adult life.

Breast feeding to induce sleep will work, but the breast milk does not initiate an effective deep sleep pattern in the brain. If it did, the new born baby would oversleep and miss the important frequency of regular feeds throughput the day and the night.

As the child gets bigger sleep is naturally induced by physical tiredness that initiates a deeper sleep essential to healthy growth and development.

Similarly the suckling reflex can be unnaturally retained when the sounds and smell of a mother breast feeding a baby sibling overwhelms the young child and disturbs his/her own level of sleep.

The pre-birth 'startle reflex' initiates a burst of adrenaline into the bloodstream. When asleep as a baby or young child this startle reflex is on high alert and that is why it is normal for adults to avoid presenting a strong stimulus when someone, especially a child is sleeping.

Babies have a strong 'Startle Reflex' that is easily triggered by sensory experience whereas adults would normally have subdued their startle reflex such that only exceptional levels of stimulus can trigger the startle reflex and accompanying fight and flight responses.

Different types and strengths of stimulus will not affect everyone in the same way. This is clearly illustrated by adults when their startle reflex is triggered by something that has not affected others in the same situation. For example one child/person may be especially sensitive to sounds within a specified area of their overall hearing range; others may be especially sensitive to unpredictable physical body contact. Strong electric lighting and some medications can also trigger abnormal sensitivity and adrenaline levels during sleep. This is why leaving a light on for a child is averse to their getting a good period of quality sleep. However, candle light and natural light are not likely to trigger an adverse 'alert state of mind'.

Before and sometimes during sleep some children self-impose an inner state of 'high adrenalin' within their body and thereby avoid a deep sleep or falling asleep; even when very tired or even over-tired. A child who is over-tired is generally unable to engage in positive activity and positive social interaction. However, even young children may produce a self-impose 'adrenalin high' using extreme forms of antisocial behaviour e.g. screaming, screeching, taunting, bullying, hitting, biting, hair pulling, sexual stimulation, and actively seeking to be physically cold or uncomfortable. The author considers that this unnaturally high maintenance of adrenaline within the body during the above three aspects of 'Baby business' can be associated with later adverse sleep issues, hyperactivity and abusive behaviour.

High adrenaline levels in the body can be triggered and maintained if the body temperature remains lower than normal for a notable period of time. For example the child who moves around a lot in their sleep may push their bedding off; then their lower body temperature triggers adrenaline and strong movements that will disturb their quality and depth of sleep. Thus the sleeping pattern becomes progressively worse and their adrenalin levels become habitually high. Poor sleep affects the child's day time performance of self-directed play and the three '*baby business*' issues remain unresolved. This can cause developmental disturbances triggered by an abnormal focus on daily survival issues (food, warmth, physical body contact resistance to deep sleeping etc.) However, these disturbances can be resolved once the underlining disturbance has been identified and suitably addressed with positive and carefully structured forms of personal and environmental support.

Parents need to discern how to give individual members of the family special periods of time away from the needs and demands of the youngest child. Each individual adult and child member of any family has their own personal needs according to their own individual personality, sensory levels of perception and developmental maturity.

When feeding is no-longer exclusive to the mother's breast then sleep, safety, warmth and comfort can be experienced from an alternative loving source/person. As a general incentive to personal development it is important to provide an alternative experience before withdrawing the mother-'*baby business*' monopoly.

Providing an 'alternative experience' can be successfully applied to any situation, in order to encourage a development beyond the normal routine into an empowering new area of independence and skills.

Helena Eastwood

When regularly sharing a bed for night sleeping, the comforting issues of warmth and companionship can be offset by limited space and restricted body movement, sensory disturbance and startle reflex triggers. While the initial stage of falling into sleep may be easier, later sleep disturbances can be notably heightened and thereby inhibit the overall quality of a night's sleep and thereby can cause a sleep deficit or a habitual shallow sleep pattern.

Mothers of babies that have undergone hospital treatment at or soon after birth often feel a desperate desire to compensate for this abrupt and unnatural separation. These mothers may feel subconsciously obligated to "never support any aspect of separation ever again!" Sadly, this can deny the child any other reassurance from father and extended family and close family friends who could temporarily relieve the mother of fulltime baby responsibilities. When a mother presents her own anxieties related to the child's safety when left alone anywhere or anytime, the child may lack confidence in personal issues of safety and resist natural development of independence with demands for constant physical body contact with the mother. Thus the mother's responsibilities are kept at a highly intense level that is ultimately unhealthy for both the mother's disposition and the child's natural progressive confidence and enthusiasm for self-directed learning.

Fortunately, the baby grows into a young child whose physical body size and weight, limit the mother's ability to stay in constant body contact throughout the day. Also, infants need a lot of sleep and eventually sleeping during the day and in the early evening provides an experience of sleeping safely and comfortably in a place separate from the mother's physical body contact. Upon waking from an alone sleeping experience it is obviously important that there is a trusted person there to care for the baby's needs – food, warmth, and comforting company by request.

Natural sleeping appears to follow the same developmental stages in every child; facilitating progression from 'mother dependence' towards a sense of individual autonomy around three years as an accompaniment to the establishment of self-directed learning activity.

When the three primary aspects of separation are processed, successfully self-directed learning, movement and mobility are achieved from a natural sense of personal empowerment. The accompanying journey from three to seven years would normally be one of a growing personal 'independence'. At around the age of seven years personal empowerment can be seen as a consecutive developmental progression:-

    a. _social interaction_ - _authentic_ personal relationships with people ;
    b. _constructional inventive activity_ with the accessible environment;
    c. _creative expression_ through artistic endeavour and original thought and language.

Sadly, some adults still illustrate an ongoing disruption within one or more of the three infant (baby) separation issues. The disruption may be illustrated as a general lack of confidence and failure to successfully engage in the self-directed activity listed a, b, and c, above and one or more retained infant reflexes.

68

Fortunately areas of developmental deficit can be overcome when separation issues are faced, as the initial developmental disturbance and a self-directed lifestyle is successfully encouraged and developed.

An adult may be able to identify:-

1. An unresolved **sleeping** issue as one of **separation**
2. An unresolved **feeding** issue as one of **exclusion**
3. An unresolved **independent play** issue as one of **isolation**.

When a child or an adult is able to consciously over-ride the source of reoccurring primal baby fears, then the accompanying emotional stress and compensatory behaviours may be identified. Any situation in which we experience discomfort and emotional stress may reinstate overwhelming feelings of separation, exclusion, or isolation. When the conscious mind can witness a 'baby business' response, we have the potential to interpret a present situation from a constructive perspective and address our responses from a real perspective of choice rather than the infant perspective of primal survival.

A New Perspective on High Functioning Autism (Previously described as Asperger's)

This area on the autism spectrum, social disability is commonly associated with high intellectual functioning. This end of the autism spectrum may remain predominantly misunderstood. Assessment remains limited to a specific classification of symptoms founded within an unknown cause. It can, for some, also include outstanding and genius levels of intellectual development. However, social interaction may remain a disturbing disability experienced as a notable deficit of social, practical and compassionate understanding of another person's perspective.

However, the author considers that all the symptoms can be attributed to a notable lack in the development of authentic and original <u>self-directed interaction</u> with the environment. Authentic social interaction is the social area of self-directed interaction. A socially orientated interaction normally accommodates each person's understanding, interactions and personal perspective.

The conscious organisation of self-directed activity is essential to personal responsibility for interaction with people, places and things. Therefore authentic self-directed activity (as opposed to copied behaviour) is essential to the development, and everyday management, of personal responsibility and active organisation of personal care and safety. Thus a notable lack of self-direction can inevitably lead to unsafe/fearful feelings and experiences. When not able to maintain a suitably controlled and predictable environment those within this area on the autism spectrum may resort to compensatory behaviours that are designed to regain a sense of safety through rigid external forms of control, copied and repetitive behaviours. For example:-

Intimacy is focused upon sensual pleasure and gratification.

Person to person interaction is predisposed to specific 'formulated' and 'stereotyped' behavioural patterns.

Interests are projected from a fixed, narrow, obsessional perspective.

<u>Fixed factual</u> aspects of life dominate over any self-directed 'live, love, learn' approach to <u>everyday variables</u>.

Without self-directed, authentic interaction with one's own experiences, any lack in understanding or compassion for another person's situation could be very difficult or even impossible.

This perspective is described in the earlier diagram on page …50…. which describes our interaction as either self-directed as 'The Director' - actively influencing the environment.

or as 'The Respondent' - fed by environmental stimulus.

The following diagram illustrates areas of development that are intrinsically linked with self-directed interaction with the environment, (people, places and things)

A Self-Directed Approach to Personal Development and Learning.

LIVE - LOVE - LEARN
Movement
Motivation
Method

Performance
Participation
Production
— PLAY

Initiative
Incentive
Independence

Learner-directed-Learning
Self-directed
Self-motivated
Self-corrected

Discovery Learning
Exploration
Experimentation
Experiential learning

Multi-sensory experience
Assimilation: Integration of sensory experience –
Replication: the accommodation of an experience, such that it can be repeated at will.
Application: a replication of an experience

Sharing Caring & Communicating
Conceptual understanding
Comprehension
Language communication

1. A working relationship with one's reality – (the present environmental surrounding)
2. Intellectual application of practical knowledge with the present environmental circumstances.
3. Co-operative interaction within a shared environment with a topic/project or schedule.

➤ Contemplate
✓ Replicate
❖ Communicate

➤ Apprentice
✓ Master
❖ Teacher

For example:
1a) Reading
2a) Handwriting and spelling
3a) Creative Writing

➤ Reception of communicated ideas
✓ Communication of skills
❖ Creative expression

Lack of consciously directed activity also fails to exercise ones conscious organisation of the working memory. In order to use our memory in conjunction with our everyday 'live - love - learn' experiences we have to establish a conscious responsibility for the way we organise the storage of information and how and when to retrieve that information in order to support one's wellbeing in future situations. The transference of information and skills from one situation into a new area of learning is essential to our human potential to learn and create. Similarly, our development of personalised <u>self-directed interaction</u> is essential to co-operative forms of social interaction with situations, people, places and animals. The living and organically orchestrated aspects of our environmental experience encourages us to develop social interactions and provides opportunities to express ourselves through authentic personal interactions.

It is especially important that our self-directed interactions embrace an empathetic and caring disposition, when we are involved with activities, places animals and people wishing to have a life and will of their own.

Developmental differences in terms of self-directed interaction, may inhibit the development of personal expression, authentic interaction, sharing and caring, adaptability, and creative expression. Without self-directed expression of 'self' the person is restricted to following the <u>directions presented by others</u> and associated levels of disinclination and impatience. Therefore they may not then attain potential levels of human consciousness associated with the ability to imagine personal consequences (normally developed between the age of 9 and 11 years) and the later ability to empathise with the feelings and experiences of others (normally developed between the age 11 to 19 years).

<u>Self-direct is an internally organised projection of doing, i.e. active interaction with the immediate or available environment.</u> When engaged in self-directed doing activity, time has no hold on us, it passes unnoticed and only becomes an issue if the activity has to be halted due to other commitments, choices or needs chosen by oneself or activity directed upon the individual by others.

When the abstract mind is dominant it may feel as if time passes very slowly and every moment might feel like it is both isolated and elongated into an unspecified length of time. This can lead to extreme levels of impatience, especially when the autistic person is waiting for someone else to do the self-directed actions s/he is not 'able' or 'willing' to do for oneself. A common example of this impatience is seen when food is being cooked, whereby waiting the allotted cooking time is a real moment by moment struggle. This total and impatient focus on the passing of required cooking time is so all embracing, that doing a bit of clearing up in the waiting period is not considered a sensible or doable option. Cooking, if it includes all the practical preparation and clearing up, can create good motivation for self-directed activity, but it can be a challenge to hold the practical as an essential part of the eating pleasure.

Adults, children and animals (both domestic and wild) can be unpredictable and intrinsically uncontrollable, however, this in itself would not normally cause a child to substitute self-directed interaction with that of behaviours focused upon predetermined specification designed to reduce environmental variables and unpredictable responses. A lack of self-directed interaction can establish an intense focus on the development of compensatory behaviours, designed to reduce environmental variables and unpredictable responses. In that external stimulation, environmental variables and unpredictable responses do not support or encourage self-directed interactive activity, it is not surprising that an autistic person develops a wide compendium of compensatory behaviours specifically designed to reduce environmental variables and unpredictable responses. Also a person without self-direct may find it particularly hard to organise their environment to suit their own 'best interests'. Associated frustration can be presented as dishonesty, cheating, and rejection of truth and denial of self-created consequences. Self-direct defines all aspects of the practical ability to project one's personal interests successfully into the environment through positive interaction.

The compensatory behaviours commonly associated with those on the 'high functioning' autism spectrum may include the following:-

- A strong reliance on copied and repetitive behaviour.
- Obsessional hobbies and exclusive areas of interest.
- Obsessional compulsive behaviours and associated needs for; -routine, repetition, fixed rules and familiar unchanging environmental surroundings.
- Echolalic presentation of language communication.
- A general lack of exploration, experimentation and enthusiasm within their everyday interactions with people, places and things.
- A personal need/desire for an almost constant exposure to external entertainment.
- A notable seeking of (primal) fear based external stimulation.
- A notable seeking of (primal) biological internal stimulation.
- Lack of empathy, sympathy and positive emotional responses.
- Exaggerated and unpredictable levels of anger and frustration.
- Extreme sensitivity to discomfort and pain.
- Notable areas of developmental immaturity.
- A love of manmade robotic devices and push button electronic controls.
- Obsessional food disorders and aversions to new foods.
- 'Exclusive' forms of repetitive behaviour that over-rides creative potential and social interaction.
- Hyperactivity – fast reactive responses to any single sensory stimulus or multi-sensory overwhelm.
- Outbursts of unwarranted emotionally charged anti-social behaviour such as abusive, excessive, verbal and/or physical reactions.
- An unnatural encyclopaedia of factual knowledge that remains unrelated to one's personal experience, preferences and beliefs.
- Irregular and unsuitable presentation of intellectual facts.
- Indiscriminate/irrelevant recall of past memories from long term memory and unpredictable, irregular, or deceitful use of recall from working memory.
- An impatient disposition that demands instant gratification and one-to-one personal attention. A preconceived outcome or result may be used as a compensation for the lack of authentic self-directed interaction with people, places and things.

- "What's yours is mine and what's mine is my own!" attitude to material possessions.
- Total and aggressive denial of their own miss conduct, adversities and addictions.

The following chart illustrates how a failure to develop self-direct within normal social interactions and skills may result in a narrow fixed definition of

(a) social perspectives,
(b) categorization of social structure,
(c) mental attitudes tailored to meet from one's own survival perspectives and personal benefits
(d) antisocial and challenging behaviour such as addictions and hoarding and associated possessive and aggressive dispositions.

Our ability to integrate our own needs and wants with that of others is defined within our self-directed interactions, choices and level of understanding. The following charts consider possible social implications presented by our superiors, inferiors and peers when viewed without the positive perspectives of co-operation, consideration, understanding and compassion.

Superiors		
Position	**Social categorisation:-**	**Social Attitude**
Employer; Boss; Landlord, Director, etc Teacher? Parent?	To be respectfully manipulated	*What does this give me*
	What does this person give me i.e. money, material benefits, one to one attention, egocentric identity	*What will get me more of what I want*

Inferiors		
Position	**Social categorisation**	**Social Attitude**
Servants, carers, employees, siblings, children,	What do I want them to do for me? How do I dominated and get control of this person. Given instructions and told what to do, when and how, as suits my needs.	*I need to insist upon what I want! I get as much as I can out of them for my own needs and desired.*
	They don't have feelings like I do.......	*I am better than them.*
	They are not important like me..... They have to do everything I want them to do without any 'whys' or 'complaints'.	*Now I am the boss. I am supposed to be a little unkind to them when I feel unhappy. I have to punish them when they do not do as I want.*

Peers		
Position	**Social categorisation**	**Social Attitude**
Possible source of entertainment.	They are socially important to my credibility as an admirable person.	Possible girl/boy friend
May be help me to attain more than I can do on my own	Is s/he willing and/or able to support my dreams, wishes, desires.	If you don't like me then I won't like you! If you like me I will like you….
Possible backup for doing new and different:- fun activities; over the edge things; taking risks for fun and excitement.	How do I make myself look 'good'/important! How can I impress the opposite sex….! How can I show myself as superior to the other girls/ stronger than the other boys!.	Look at me Look at how special I am. Look at how much better I am than you. I need you to look up to me! Please don't criticise me about anything I do or try to make me look weak or stupid.
	Does this person share my obsessional activities/interest? What hobby/project of interest do we have in common….?	Are we a 'tribe'/'team' /'pack'. Can we go hunting together for pleasures e.g. food, clothes, desired possessions, entertainment, exciting adventures and challenges, members of the opposite sex.

Glossary of Specialised Use of Words and Phrases

Multi-Sensory Integration

This describes the combined reception of different sensory information (e.g. auditory, visual kinaesthetic etc.) This phrase describes the ability to work with several or all sources of sensory information. The integration of multi-sensory information is essential to our ability to accommodate the combined input of sensory information in any given situation/task.

Many tasks require a focus on one or more specified fields of sensory reception. Sometimes the learning of a skill is dependent upon our ability to prioritise one specific area of sensory information and tune out of all other areas of sensory information. In contrast to this single Sensory Focus, the integration of Multi-Sensory information involves an ability to regulate and integrate all sensory input, at any given moment according to the given task and/or desired result; therefore, multi-sensory integration is inter-dependent upon our ability to regulate and prioritise sensory information. Multi-sensory integration is opposed when we prioritise one favoured sensory input, above all others. Multi-sensory information facilitates our ability to network and organise our integration of sensory information. How we organise and integrate multisensory information helps better understanding and facilitates a successful application of sensory information within self-directed activities.

Sensory-Regulation

Sensory-Regulation is critically important to our ability to select and prioritise one area of sensory information above all other sensory input, at any given time. Our individual ability to tune in or out of the sensory input at any given moment and situation, defines how well we can apply and accommodate sensory input relevant to our present chosen activity. In order to focus on a self-directed learning experience, it is essential that we turn down our sensory input on some aspects of sensory perception, while at the same time we turn up our focus on other areas of sensory information in order to successfully accomplish a given task, new area of learning or the development of a new or extended skill. Thus, sensory regulation can be thought of as similar to when we tune a radio into a certain channel. However, the radio will only tune into receiving one channel at a time, whereas we have the capacity to tune into or out of any specific sensory perceptual information and have a level of intelligence that can discern and prioritise which sensory information is required for

- ✓ Maximum levels of learning.
- ✓ Successful organisation of our surrounding area.
- ✓ Positive influence upon our environment.
- ✓ Personal interaction with the environment and those around us.

Thus sensory regulation is essential to self-directed activity.

Self-directed activity is an essential part of play and discovery learning.

Play and discovery learning are essential to creative expression.

And creative expression is an essential part of everyone's sense of living as a unique individual engaged in a 'live, love, learn' lifestyle.

Imitation

Imitation, unlike rote copying has to have an element of purpose and personal endeavour. Imitation is not an automated response founded within the subconscious areas of mental activity and influences. Imitation has an aspect of respectful admiration and dreamlike desire to gain what is seen as a desirable outcome. Imitation may include a personal application and aspects of creativity.

Copying

Copying may to the onlooker appear to be a form of imitation, however, to copy is notably different in that personal, emotional and social elements are not intrinsic to any type of copied activity. To copy is to remain neutral and unquestioning, while producing an action that replicates what another person has done. Copying does not include personal application or aspects of creativity.

Repetitive occupational activity

Repetitive occupational activity that is notably unrelated to the environmental geography and events. Thus the same repetitive physical activity may be resumed in different situations and remain unrelated to the present environment and actions of those around at the time.

Play

Play is used to describe those activities that involve exploration, experimentation, personal enthusiasm and wilful endeavours. Play often involves a personally unique combination of fantasy, imagination and creativity. Play is founded on a multi-sensory awareness of the immediate environment; and a desire to prioritise certain areas of sensory information in order to focus on a specified endeavour, an identified desire, goal, result or achievement.

Self-direct

All self-directed learning is dependent upon one's sensory perceptual abilities and one's ability to direct and internalise sensory integration skills.

Self-directed learning normally develops progressively between the age of three (willed self-direction) and seven years, when learner-directed learning starts to integrate the will with goals and personal interests.

Self-direct describes the ability to use *willed* interaction with people, places and things as a means of facilitating one's own learning potential in any given circumstance. Self-directed learning follows as a natural development *after* parallel play, imitative play and the development of automated skills. Self-directed learning is prerequisite to creative expression and discovery learning.

Learner-directed learning is founded by 'play', 'creative expression' and 'discovery learning'.

The author considers the autism spectrum as a lack of self-directed activity and the subsequent lack of constructive interaction with people, places and things (i.e. one's personal reality) in any given time and situation. Some people with autism may show a notable inability to organise or alter the physical environment in order to meet practical issues of personal wellbeing. Autism manifests as a notable lack of consciously organised and premeditated interaction with one's reality. This lack of consciously organised thinking and learning, leads to the development of specified subconsciously organised compensatory brain activity. This may be seen as a predominance and focus on abstract mental activity, whereby the brain actively ensures that primitive survival instincts and primitive reflexes direct one's safety during essential environmental interactions. A notable lack of self-direction also leads to an unnatural focus on repetitive and echolalic, activity along with a desire for extensive periods of external entertainment.

Later in life the ever growing desire for extended periods of external entertainment can evolve into one or more types of addiction. Psychologists are now acknowledging that addiction is initially related to lack of self-confidence and thereby associated with a lack of self-direct and negative or unnatural social interaction. Thus, addiction could be seen as the escalation of an abnormal level of dependence upon external sources of entertainment, because these external experiences accommodate the above deficits and compensate for the individuals lack of personal motivation, authentic social interaction and constructive endevour.

Addictions are often associated with reckless and provocative behaviour designed to create high adrenalin and associated exuberant feelings of pleasure and/or excitement; e.g. Pornography and masturbation; horror films; dangerous sports; alcohol; recreational drugs; obsessional project based activity; computer screen activities; shopping, gambling etc. In this way the lack of self-direct and social interaction is substituted for internal feelings of excitement and pleasuring obtained from external sources of entertainment. The lack of self-directed activity and willed directives ensure that addiction remains out of control and thereby detrimental to the persons general wellbeing.

Abstract mind

The author uses this phrase to describe the activity in the mind that is not consciously related to the person's practical reality. The abstract mind deals with primal survival and thereby this aspect of mental activity cannot take in to account any other person's perspective outside of that directly related to one's own needs and wishes. The abstract mind is linked to personal survival and therefore only considers one's own wellbeing; caring and sharing of objects with others is defensively restricted to one's own best interest; this can lead to selfish motives such as possessive and excessive types of hoarding and jealousy. The abstract activity in the mind is usually unconsciously directed, because it is designed to prioritise one's own survival and wellbeing.

Thus 'high functioning autism' is considered, by the author, to be an abnormally dominant use of the *abstract mind* which is commonly seen to favour high levels of:-

Adrenalin in the body.
Primal survival abstract thought processes.
Hypersensitivity.
Fear based instinctive responses.
Automated and repetitive activity.
Retained 'Startle Reflex'
Dramatic perspectives that are notably not related to one's own 'reality' i.e. ones present of past experience
OCD (Obsessional-Compulsive-Behaviours defined as an Obsessional-Compulsive Disorder)

If the abstract mind related compassionately towards another's perspective, this distraction would be thought of as certain to jeopardise one's own ability to prioritise defending oneself from adverse external conditions. Indeed when those around insist on compassionate behaviour and social interaction, the abstract mind may perceive 'social guidance' and 'boundaries' as a threat. This perspective is commonly expressed as phrases such as "You are hurting me!"; "I hate you!"; "You are making me hate you!" and "Why are you being unkind/cruel to me?" etc.

This perspective on social interaction can quickly lead to a habitual projection of *blame*. Whenever anything is seen as adverse to personal ideals or desires the blaming response may be as follows:-. Why did you do that?" "Why did you let that happen to me?!" "Why didn't you stop me doing that?" "Why didn't you stop that from happening to me?" Traumatic experiences, at any age, may be processed by the abstract mind as adverse to our future safety because of 'a relatively minor aspects of similarity'. Survival/wellbeing and fear based negative reactions may thereby trigger a dominant feature, when any present circumstance stimulates a memory of related sensory experience.

Alas, the presentation of TV dramas, films and computers has exacerbated the amount of stimulus presented to our *abstract* thinking minds. The sensory input from screens is devoid of any experience in relation to one's present reality. Thus media based drama, both fiction and non-fiction, entertains the abstract primal mind. The dramatic visual stimulus is classically categorised as one of three primal survival issues - separation, exclusion and isolation.

High Adrenalin Levels

The dominance of a survival perspective causes the adrenalin in the body to rise, but a weak sense of reality holds the person from any natural physical response i.e. movement designed to protect one's wellbeing. Media entertainment is generally designed to give a good feeling by stimulating a raised adrenalin level in the blood. However, media entertainment is not designed to include physical activity and strong body movements. Therefore, the extra adrenalin rush in the body remains unused by fight and flight movement and is maintained at an abnormally high level. In order to address a prolonged high level of adrenalin in the blood the body may channel the fight and flight energy into a general state of 'hyperactivity'. This hyperactivity may lead to an abnormal addiction to high adrenalin levels. Extremes in the body temperature i.e. too high or too low, can also support abnormally high adrenaline levels. It is not unusual for those with Asperger's autism to become fixed on high adrenalin levels in the body and a constant desire to seek ways to maintain and increase abnormal levels of adrenalin. High adrenalin levels are seen in both children and adults with a hyperactive disposition and diagnosed ADHD or DCD. Hyperactivity is the natural way in which the body deals with high adrenalin levels. Hyper-activity includes a state of hyper sensitivity and the infant 'startle reflex' retains an abnormal level of dominance over self-directed activity.

Difficulty and Learning Differences

It is easy to identify the nature of a disability when a specified sensory organ is damaged. For example the eyes of a blind person do not see; the ears of a deaf person do not hear and the vestibular organ of balance does not work very well for a drunken person. However, sensory impairment can also be caused by damage in the brain. Unseen sensory differences When the brain is unable to receive and interpret sensory information learning differences and difficulties may be very hard to see and understand for everyone, even the person with the difficulty may not perceive or understand what or why an specific area of development and learning feels especially difficult. Some aspects of perceptual difference [caused by specific areas of brain dysfunction/ damage] are now acknowledged and partly understood e.g. dyslexia, dyspraxia, dysphasia and proprioceptive disorder.

The cause of these sensory perceptual differences may be difficult or even impossible to specifically identify or trace to a specific area of brain damage. The brain is a very complex and intensive aspect of our human disposition and much remains to be fully understood.

The author has found that when working on an intense one to one individual program, a child on the autism spectrum may also illustrate a specific learning difficulty that may have contributed to the lack of self-directed learning and subsequent compensatory autistic behaviours. For example one young child could copy word for word all the spoken sound track of a favourite film but when he tried to communicate for himself he spoke in a jumble of meaningless sounds and illustrated a severe form of dysphasia. He did learn to speak for himself but it was a prolonged process using a unique sound by sound, word by word, and later phrase by phrase approach that demanded exceptional effort and intellectual patience for all concerned. Other autistic children have shown different areas of specific learning difficulty such as a proprioceptive disorder and/or retained primitive reflexes, auditory integration difficulties and other uncategorised differences unique to each child.

Compensatory behaviours

The author considers these behaviours as specific to each individual persons way of accommodating areas of personal care and creative expression left in deficit when authentic personal development of self-directed activity has failed to accommodate self-directed learning. Self-directed activity is superior and dominant over pre-birth reflexes, *abstract* mental activity, and other *subconsciously* organised survival strategies. Compensatory behaviours could be specifically designed to accommodate areas of personal care and creative expression when normal development of self-directed activity has failed to be established. Compensatory behaviours may also help to establish a sense of personal identification. Those who lack a sense of personal identity may focus on imitation of others, following as one of a predetermined social group, fashion or cult. Lack of an inner sense of personal identity may lead to seeking a sense of self through mirrors and self-portraits using digital media formats.

Area of Difficulty	Disposition	Compensatory behaviour	Recommended activities
Lack of social interaction	Avoidance of physical contact. Quick to anger and defend one's personal space with physical aggression.	Reading as an exclusive behaviour. Excessive demands for external entertainment. Alcohol Addiction	One to one sharing, Creative listening and Special Time.
Difficulty regulating sensory perception.	Avoidance of eye-contact. Reluctance to try anything new i.e. a fixed desire to keep things the same and avoid any form of change.	Negative responses to all new opportunities/ situations. Eating disorder/obsessions for things to always stay the same. Extreme and obsessive control issues.	Outdoor pursuits; camping; hiking; trampolining; (except cycling –biking which encourages a predominate use of automated reactions and skills)
Poor or inappropriate sensory integration skills	Lack of physical exercise and minimal engagement in physical activity	Excessive cleaning or other OCDs.	Cooking; pottery; gardening, climbing
A poor sense of practical needs and environmental organisation. limited structural thinking skills	Unable to organise ones environment to suit one's own practical needs.	Unable to keep things clean and tidy. Hoarding, Addictive shopping usually on line. Habitual eating of set 'take-away'-meals	

Seeking external directions and limited presentation of creativity through interactive forms of creative expression.	Obsessional interest in the acquisition of encyclopaedia styles of intellectual knowledge	Detailed and pre-directed craft activities e.g. Small Lego kits, puzzles, knitting patterns, cross-stitch picture kits etc.	Knitting; juggling; swimming; canoeing; sailing; rock climbing; badminton.
Lack of self-directed interaction with people places and things.	Sensory overwhelm, limited authentic interaction with people, places, natural environments and	Repetitive-obsessional activity. Reluctance to act according to anyone else's advice or instructions. Unable to receive any form of external help or guidance. Excessive desire for control and domination over people and objects.	Interactive games; outdoor adventures; Musical activities and dance.
Lack of personal communication	Obsessional and thereby exclusive topics of interest	Computer (screen) based occupational internet activity.	Playing a musical instrument; signing; dance; drama; horse riding.
Lack of compassion – unable to imagine a realistic view of another person's situation	Social Isolation and rigid approaches to parenting.	Criticism and blaming others for personal stress levels.	Working with animals especially those in need of help.

Libertarianism

The libertarian approach to parenting releases the parent from carer responsibilities related to the safety and wellbeing of others and the surrounding environment!

The libertarian parent may not want to know "Where the child is and what the child is doing? or With whom, how and what the child is relating to"? This extreme level of freedom can thereby lead to a lack of parent child interaction and sharing of interests.

Social interaction is an essential part of learning and social development for every child. If freedom also instates a deficit of interaction between parent and child, then an important realm of adult and child learning will be omitted form the child's everyday learning experiences.

This is a child centred approach to childcare and parenting, whereby the child is not given any boundaries for their behaviour i.e. no boundaries for their physical safety; no boundaries for their social interactions with family friends and public; no boundaries on their use of the environmental geography, objects or materials and resources. In theory the young child quickly learns that certain behaviours create adverse responses. However, different children respond differently. Some children may do well with the libertarian approach, while others may be overwhelmed and intimidated by the level of responsibility and the opportunities to establish habitual anti-social behaviours and consequential limitations on their development of compassion, for their own wellbeing and that of others and their environment.

When a young child does not have the developmental resources to independently direct and realistically assess their own responsibility and compassion as a member of a community, this parenting approach can be unsupportive. Natural development is intrinsically linked to care received. In a natural environment, nature directs basic boundaries and lessons of consequence. However, in our modern day environment, libertarian parenting can leave children at the mercy of screen entertainments and other occupational obsessions and other unhealthy aspects of diet and primal defence. Children learn by example and if there are no boundaries, the example may become one of 'the strongest gets all' and the child may become either a social bully or a victim to feeling of no importance. When children are at the mercy of primal and anti-social patterns of behaviour, excessive levels of competitive and defensive survival are established to compensate for the parents' lack of authority and protective care. The author considers this a system of care overwhelms the child with adversities such as:- unsuitable levels of both seen and unseen responsibility; overwhelming extensive ranges of choice within everyday situations; lack of rhythm and familiar routines; and lack of social guidance and learning through example and social guidelines. For a child with poor levels of self-directed interaction, the libertarian environment can promote unpredictable and frightening experiences, emotional instability, generally over-defensive fear based responses, and an intense focus on the development of rigid control and manipulation of objects and people.

Eventually, family members, schools and others in the community may take on responsibility for setting a positive/good example and deterrents designed to enhance positive social interactions. Later, the community as such will present boundaries designed to deter and prevent anti-social behaviour that is adverse to the well-being of others, their personal property and physical safety. However, community boundaries are not accompanied by any genuine personal care for the individual. Whereby, what the child's social learning does not necessarily accommodate areas of deprivation created by social-emotional difficulty and obsessional behaviours. Libertarian parenting can promote obsessional use of media entertainment and thereby fail to promote self-directed endeavour that accommodates care for others and the environment.

For those who seek to love unconditionally, 'boundaries' are a natural and essential part of one's responsibility as a parent or community of people whose everyday living influences the quality of life for others. Adults have a wider overall understanding of consequences beyond the immediate perception of cause and effect. E.g. a person may drive extra fast to get somewhere all the sooner but any mature adult will also acknowledge that the greater the speed, the greater the risk to driver and everyone else.

Ideally, all boundaries would be based upon an adult sense of perspective and their desire to *change the environment* to accommodate the behaviour in a positive illustration of reality and consequences. For example, a parent may remove a screaming child from a café of noisy strangers in order to provide a more appropriate child friendly space (less noise; space to run around, one to one contact with a trusted adult etc.) Ideally, boundaries should not be governed by any desire to establish external control through punishment or external intimidation or other forms of oppressive control. Inevitably punishments, disciplines, intimidation and physical domination are intrinsically based on the creation of intense survival issues related to feelings of isolation, separation or exclusion. Some controlling behaviours may be based on the instigation of some form of genuine survival fear, related to innate issues or past experiences. Some boundaries may appear to instate one or more of these scenarios, without causing undue stress. For example, removing a toy central to an anti-social outburst could rightly be conceived as exclusion of a toy, this is a practical solution, and the element of exclusion is thereby not related to personal survival issues. Similarly if fighting and hurting another person means that one or more children are sent to their room for 'time out', the issue of separation provides a helpful *cooling down period* and an opportunity to *reflect* and determine *a better way of sharing* time together. If however, the time out is a period when a child is locked away from contact with their family for an unlimited or undefined length of time then survival issues of separation/exclusion/isolation may become detrimental to the child's future wellbeing and future development of positive social behaviour.

Concluding Summary

How can we balance positive abstract media entertainment with concrete self-directed interaction?

Autism is generally perceived as a specific disability, seen to disrupt early social development and self-directed learning. The development of consciously organised interactions with people, places and things is motivated by a person's will to explore, interact and influence one's present environment.

Normally 'will' based activity develops between the age of two and a half and three and a half. This age is notably associated with tantrums. These tantrums illustrate the child's frustration when things directed by themselves or others do not go according to their wishes. It is natural for human responses to reflect the present level of interaction. During these early years the child's wilful presentation of wants, needs and exploration supports and motivates their interaction with people places and things. For example we may crawl on the floor with a baby when s/he is learning the crawling movements; we may sign to a deaf child with expressive body language, or physically guide a blind child to a desired destination. These approaches are generally natural and admirably helpful. Thus the first level of reflective interaction is one of sharing where the child is at present. This is a first level of social sharing and communication. With a young child or specifically handicapped child, adults may override a natural reflective response and optimism with what the adult considers an easier and more appropriate form of interaction. For example, if we reflect the autistic child's isolation and exclusive monotonous repetition of a fixed activity; our reflective interaction is never going to encourage self-directed interaction with the environment or motivate social interaction or exploratory behaviour. In these situations our behaviour reflects what the child is doing and can already do. However, development and learning involve a system of encouragement designed to encourage a successful approach and scaffold new areas of progress.

Thus it is essential that our interactions during special time are not simply a copy of the child's present behaviours. Special time needs to include an element of reflective activity with authentic interaction that illustrates the individuality of both the child and the adult. This allows the adult to organise appropriate motivational scaffolding and incorporate small steps to motivate new levels of activity. This can help the adult to organise appropriate motivational interactions that present a guided series of small attainable steps, as helpful scaffolding, for previous areas of failure.

Every self-directed action is initiated from a focus of choice.

The simple standard of basic choice may be the same in every situation and for every person; the initial key to choice is action or no action. Once the motivation has engaged in a positive 'will' filled connection, then the choices may be simply this or that, or a kaleidoscope of variable options: *different directions, *alternative choices, and additional choices based on who, how and why, motives associated with a specific person and predetermined agenda...........

Four things that compound a lack of self-directed interaction

1. Lack of social interaction. Lack of authentic interaction from the autistic person discourages those around from responding with their own authentic interaction. Lack of social interaction can suppress motivation within a Live, Love, Learn approach to daily life and interactive activity.
2. Lack of motivation and environments that fail to meet the present level of interest, ability and competence. Even an adult may feel disturbed by certain environmental circumstances that do not respond to their own interests, wishes, and circumstances that change unpredictably.
3. Overwhelming levels of sensory stimulus and/or external interference that override the conditions that support the person's ability to express personal choice, need, desire or perceptual understanding.
    Lack of self-directed behaviour eradicates motivational incentives.
    Adverse environmental conditions are likely to produce anti-social defences because environmental changes and unwanted responses or events may be unbearably challenging and disempowering. This may cause the autistic person to feel powerless and unsafe.
4. A false social environment is going to produce antisocial defences. Authenticity is essential to wellbeing and even adverse reactions that are not received well can be better than an underlying intuitive sense that there is something wrong and the adult is likely to express unmanageable adversity. Autistic children are especially disturbed by unpredictable and subtle forms of defensive behaviour and unfavourable social interaction.

For an autistic child, environmental changes and unwanted responses and events may be very challenging because their personal lack of self-directed action leaves them unable to look after their own interests. This may instigate that the child feels powerless and thereby unsafe. Thus a repertoire of controlling behaviours may be essential to the child's personal sense of wellbeing and preferable to any courageous and clumsy attempts at self-directed interaction. Alternative routines and unchanging environments may seem favourable and safe, but *routines* do not motivate self-directed personal responses.

Similarly, emotional defences may predetermine antisocial behaviours and thereby block any possibility for social interaction. Primal and survival behaviours such as throwing, sucking/biting, hitting, pushing and snatching are generally tolerated from babies but if this early behaviour fails to develop into normal co-operative forms of social interaction those around the child are inclined to feel rejected or disturbed. This may understandably cause those around the autistic child to withdraw their 'normal' social interaction. This isolates the autistic child and s/he fails to experience the co-operative interactions that can help the child to develop self-directed interaction. Encouragement to interact within a learning environment is mandatory to self-directed learning and authentic social interactions. Lack of normal social interaction and associated learning is essential to child development.

A blind child has their interaction with the environment disrupted by their lack of visual information. However, young children have little or no understanding of why the blind child's behaviour is different and they interact as positively as they can without necessarily altering their social interactions towards the blind child; thereby their social interactions and levels of encouragement are not lowered unnecessarily.

Unfortunately, lack of self-directed interaction combined with social withdrawal creates a barrier of unknown and misunderstood limitations. Those around may feel that normal social interaction is too difficult to maintain without appropriate responses of exchange and encouragement. The autistic child may have a difficulty with cooperative sharing similar to that of a blind child; however, his antisocial reactions and peoples' lack of understanding may shut down social interactions. If adults treat the autistic child with the same unqualified level of positive and playful companionship that they might present to a blind; then the just as the blind child learns in spite of his blindness so the autistic child may learn in spite of his lack of self-directed social interaction.

When children play together they do not put much importance on how well their play mate performs, and thereby a simple request may be enthusiastically repeated even when the response is not according to their wishes. Children and adults may be so disturbed by the autistic child's isolation and strange forms of interaction e.g. vocal noises, rocking etc. This may encourage adults and children to give up on natural playful interaction because of their own lack of empathy with the autistic child's area of learning difficulty and lack of social response.

If we want to play catch with a blind child or a child with physical co-ordination problems we would keep on trying to find a way to make the game work. Successful scaffolding could be formatted as spoken clues denoting the moment the ball is thrown or a verbal warning of when and from where the ball is coming into their area of reach. Also the ball may be changed in size and density e.g. a very large very soft ball or cushion. Thus environmental adaptions can promote that a blind child can participate in a game of catch. The Helen Keller story describes a successful approach to teaching a deaf-blind child. An autistic child, like Helen Keller may not be able to organise cooperative responses. Therefore it is up to us to organise an environment of personal interaction that encourages self-directed co-operation with enthusiasm and perseverance. We need to develop a supportive learning environment as carefully as we can. If we can do this successfully, the autistic child can learn just as the deaf-blind child can learn, but the level of effort and grace required is not to be underestimated. It will take effort, interaction and compassion to establish a positive environment of social interaction designed to promote self-directed responses and subtle forms of communication.

The human capacity to overcome severe disability and heal areas of brain dysfunction is known to be outstanding. However, the isolation caused by a failure to develop normal self-directed interactions may cause those around to give up normal levels of interaction and enthusiastic encouragement for interactive play and learning. We may not limit our willingness to attempt to communicate with a deaf-blind child through touch or to dance with a blind child etc. Equally lack of social and self-directed interaction should not necessarily weaken our own willingness to interact co-operatively with an autistic child. Thus

Every learning experience needs to successfully address –

1. firstly what the child can already do,
2. secondly what they may like to do
3. and thirdly what they have previously failed to do.

Without a natural development of cooperative interaction, carer's naturally resort to repetitive and routine social responses. This compounds the likelihood that interaction is either avoided or packaged into predetermined and restricted routine responses.

Compromised and stilted responses do not ensure that the autistic child is happy or supported according to their special disposition. As adults we need to be aware of the dangers of unnatural responses simply because we do not feel our social interaction has been appreciated. Hopefully when we interact with a baby that cannot give specified response or when we interact with a physically disabled person in a wheel chair, we do not give up our inclusive and interactive activity even when a standard response is unlikely or impossible.

For example, when a young child bites some-one due to frustration, a responsible carer would try to change the environmental situation in order to deter any further biting. Similarly if a child fails to learn to walk, we give them a walking frame to help them stand and strengthen their legs and give them an experience of independent mobility according to their own motivation for desired experiences.

When adjusting the environmental surrounding has been organised to address safety issues and risk assessments, we encourage a blind or deaf child to develop self-directed activity even if it is very difficult for them to address their objectives. The lack of self-directed interaction in the autistic child, distracts us from structuring the same level of environmental support and encouragement. Without a will based development of constructive and adventurous interaction, carers can easily fail to provide a *'special'* environment focused on social interaction and supportive environmental encouragement. A successful learning environment would normally provide forms of interactive encouragement that invites self-directed activity.

The autistic child who does not display self-directed behaviour is most in need of suitable interactive environments and experiences tailored to meet the issues presented as 1-3 above. This scenario is similar to that of 'the unloveable child is the one who has the greatest need to receive our love; even if they reject our loving interactions, we can be confident that it is important we do not give up showing them our love in the best and most caring way. If we curtail to their emotional withdrawal and unresponsive behaviour we are ignoring their greatest need to be loved. We do not give up on a blind child because they do not move because they cannot see. We still encourage the blind child and the deaf child to interact with people, places and things.

The isolated exclusive nature of an autistic child illustrates that they have the greatest need for authentic social interaction. Adult carers need to create motivating environmental experiences that meet what they can already do and encourage them to make choices of their own. We need to challenge the isolated and unresponsive child with choices, invitations, and, above all, normal levels of social expectation. The autistic child is the one who most needs to be challenged with expectations founded by needs and opportunity. Neither, living within a safe static environment or hiding from a chaotic over stimulating environment will encourage social interaction or self-direction.

Survival issues can in suitable situations provide a strong motivation for self-directed behaviour. For example within a safe natural environment the autistic child's normal desire to run away from the adult carer may change to wanting to stay with the pet dog that is tracking them;..... alternatively within a large enough safe space an adrenaline survival tactic of running away may ultimately change to a survival issue related to not feeling safe when alone and separate from everyone. Under special situations abstract survival issues related to aloneness can override 'fight and flight' reactions. These special conditions can thereby change the triggers for antisocial behaviour into a desire to be with a person. This self-motivated and consciously chosen response can change running away from human companionship into a disposition that is seeking and accepting human or animal companionship. The author has set up safe situations where a child can run away from adult care and thereby gain a real sense of aloneness and vulnerability that then motivates that they seek to find companionship. We all feel safer and comforted by caring adults and when allowed to run away for as long as they wish ..... Even an exclusive autistic child can seek companionship, of some sort, to avoid basic survival issues of aloneness, separation other exclusive social dispositions.

Recommended Resources on Autism

FILM 'Son-Rise; a Miracle of Love. The Option Institute USA pioneered a way through autism. Raun Kaulfman is the author of the book 'Autism Breakthrough

<u>FILM</u> 'The Horse Boy' This documentary film is about one family's journey to cure their autistic son, Rowan.

<u>MAKATON</u>

Within our everyday life we may choose on occasions to indicate communication using body movements instead of spoken directives. The author has found that those on the autism spectrum often do better with simple and minimal verbal communication and/or signed communication.

The abstract nature and excessive delivery of verbal communication may overwhelm the autistic person. This may be because they lack the ability to gain a clear understanding of the context and conceptual meaning of any given verbal communication. This limits their ability to organise an appropriate response. Indeed slow or weak responses inevitably encourage the person speaking to repeat and present additional verbal communication which again distracts the autistic person from processing what was originally said.

Makaton is a simple everyday signed vocabulary that can be used to enhance and replace verbal communication. It provides a signed system of communication through body movement that is a suitable addition to every aspect of family life and all ages and abilities.

Signing encourages a more practical relationship with communication, as well as, a multi-sensory mode of expression. Body language has been established within the arts as an expressive form of enrichment that incorporates kinaesthetic movement with both visual and auditory systems of communication.

Recommended Book: A Line drawing illustrations for the revised Makaton vocabulary. Published by the Royal Association of the Deaf and Dumb.

Appendix 1

PART 1 – UNDERSTANDING AUTISM

<u>Poetry and Prose</u>

<u>Deep within the night,</u>

When the silence of darkness, holds everything in stillness.
Frustration burns a hole in my lonely heart.
Yet still I think and pray for you and me.
I wonder and wish it had ended differently…..
I know the truth is much bigger than the world would believe…
For who, not even you or I, can say?!
What illusions are helpful to the fulfilment of a dream?
According to Gods mercy and known only to Him.
Concluded at some future date, as a fulfilment to the dreamer….
A future written in the stars, may have some resemblance to the illusive fantasy,
When? and with persons of reality!
Thus the dreamer greets that which has run away into an elusive room,
Where new ways forward are created from the colours of the heart,
And are breathed out as a 'good life' and 'peaceful mind',
Greeted and shared as love and light divine.
Found by those children of God,
Living within a new promise,
A kingdom of peace and harmony.
A reunion with the prince of reconciliation,
Son of the father creator of all life……Amen
For time is but a shadow of potential
And 'now' is a ghost of the future,
Yet, love is an eternal energy that flows from the soul into the goodness of the heart.
And every last goodbye seeds a new beginning and further joy seeps in through the cracks of grief, to mend the past and heal the broken heart….

I am falling down

I am falling down a narrow ungodly abys down and on down
Fortunate am I that God is everywhere, even in this ungodly place.
Our lifetime is only a game of contrast and opposition
Of little importance, observed by God's infinite care and eternal mercy.
Witnessed as the consequence of our own free will, the results of our own doing,
With childish perceptions and immature needs.
So far from our true potential as children of God;
So confused our scrambled minds create disasters,
Our hardened hearts fill with resentment,
Our disturbed bodies are born to die.
Why to die is Gods biggest gift –
A peaceful release from our world of despair;
Without death we would live eternally in our own disruptions:
Anti-life attitudes, negative lifestyles, unforgiving torments of destruction.
Locked into a '*misery*' mentality, that seeks to be rescued from our own unhealthy choices, - Loved even though we are unlovable.
The snake still guides us away from the one love that can overcome every rejection of life.
Are we still so very far from our original divine nature,
Our 'light' nature has been wilfully buried, lost for ever!?
Redemption is our only hope; we must stay focused on this,
The way, the light and the truth beyond all deceptions.
And live in association with the Son, the Good Shepherd – our 'redeemer'.

Like a misshapen vegetable!

I feel all wonky like a misshapen vegetable
Living and growing according to a defected programme
Within a nutrition deficient environment,
Isolated within an uncomfortable confinement.
Wearing a protective coat of withdrawal,
Sewn together with censored communications, and limited personal movement.

Personal exploration From How to awaken the fearless Heart (Tara Brach)

- Identify judgemental messages presented by the mind.....
- Then ask questions to clarify the reality behind the judgemental messages.
- Who would you be if you did not believe there was something wrong with you?
- What are you unwilling to feel?
- Turn around and face the fear see the disruption as a fear of failure; a not good enough to be loved - unlovable; undeserving;
- Identify areas of insecurity and self-doubt, distortions to your sense of truth and disruptions within your faith.
- Challenge the beliefs with the question 'it may be real, but it is possible it is not true.'

If someone keeps treading on your toes eventually you will want to kick them

If a man uses a woman's body to provide a superior sources of masturbation, ultimately she will want to knee him in the **** and if that is above her moral sense of appropriate behaviour, she will run away and leave him for good.

Money

Only the wisest person can swim successfully in monetary waters without drowning in need and greed.....

Those who paddle in lakes of gold know how to stay open-hearted.

Those who give to those they love, will thrive in a river of joy.

Those who collect the golden water for themselves, lose their mind to childish entertainments and infant comforts.

Those who help others to prosper will not be forgotten.

Those who are patient with the needy will float safely in stormy waters.

Those who experience life as a challenging journey of hope and faith, can sail a tall ship around the world.

Pennies are like raindrops, only felt as a free falling abundance when one is happy to get wet.

True riches are like the moisture in our air – unseen yet essential to our wellbeing.

Gifts and fruits like 'pooh sticks' playfully float under bridges constructed over the river of life.

We can only appreciate getting more, when we truly appreciate what we have already.

The biggest experiences of life are in the smallest and simplest exchanges.

Wisdom is scarcely seen in the air

Rejuvenation is gained from the taste of fresh spring water.

Redemption is buried beneath every mountain of gold.

My body feels clumsy

I am awake but the night is still strong

Time is asleep awaiting the dawn

My body feels clumsy

My spirit is unanchored. I am here, yet, somewhere unknown

The rain water gathers in its noisy departure down the drain

Or in single drips slides down the window pane

The road is silent and forgotten.

The wind has retired back into a sheltered corner of the garden.

Life is like a marshmallow, tantalising to the senses with soft sweet promises;

Condensed for our consumption, then melted beyond recognition

Remembered as a flavour of hope

Taken on trust without any regret.

At last I have humbled my survival plight to one of simple living;

Transferred my designs of escape into a living expression of sweetness and appreciation.

A poem about truth- the simplest of stories –

I am a chameleon

I am a comedian

I am invisible

I am strong

I am steady and safe

I am a carer

I feel soft in the middle

I try to bend in every direction

This marathon feels an ever lengthening journey that can not end until I free-fall over the edge, with all my pieces broken apart shattered in all directions.

The grief that shakes the inner core of my being......and teaches the true meaning of life.

The aloneness of separation that strengthens me in the void.

No more is my story stuck to me

This is a form of celebration without dramatic entertainment or mundane bribes and comforters.

I am a Jesus' disciple held safe on my pilgrim way.

Blessed in a growing knowledge of the real me and my own divinity.

Gracefully parented by God the father of my creation.

Held sweetly in peaceful harmony within the flight of a bird,

Energised by the rivers endless journey

Purified within the silent strength of the forest.

Whatever disturbs my demeanour is powerless against these my redemption.

When the safety line of hope begins to fray

The fall of escape looks me coldly in the eye.

And I dream a distant promise of a peaceful descent

Yet I am held firmly within His hand

My fragmented mind calms within the knowledge of His love

I surrender my way as He guides me through the next day.

Alone I am walking my endeavours, and whispering my prayers;

In company, but alone, without companionship -

Still trying to please, but like an empty cave, life echoes with the sounds of unresolved isolation.

Memories of my home, broken pieces that hardly fit together.

My life appears faded out of recognition, lost in the 'carer' calling

Overwhelmed by the dawning of this day and the next.

The bell has rung the secret silence has begun

I die alone and seek the love I pushed away

Kept at bay

I who had lost my way

I was afraid to prey in his name

For my own redemption

I have done with my living and dying for the daily life of another

My living happiness cannot be given to a negative responder without us both dying unloved

We only have God to call upon,

And if that calling is a miserable affair, God will know how to handle it with love. God always knows what to do and always finds a loving way through.

For unloved is the expression of unable to love

Un-loveable is the expression of resistance to receiving love.

Giving love is a misadventure if receiving love is absent from the equation.

> The song is sung
>
> The bell has rung
>
> I die alone
>
> And seek the love I pushed away
>
> Kept at bay
>
> I had lost my way
>
> Afraid to pray in his name for my redemption

The sunlight shines warmly on our lawn of reconciliation

And blesses the flowers that colourfully celebrate our redemption

The moments of sweetness that I have so longed to feel, slip into my heart through a crack in the door.

This flicker of light creeps into our sharing without invitation, smiling upon the silent moments of hesitation.

Everything will be alright in the end and if it is not alright then it is not the end.

Some things don't happen as planned but what happens instead may be just as good or even better.

The measure of success is how well we cope with disappointment.

If we are doing our best nothing else matters.

If you don't pause to listen then you won't hear the music and if you don't hear the music we won't be able to dance.......... to dance is to express one's joy and joy grows from gratitude. Have faith - dance through the 'live, love, learn' processes of life.

Life is not about perfection it is about redemption....'The purpose of my instruction is that all believers would be filled with love that comes from a pure heart, a clear conscience, and genuine faith(Timothy 1:5)

Maybe

It would have been better to just cry my way through the scary bits of my life, but insecurities make crying too vulnerable, so I generally prefer to hide. Fortunately I am especially easy going and positive about life's roller coaster rides….big smile and everyone seems to like my company, even sad people and those adults and children who are considered challenging! I think God is always blessing me with 'His love' and encouraging me to take on difficult situations and fill them with 'His love' and the care of the angels…. More recently aloneness and isolation has felt more difficult to manage than any of my previous wild and courageous challenges that I have been blessed to be successful with in the past…

A real kiss comes with an everlasting breath and endless blessings

A true kiss is a precious blessing

Real kisses can only be given

Smile a lot

Find a safe place for your playful self

And share an everlasting kiss.

Embrace your life with silent kisses and hear the music of the soul

Live love Sparkle Live from the original innocence within 'for you are all children of light, children of the day.' (Thessalonians 5:5)…..

Whoever humbles himself like this child is the greatest in the kingdom of heaven.(Matthew 18:4)

"For I know the plans I have for you" says the Lord "They are plans for good and not for disaster, to give you a future and a hope. In those days when you pray, I will listen. If you look for me wholeheartedly, you will find me." (Jeremiah 29:11-13)

Appendix 2

PART 1 – UNDERSTANDING AUTISM

<u>AUTOBIOGRAPHIES</u>

Although autism continues to be presented as a social emotional handicap that is predominantly considered incurable, many individual stories continue to illustrate a successful way forward that alleviates the characteristic difficulties that constitute a diagnosis on the autism spectrum. The following books present inspirational stories of how some have found successful natural approachs to *curing* autism.

Lovely by Mary MacCracken. Published by Andre Deutsch; 1977. Also by Mary MacCracken 'A Circle of Children'.

Breakthrough of an autistic child - Bobby by Rachel Pinney; Harvill Press 1983.

To love is to be Happy with by Barry Neil Kaufman. The first book of the Option Process.

Son Rise by Barry Neil Kaufman. The original story of how the Kaufman family overcame their son, Raun's, autism

Son Rise: The Miracle Continues. This book describes how the Son Rise family programme presented at the Option Institute USA www.autismbreakthrough.com/recoveredkids.

Autism Treatment Centre of America: The Son rise Program.Autism Breakthrough by Raun Kaufman:2014. This book is written by Raun himself about his own recovery and his adult work within the Son Rise Program at the Option Institute. Raun has many years of experience helping autistic children to 'Break through Autism' using the same approach used by his own parents for his own recovery age five. If you only want to read one book about the Son Rise Program this is the one to choose.

Let Me Hear Your Voice – A Families Triumph Over Autism by Catherine Maurice 1993

The Horse Boy – by Rupert Isaacson. The true story of a Father's Miraculous Journey to Heal His Son (At three years old Rowan was diagnosed as Autistic).

The Long ride Home – also by Rupert Isaacson. The Extraordinary Journey of Healing that Changed a Child's Life. Rupert discovered new ways of connecting with autistic children. Through the process of healing Rowen and using his Horse Boy Method, he learned to unlock children from the most sever autistic symptoms.

The Autistic Brain – exploring the strength of a different kind of mind by Temple Grandin and Richard Panek

The Spark – A mother's story of nurturing genius and autism by Kristine Barnett

Look me in the eye – my life with asperger's by John Elder Robison

Eating and Artichole – A mother's perspective on Asperger Syndrome by Echo R. Fling

A Real Person-life on the outside By Gunilla Gerland

Drug-Free approach to Asperger Syndrome and Autism by Judyth Reichenberg, Robert Ullman and Ian Luepker. Also authors of the book 'Ritalin-Free Kids'.

Caged in Chaos a Dyspraxic guide to Breaking free. By Victoria Biggs aged 16

Doran a child of courage by Linda Scotson

The Other Child by Linda Scotson

PART TWO

A LIVE LOVE LEARN APPROACH TO AUTISM

Now the birds fill the woods with their springtime songs,
While winter commands a cold obedience over nature's optimism,
And wanders and wails among the silent trees
That stand strong and tall - meditating upon our playful ways.
The children came again for a while to play and roam among sticks and stones.
They remembered your presence,
Played with the dogs, walked along logs and fell in the bog.
They watched the mist creeping into the valley as they left
Carrying woodland contentment and wearing moments of peace,
Holding something special.
With love and thanks to you from all of us, those before us, and those yet to come.

The natural environment appears to provide freedom which actively encourages children to develop their fullest functional potential within a *living curriculum* of effective educational resources that organically nurture the children's enthusiastic social disposition and curiosity about life. (Montessori,1967:50; Bradburn,1976:55.)

Contents

Spinning the Wheel of Life

Our ability to <u>perceive</u> and <u>integrate</u> sensory information from all areas of sensory information is essential to our ability to direct our external environment and internal learning.

> During the early years the child subconsciously selects how s/he responds to sensory information and environmental stimulation. By the age of three a child would normally have established self-directed play whereby the conscious *'will'* can organise unique personal responses to environmental sensory stimulus.

Multi-sensory integration may be used to support and inspire:-

- ° Broad spectrums of creativity and aesthetic appreciation,
- ° Development and mastery of skills,
- ° Self-correction,
- ° Co-operative social interaction and play,
- ° Internal motives and associated self-discipline.

Our sensory perceptions help us to recognise elements of our reality that can support inner motivation, personal assessments and discerned judgements. Steiner presented that this area of development becomes actively present from the age of seven. '....thus you can now comprehend judging as a living bodily process that arises because your senses present you with a world analysed into parts.....Here the act of judgement becomes an expression of your entire human being.' (The Foundations of Human experience, Steiner 1996:page144-145)

When consciously looking at our reactions and interactions, we can consider all aspects of life as part of our way forward to higher levels of intelligence and consciousness. We may thereby acknowledge a greater sense of responsibility for how we relate to the worldly environment i.e. what we bring towards ourselves; what controlling strategies we use; and when, why and how we chose to interact with people, places and things.

Multi-sensory activities do not necessarily have a predetermined goal or measure of achievement. Sensory integration may embrace a spectrum of intelligence that is not necessarily acknowledged; especially when learning is:-

- • held within an specific area of dominant sensory information,
- • or predetermined by an agenda of specified results.

Multi-sensory activities embrace a wealth of sensory experience, whereby motivation and focus are intrinsically directed by environmental scaffolding. An expansive relationship with an indefinable potential, presents qualities of creative engagement, and support future development of awareness. However, distinction between multi-sensory learning experience, enrichment, sensory overwhelm and sensory perceptual <u>chaos</u>, may essentially be unique to each individual person. Self-directed learning is notably supported by each individuals capacity to integrate, organise and discipline sensory perceptual integration through self-directed interaction with people, places and things.

Steiner approached the three sensory issues of overwhelm, chaos and distraction by structuring learning with natural materials, natural environments, and a specific approach to presentation from the teacher to the pupil. The three part lesson could be as follows: a presentation of <u>information</u> on the first lesson; a <u>directed activity</u> using the information on the second lesson; and finally an invitation to integrate what has been learned from the previous two lessons as the basis of a personal, creative presentation.

When knowledge and skills are presented as qualities of enjoyment and social interaction, the pleasures of participation and fruitful learning can be acquired through exploration and discovery. Then creative consequences can range like a gift, beyond perceived normal boundaries, and over-flow into new domains. Thus each individual's unique human design is nurtured as a tender seedling of creative expression.

<u>Dharma: Spinning the Wheel of Life</u>

A balance between the three spokes of the wheel presents a possible description of how well the wheel of creativity spins within our daily lifestyle of choices.

Imbalance between the three spokes may slow the wheel and thereby allows for:-

- a change of speed and direction;
- spring cleaning, maintenance, and repairs;
- safe systems for releasing unwanted baggage.

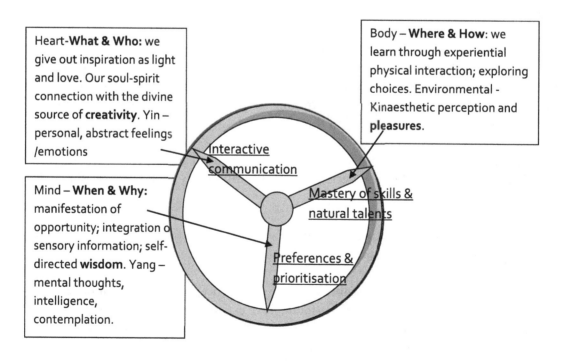

❖ Creativity is the gift of movement,
         Joy is the gift of love.
         Happiness is the gift of being present,
         Peace is the gift of calm contemplation.
         Gratitude is the gift of sharing,
         Devotion is the gift of life.
         Reverence is the gift of humility,
         Patience is the gift of time.

Neale Donald Walsch describes 'a new understanding of life and how it might be most joyfully and wonderfully experienced.

Life will not be lived with an eye toward the Afterlife, but with an eye toward what is being created, expressed, and experienced at many levels of perception in the Holy Moment of Now. Humans will become increasingly aware that "now" is The Only Time There Is (TOTTI).' [What God Wants by Neale Donald Walsch; Hodder Mobius, 2005:159]

The Interactive Wheel of Life

The human powers of association are pre-dominantly guided by the three levels of consciousness: *subconscious, conscious* working mind and *higher consciousness*. The way we energetically engage (give attention to) different aspects of sensory experience could be described as three energetic choices of interaction –

1. <u>Reflective</u>: Reflective experiences are those that are experienced as similar to, or the same as, something related to the individual person. This 'same or similar' perspective is described from a consequential perspective in catch phrases; 'what is put out, comes back' and 'like attracts like'; negative attracts negative and positive attracts positive.
2. <u>Complimentary</u> - Complimentary experiences are those that are found on either end of the issue, whereby the centre point presents balance. Complimentary experiences can be seen as influences that aid harmony, balance and holistic perspectives. For example, opposites: Yin and yang, day and night, happy and sad; attraction to love and avoidance of danger. Appropriate complementary differences can bring neutral status, or balance i.e: action and reaction; cause and effect; magnetic polarisation; abstract and concrete; thoughts and feelings; creative talents and practical skills
3. <u>Associative</u>: The will – the *'ego'* the *'I'*, has an authoritative power over what association we seek and how we engage with chosen areas of sensory perception and responding interaction. What gains our attention and subsequent areas of endeavour initiate our human capacity to interact and contemplate.

A simple example of the above 1-3 can be observed if a person notes what catches his/her attention when walking through a crowd of people.

1) Reflective: We may notice a particular person's dress colour because it is a colour that we like or wear ourselves; reflective of our personal choice.
2) Complimentary: We may also note the sad expression on a person's face because it presents a contrasting opposite to our own happy disposition; illustrating a complementary opposite.
3) Associative: Alternatively something that aesthetically pleases, may bring us to a pause for a few moments of internal contemplation and deeper focus of internal association.

When we experience things that happen in our environment as impersonal, and unrelated to our personal growth, we may miss opportunities that can help us attain personal understanding and thereby invoke our humanitarian potential and empowerment. Our individual potential may be influenced by:-

(a) How we use our free will,
(b) Development of personal intelligence,
(c) Our relationship with natural resources presented on planet earth.

Our lives are suspended in an ocean of interactive experience. The three types of interaction and endeavour previously described 1-3 are 'key' to all our interactions and relationships as spokes on the wheel of life. When these three spokes are evenly distributed and of equal strength, the wheel spins with balance and a steady momentum which can support our sense of wellbeing and encourages patience, creativity and harmony.

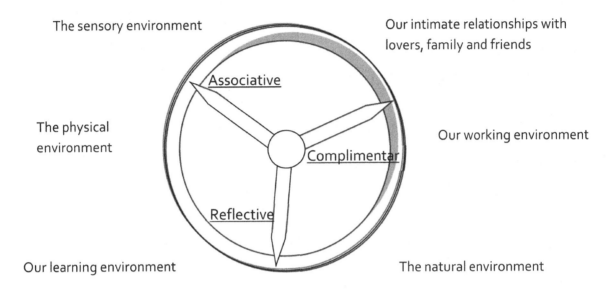

If the three spokes are uneven in their influence, the wheel can become very wobbly and thus lose its stability, momentum and versatility.

For example:-

1) <u>Reflective</u> The Autism spectrum could be considered a predominance of a reflective relationship with the environment which leads to a focus on imitative and obsessional behaviour patterns. The dominance of copied repetitive forms of behaviour excludes the possibility for successful development of self-directed learning, creative expression and personal independence.

2) <u>Associative</u> A parent can share authentic imaginative play and creativity with their child. However, if this imaginative play becomes the main style and focus of interaction, the parent could ultimately lose contact with their *adult carer* responsibilities.

3) <u>Complimentary</u> When an adult partnership within an intimate relationship, involves a predominance of opposites their styles of interaction, strengths and issues of priority, may be felt as an adverse form of separation. The couple may therefore over a period of time suffer from a lack of confidence in themselves as individuals. When we can share things together from a similar perspective this helps us to appreciate who we are, and we can gain a comfortable feeling from those aspects of life that are easiest and familiar.

> When I feel love I see beauty.
> When I feel grace I hear comforting sounds.
> When I feel gratitude I perceive mercy.
> When I have faith I feel the compassion of His love.

Acknowledging Our Daily Experiences.

Love, freedom and safety,
The foundations for movement.
Movement - The Foundations for Play,
Play - Foundations for Learning.
Learning - Foundations for Intelligence
Intelligence - Foundations for Personal Empowerment
Empowerment - Foundations for Heart-full Living
Heart-full Living - Foundations for the Engagement of the soul.
Engagement of the Soul – Revival of Higher Consciousness
Higher Consciousness - Foundations for Communion with God
Communion with God – The Supreme source of Love and Light
Love and Light – Living the Dream of Heaven on Earth

A Natural Order of Priority for Maintaining our Human Potential.

Sleep - a comfortable, safe, quiet environment for the required length of time.
Food – adequate amounts of food, free from stimulants and artificial additives, containing the required nutrition.
Movement – a safe and suitable quality and size of space.
Free play – uninterrupted activity within a suitable free play environment.
Creative activity – self-confidence, enthusiasm, imagination.
Authentic social interaction
Intimacy
Devotional service to *'Highest Good'*.

Sharing, Caring and Creative Parenting

The human capacity to engage in intimate exchanges is directly related to the above order of needs. Our loving relationships are initially founded upon bonding cues, related to our primary needs, originally presented as infant care. [see the list of 21 Bonding Cues described by Marnia Robinson in 'Cupid's Poisoned Arrow; North Atlantic Books, 2009:page 178.]

The development of adult relationships is founded upon biological makeup, inner emotional development, conscious development and other aspects of adult maturity and understanding.

From a purely biological perspective our relationships are especially influenced by the two hormones – dopamine and oxytocin.

Dopamine induces a state if high excitement. In order to accommodate high levels of dopamine the nerve cells in the body decrease their sensitivity and our mood can change to one of lethargy and disempowerment. This low state is susceptible to an unnatural desire to seek and create another hormonal dopamine flare.

Thus the dopamine story involves extremes of high and then a low, that leave the person keen to engage in any activity that will stimulate the dopamine level to rise again and initiate feelings of excitement, passion and challenge. This feeds an ongoing competitive disposition based on contrast between Dopamine excitement and basic survival issues.

In contrast, the hormone Oxytocin has the opposite effect. This hormone induces a calm mood of happiness and contentment. These feelings are often associated with caring dispositions, optimism and trust. The more oxytocin produced the more sensitive we become, because our nerve cells activate additional oxytocin receptors. Good feelings predominate and we may feel satisfied and contented.'

Knowledge and understanding of how these two hormones affect our interaction with those we love can be very helpful, and encourage those bonding activities related to oxytocin production, such as gentle physical interaction, eye contact, smiling and cuddling.

The order of development

The young baby first learns to move its limbs while in the confines of the womb. Some babies learn how to put their thumb in their mouth in order to suckle on their thumb. This illustrates the primary importance of movement, as key to our sense of wellbeing, whereby kinaesthetic and sensory experiences are usually superior to 'thinking' processes especially during early development.

1. Movement
    In order to engage in personal and self-directed interaction with our environment, we have to relate to our physical body and those sensory perceptions gained through body movement.

2. Sensory Perceptions
    Our perceptual awareness through movement facilitates our ability to accommodation and integrate sensory perceptual information.

3. Co-ordination.
    Movement and sensory perception, combine as mental activity in the brain to facilitate co-ordination skills and personal responding interaction.

4. Pre-determined actions
    Co-ordinated interaction with the environment promotes co-ordination of thought and movement. This provides opportunity for exploration and experimentation, which may also initiate social interaction.

5. Interaction
    Personally motivated interaction supports communication skills and social development.

6. Investigation
    Investigation supports inventive influences over the environment, discovery learning and self-directed learning.

7. All the above combine to develop cognitive intelligence, positive behaviour patterns, personal preferences, and authentic aspects of sharing and caring.

A brief look at Steiner's perception of child development

0-7 years. [Physical growth and sensory perceptual development]
Steiner described the early years from birth to seven as predominantly a time of:-

o   Physical growth,
o   Co-ordination of movement,
o   Reception and accommodation of sensory perception.

The focus during these years is one of gratitude that can also initiate an innocent and natural love of God

7-9 [Metamorphosis of Thinking]
Steiner presents these years as *the metamorphosis of conceptual thinking*. The child's inner world of Imagination becomes a key influence to the development of conceptual thinking and a notable disposition of happiness, balance and harmony may prevail.

9-12 [Metamorphosis of Feeling]
Steiner presents that the child now becomes aware of aloneness and one's individual disposition. The growing awareness of inner feelings is generally kept within and the child may feel exposed and vulnerable within a strange and often socially over demanding world. However, the will to

'live, *love and learn*' is awakened and blossoms within these early years of pleasure, positivity and purity.

12-14 [Metamorphosis of Will]
The child now addresses a personal quest to succeed and do well within their worldly surroundings. This is supported by their growing ability to think of a situation from another person's perspective. The developmental focus is on social interaction, social structures and an awakening of social responsibility. Creative endeavour and craft skills can now be developed from a personal inner sense of aesthetic appreciation and inventive potential.

13-15 [Synthesis of Thought]
The focus is on gaining knowledge of *the self* as an individual and learning to co-ordinate the inner self with the outside world. The adolescent may gain a sense of self-worth through a confrontational attitude, and associated struggles.

15-17 [Synthesis of Feeling]
Now the focus is to find and establish a natural and authentic presentation of the true self. The lower nature is revealed outwardly while the higher nature develops within inner feelings of a maturing personality and a *love of life*.

17-21 [Synthesis of Will]
The adolescent matures into adulthood. These years initiate genuine consideration of the three questions: Who am I? Where have I come from? Where am I going?

Abstract Mental Processes and Survival Issues

Abstract mental processes have minimal influence over our development of movement and self-directed learning.

Abstract mental processes create a dominance of *survival issues.*

Abstract thinking gives priority to survival related mental and physical activity. This dominance can disrupt learning and relationships, and thereby restrict the development of human consciousness.

Dominant survival issues may inhibit a person's ability to engage in a positive and useful lifestyle

Abstract mental processes relate to sensory information from primitive responses, based on fears related to survival. If imagination is given priority over every day living and learning, then occupational abstract thinking may dominate the person's activities and state wellbeing. This survival mode of abstract thinking motivates primal behaviour. This may then block the development of appreciation and conscience. Thus limiting the following aspects of development and maturity:-

1. One's ability to integrate sensory information with conscious brain functions.
2. One's awareness of physical consequences.
3. One's ability to predict the results of a specific action.
4. One's ability to integrate abstract and concrete thinking and thereby engage in creative activity.
5. One's ability to engage in self-directed learning.
6. One's ability to communicate and cooperate with others.
7. One's ability to engage in *positive* social activities, (as opposed to negative anti-social behaviour).
8. One's ability to express compassion and empathy within a sharing/caring context.

Our ability to reflect and witness both our inner disposition, as well as our relationship with the world around us, is fundamental to our level of consciousness and personal sense of wellbeing.

Through our conscious awareness of being witnessed by others, we develop our own inner ability to witness ourselves, and later, to be the witness for others.

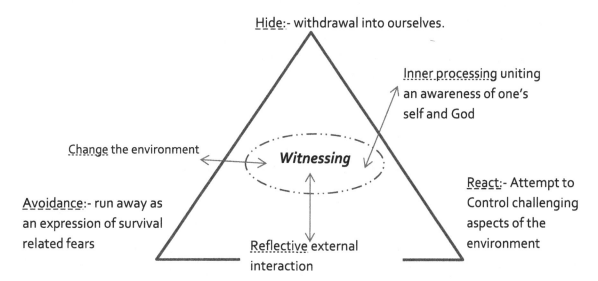

Hide:- withdrawal into ourselves.

Inner processing uniting
an awareness of one's
self and God

Change the environment

Witnessing

Avoidance:- run away as
an expression of survival
related fears

React:- Attempt to
Control challenging
aspects of the
environment

Reflective external
interaction

Stage ONE

Through our <u>physical sensory system</u> we witness the physical qualities presented by the world around us. From this we develop and learn to integrate ourselves with our environment.

> A child before the age of three relates to him/herself as a part of the world; like a bubble in a glass of water which is separate from the water yet the bubble is unable to establish it's self autonomously because the water gives the bubble its form and directs its movement.

The young child <u>before the age of three</u> actively employs strategies of copying and repetition that engage them with their environment through movement and the associated sensory experience. This age is predominantly one of sensory exploration.

The young child from <u>three to seven</u> actively seeks sensory entertainment in order to assimilate extensive amounts of sensory information within the simple structures of copying and repetition. This is the age of wonder and joy, experienced through the three E's Exploration Experimentation Enthusiasm; celebrating free will and the ability to utilise the predictable aspects of cause and effect. The young child now develops their own enthusiasm for life and fundamental understanding of physical structures of order both natural and manmade. At this stage **order and routine** are used to establish the inner assimilation of sensory perceptual knowledge. Subsequent skills are essential to the development of one's ability to creatively influence the environment through physical activity and imaginative presentation.

Helena Eastwood

Stage TWO

Through <u>social interaction</u> we witness the human capacity to feel emotions. From this we develop and learn about our own inner feelings and emotions.

Stage THREE

After the age of seven, we may develop the ability to witness from an independent place of consciousness. We witness what others do and integrate what we see into our own experiences and levels of intellectual understanding. We develop an ability to engage in discovery learning.

Traditionally this is considered the beginning for potential God consciousness i.e. a heart soul-spirit connection within promotes aesthetic appreciation and joy for life through discovery learning.

From the age of nine, we may develop the ability to witness ourselves and how the environment affects us and those around us. We learn how we can influence others through sharing and caring or even lying, people pleasing and challenging attention seeking behaviour patterns.

Creative endeavours can now integrate imagination with self-directed organisation of interaction with others and the physical environment.

11-14

During these years of development we may consciously organise sharing and caring from an empathetic disposition.

14 and onwards.

Now we may develop the ability to relate to how we witness ourselves and others, and incorporate this as an aspect of our personal development and social awareness. We develop and learn about consciously embracing issues associated with and related to <u>change and transition</u>. We learn how to consciously process responsibility and integrate the actions and feelings of others consciously within our own situation.

Empowerment is Compassion / Compassion is Empowerment

Empowerment without acceptance and compassion is competitive and controlling. This leads to or comes from an anti-life attitude and interactions that 'trash' and/or 'sabotage another person's well-being. For example

- An aggressive rejection of another person's genuine act of kindness
- Lack of forgiveness caused by resentment

118

- Resentment may cause a person to bully others as a way of expressing unresolved objections. Resentment is founded upon a fear that not having a desired influence of control will adversely affect the quality of one's life.
- Many people can feel unsafe when they experience a form of rejection and/or negative attitudes and negative interaction.
- Resentment can lead to depression or anger.
- Both anger and depression are caused by an underlying issue related to an unresolved survival issue; i.e. when an issue appears to oppose our potential safety.
- Ignoring someone is a negative response, a guarded pushing away.

> Acceptance without compassion can lead to a victim
> perspective and a defensive disposition.
>
> Compassion without acceptance can lead to a competitive disposition; a
> desire to be a powerful leader instead of an empowering influence.

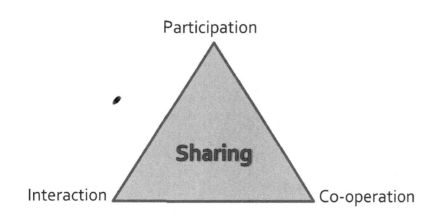

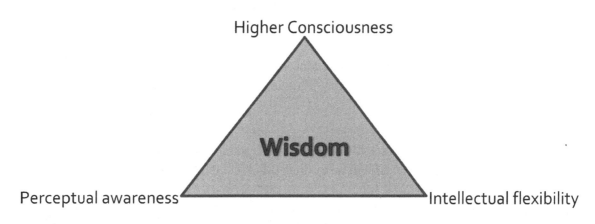

Empowerment – Spinning the yarn for life's Knitting!

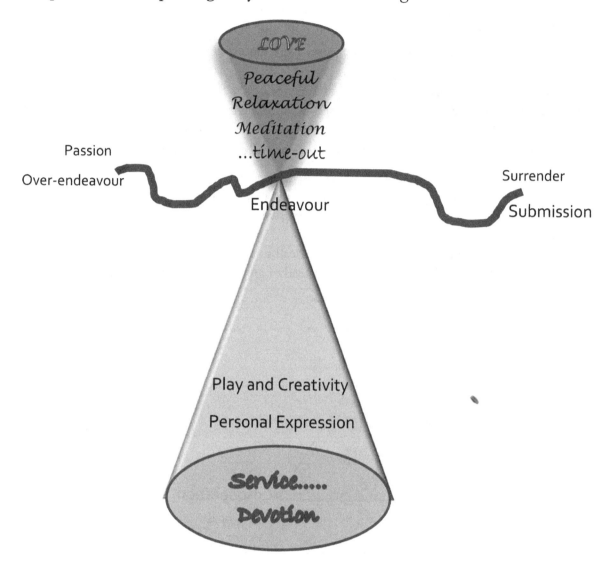

It seems to have come to pass that human consciousness has evoked that "Mans' will be done on earth, while *God's will* is done in heaven. This attitude has separated man from God and the heavens!

'Whoever exalts himself will be humbled and whoever humbles himself will be exalted.'[Matthew 23:12]

My inner feelings create my thoughts; my thoughts create my inner reality and my inner reality creates my external experience.

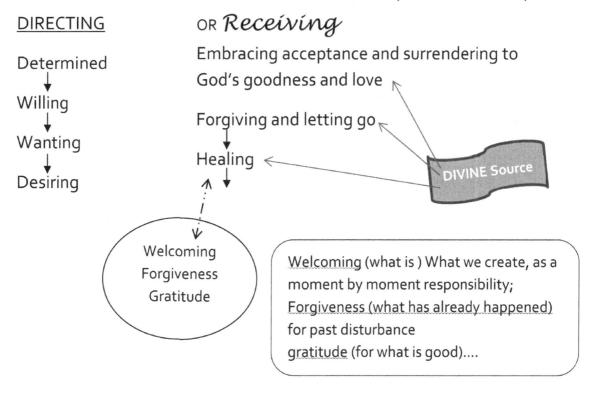

DIRECTING

Determined
↓
Willing
↓
Wanting
↓
Desiring

OR *Receiving*

Embracing acceptance and surrendering to
God's goodness and love

Forgiving and letting go

Healing

DIVINE Source

Welcoming
Forgiveness
Gratitude

Welcoming (what is) What we create, as a
moment by moment responsibility;
Forgiveness (what has already happened)
for past disturbance
gratitude (for what is good)....

Moving into creative levels of consciousness requires that we integrate the two principles of existence and growth described below as action and allowing.

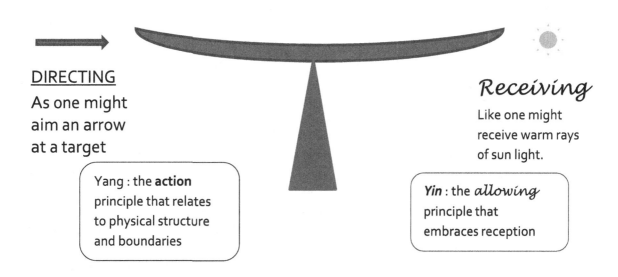

DIRECTING

As one might
aim an arrow
at a target

Yang : the **action**
principle that relates
to physical structure
and boundaries

Receiving

Like one might
receive warm rays
of sun light.

Yin : the *allowing*
principle that
embraces reception

Creative freedoms

Creative freedoms

Those adults who hold a position of authority and pastoral care over others, especially children and teenagers, may need to establish a more conscious assessment of how and what and when they take on active responsibility for:-

> Boundaries,
> Supporting materials and environments
> Natural consequences.

The author presents the following areas of consideration as fundamental and therefore supportive to any adult role of responsibility.

Empowered authenticity

Emotional honesty that avoids a projection of external expectations or demands and/or primitive survival issues. For example:- you have had an upset with your partner and there is a remaining level of emotional upset. When you are asked if you are upset you could explain that you have emotional feelings that are disturbing your sense of happiness and will therefore need some time to process and establish a personal recovery

Integrated Boundaries of Integrity

For example:-

○ You get a text from the in laws inviting the family out to lunch, however, you do not feel this is a suitable family outing for that particular evening. When your child asks what was said on your text you simply reply: "it was an adult to adult text and it was not anything for you to be concerned with."

Appropriate Adult Responsibility

For example holding children and young dependent adolescents, free and/or separate from unsuitable and unnecessary levels of responsibility and decision making. E.g:

○ Driving the car when, where, and at what speed;
○ How to address money issues related to bills, provisions, safety etc.
○ Adult to adult communication in private to avoid unsuitable levels of dramatic entertainment or fear related anxiety and worrying;
○ Consciously organisation adult presentation of information, questions and choices tailored to suit the listener's individual personality, level of ability and maturity.

Simple structures of communication

It is the very nature of simple communication that provides successful scaffolding that can deeply nurture seeds of encouragement and meaningful experiences with an accompanying sweetness of personal empowerment. This may wisely support our evolution into higher realms of consciousness.

Through the power of unconditional love we can provide an abundance of creative opportunity for personal empowerment and self-directed learning.

Creativity and co-operative interaction are the foundations of learning. Multisensory integration creates depth and richness to our interaction with the world around us. Thus when multi-sensory information is framed within areas of creative freedom and passionate interaction, learning can be experienced as personal discovery within an infinite potential for meaningful expansion.

Creativity, multisensory learning, aesthetic appreciation and divergent thinking plus some heart magic, are born when ideas, feelings and experiences flow togerther like the water within a stream. Whereby an infinite freedom is continued within the boundaries of the geographical terain and the earthly laws of physics.

> As the daylight dissipates the darkness of the night
> The sun's rays shine across the land,
> My soul leaps in the hand of the Lord's goodness.
> As we share in the light of this new day
> Our gratitude and reverence for work and play.
> We give thanks for the divine grace that shines within us,
> Our individual personalities that enrich our sharing,
> And the joy of creativity that guides our learning together.

In her peace message Amma (Sri Mata Amritanandamayi Devi Geneva 2002) spoke the following words "What everyone needs is peace, but the majority want to be king. No one wants to be a servant. How then can there be peace? Won't there be war and conflict? A true servant is the real King. Isn't the milk from the black cow, and the white cow, and the brown cow, white? Similarly the essence in every person is the same. Peace and contentment are the same for everyone. Those who desire them should work together."

Our fullest potential is present within the very essence of our being from which we express our original nature, the very essence of positive and joyful living.

In her peace message Amma (Sri Mata Amritanandamayi Devi Geneva 2002) spoke the following words "What everyone needs is peace, but the majority want to be king. No one wants to be a servant. How then can there be peace? Won't there be war and conflict? A true servant is the real King. Isn't the milk from the black cow, and the white cow, and the brown cow the same?"

Similarly the essence in every person is the same. Peace and contentment are the same for everyone. Those who desire them should work together."

Our fullest potential is present within the very essence of our being, from which we express our original nature, the very essence of positive and joyful living. The diagram below presents a simplified consideration of how we can express the sweetness of our unique potential out into to the world around us.

The following diagram presents a simplified consideration of how we can express the sweetness of our unique potential out into to the world around us.

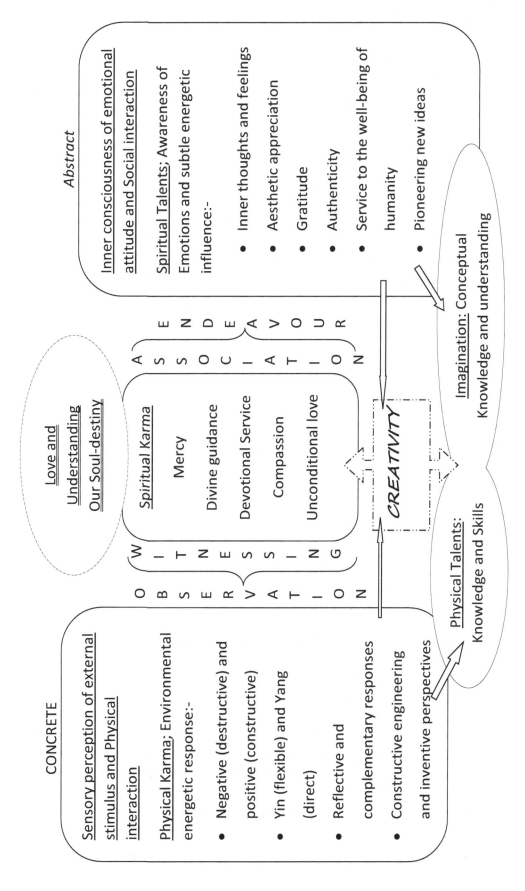

Outdoor Play Every Day

Now the birds fill the woods with their springtime songs,

While winter commands a cold obedience over nature's optimism,

And wanders and wails among the silent trees

That stand strong and tall - meditating upon our playful ways.

The children came again for a while to play and roam among sticks and stones.

They remembered your presence,

Played with the dogs, walked along logs and fell in the bog.

They watched the mist creeping into the valley as they left

Carrying woodland contentment and wearing moments of peace,

Holding something special.

[With love and thanks to you from all of us, those before us, and those yet to come.]

The natural environment appears to provide freedom which actively encourages
children to develop their fullest functional potential within a *living curriculum* of
effective educational resources that organically nurture the children's enthusiastic social
disposition and curiosity about life. (Montessori,1967:50; Bradburn,1976:55.)

The Wonders of the Earths Creation

The Christian faith is guided by the text in the Bible which describes the activity of God initially
as the creator of the universe,

He commanded:- "Let lights appear in the sky to separate day from night.". So He made the sun to
rule over the day and the moon to rule over the night; he also made the stars..... Then He commanded
"Let the waters be filled with many kinds of living beings and let the air be filled with birds.".......
"Let the earth produce all kinds of animal life."....... Then God said "And now we will make human
beings.... They will have power over the fish and birds and all animals domestic and wild, large and
small."....... He said, "I have provided all kinds of grain and all kinds of fruit for you, but for all the
wild animals I have provided grasses and leafy plants."............ Bible - Genesis1-2:3-5(Elass,1997:3-5)

The popular children's songs *Morning Has Broken* and *All Things Bright and Beautiful* [as shown below] praise the creation of our natural world. However, in our present day life style within comfortable buildings, children have relatively few opportunities to experience 'intimate contact' with nature and experience the natural cycles and rhythms presented by life and natural phenomena.

Morning Has Broken

Morning has broken, like the first morning
Blackbird has spoken, like the first bird
Praise for the singing, praise for the morning
Praise for them springing fresh from the world.

Sweets the rains new fall, sunlit from heaven.
Like the first dew fall, on the first grass.
Praise for the sweetness of the wet garden,
Sprung in completeness where His feet pass.

Mine is the sunlight, mine is the morning
Born of the one light Eden saw play
Praise with elation, praise every morning
God's re-creation of the new day.

All Things Bright and Beautiful

All things bright and beautiful,
All creatures great and small,
All things wise and wonderful
The lord God made them all.

Each little flower that opens,
Each little bird that sings
He made their glowing colours
He made their tiny wings.

The purple headed mountain,
The river running by,
The sunset, and the morning
That brightens up the sky.

The cold wind in the winter
A pleasant summer sun
The right fruits in the garden
He made them every one.

He gave us our eyes to see them
And lips that we might tell
How great is God almighty
Who hath done things all well.

Pioneering Outdoor Play in Childhood Education

Montessori wrote 'the aspiration to know, to love and to serve' is the 'trinomial of all religions, but the child is the true maker of our spirituality'; that a small child has a tendency which can best be described as a 'sensitive period of the soul' when they need 'freedom and intense activity in accordance with the laws of life,' and thereby, teachers can use the plan of nature to 'give form' to the 'development of conduct and personality'. Montessori presented free access to an outdoor garden was an essential part of early childhood education.(Montessori,1988:201&1967:172) '.......
However Hobday presents that 'Since the 1950s much more emphasis has been placed on creating comfortable indoor environments than on promoting wellbeing,'

Steiner considered that learning during the early years is especially well supported by the natural environment because the human being is a mirror of the universe and 'all the elements of nature'. (Steiner,1997:84) Children 'live and work in the element of life.....as part of a living world', and intuit 'that behind every physical occurrence there is a real spiritual occurrence and both together form a whole'.(Steiner,1988: 58,18-19)

Froebel (1782-1852) encouraged 'children to grow up in harmony with nature', he nurtured their 'spiritual awareness' (Garrick,2004:17) and pioneered free-play as learning, and outdoor play as central to this'. (Knight,2009:62).

Over the last century 'British traditions of multi-religious education' (International Froebel's Society conference,2004:21) have developed alongside a growing endeavour to incorporate radical educational practice and theory presented by Froebel (1782-1852), MacMillan (1860-1931), Steiner (1861-1925), Montessori (1870-1952), Forest Schools, Reggio Emilia (1946) and the recent Welsh Foundation Phase (2008), which have culminated in to emphasising the importance of free play in an outdoor environment (the *Kindergarten)* as a resource for children's wellbeing, natural development and early years education, alongside natural materials and aesthetically pleasing surroundings.

> 'Nature is a curriculum' "The natural environment offers a wealth of play potential for young children with trees and small patches of water the most valued elements.' (MacMillan,2008:7-8)

> Moyles, (2007:173) suggests 'children have the right to be outside because, besides being a wonderful springboard for learning, that is where they want to be most of the time.'

> Elinor Goldschmied 'inspired encouragement to give young children natural objects or objects made from natural materials to play with and explore.' (Cited in Roberts & Featherstone,2002:5-7)

The *natural curriculum* is thought to promote 'spontaneous freedom of action' within a framework of 'play and self-chosen activity' that embraces the interconnected nature of all living things rather than intellectually formatted thinking. Natural materials and free-play in natural environments encourages intuitive and compassionate perception, that is *felt understandings,* alongside an inner sense of confidence and wellbeing. (Montessori,1967:68-69)

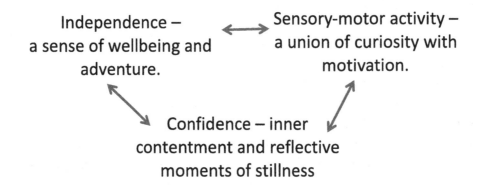

The Importance of *'Free Play'*

Some Early Year's education theorists and psychologists have presented the importance of free play activity as a prerequisite foundation for learning (Einarsdottir&Wagner,2006:208) The work of Macmillan (Bradburn,1976:57-58), Montessori(1967:173), Steiner(1981:51-54) and Goldschmied (Goldschmied&Jackson,2004:97-99) suggest young children are spontaneous observers of nature and can gain a wealth of perceptual skills and detailed awareness of discrimination and differentiation (Montessori,1967:70-71.) long before this information is consciously structured, categorised, calculated or manipulated as an academic understanding through formal thinking operations. The freedom to play and explore the abundance of materials and possible activities given by a natural outdoor environment can encourage and support the unlimited aspects of human potential - 'physical performance' related to 'physical intelligence', the mastery of integrating thoughts with actions.

> 'Essential changes take place in the development of a child's motivation under the influence of play.' (Einarsdottir&Wagner,2006:214citing El'konin (1978/1999))

Play seems to embrace a purity of thought that perceives truth without educational interference and thereby initiates the powers of thought within a cycle of dream-thought- action and the development of talent.

'...even a small child should not be distracted from what he's doing, in other words the operation of his thought should not be stopped......education ...begins with the correct presentation of questions whereby children are encouraged to think for themselves and make their own independent decisions.' (Megre Book7;49)

Pioneering educators that advocate the young child's affinity with the *natural* ecology, considered the natural environment a stimulating and nurturing resource for all aspects of the young child's physical, mental, emotional and spiritual development.

Helena Eastwood

An enrichment of sensory and aesthetic experience.

Direct contact with the natural world -'..stimulating all the senses in a natural world rich in things to be discovered', *(Trevarthen cited in Mortan & Zerbato Eds.,2008.)*
'-not only involving meticulous observation but listening and smelling, touching and tasting to bring us in touch with the land and its biological processes.' *(Thoreau(1906) Cited in Mortari, L& Zerbato, R, Eds. 2008:108)*

Visual - focus, tracking, distance (near, middle, far) shape, pattern, shades and shadows (light-dark),colours ,shapes and aesthetic beauty.

Auditory sounds -.
Auditory - frequency of sounds (hz), location, vibration, pulse, intensity, rhythm, melody, e.g. the songbirds sweet melodies, the sound of the running stream.

Smells and fragrance - minty, floral, ethereal, musky, resinous, pungent, putrid.
(Ceppi et al. 1998: 86)

Tactile – senses of touch, movement, texture, temperature, viscosity, density (soft-hard), structural shape.

Children 'live and work in the element of life.' *(Steiner,1988:58)* In the outdoor environment young children celebrate the life force that maintains our lives and that of the natural world around us.
Research has also presented strong evidence to support observations that illustrate that a child who has less opportunity for sensorial activity remains at a lower mental level:

'A child needs to live naturally and not simply have knowledge of nature.' (Montessori,1967:67,172) (Montessori,1988:200)

In the Norwegian nurseries the '**children experience wooded areas with rivers and streams every day**'(Curruthers cited in Moyles,2007:176) Lasenby describes *weather* as 'one of the most valuable resources' which provides experiential experience that increases children's 'knowledge and understanding of the world in which they live.' (Cited in Ouvry,2003:24) In Finland the outdoor Forest School approach presents the wild natural environment and the changing seasons as the curriculum and the teacher for children up to the age of six; Finland is regularly placed in top positions in the Organisation for Economic Cooperation and Development's 'prestigious world rankings for educational performance and literacy'. (Honore, 2004:25)

Forest schools present a belief in 'the holistic benefit of natural experiences' and consider the natural environment as 'awe-inspiring' for young children. (Moyles,2007:177) The Danish Early

Years curriculum describes the Natural outdoor Forest School environments successfully meet the following six areas of learning required 'to create a competent child':-

- Language,
- All round Personal development,
- Body and movement,
- Nature and natural phenomena,
- Cultural expression and values,
- Social development. (Austin,2007:64;)

The natural environment is very supportive during early learning, especially during the important *'Sensitive Periods'* of learning. Montessori identified the 'sensitive periods' as the following areas of the young child's development:-

Language,
Order,
Sensory-motor activity - refinement of *the senses,*
Walking (postural reflexes),
Small objects,
Spiritual awareness.

(Montessori,1988:201;Montessori,1967:172;Goddard 2004:94&Meadows,2006:336)

'Research....suggests that children seem to have a special affinity, or connection to the natural world – that they experience a kind of 'primal seeing' which allow them to 'experience the natural world in a deep and direct manner, not as a background for events, but rather, as a factor and stimulation.' (Sebba cited in MacMillan,2008:10)

Nature's curriculum is one of open ended activities with open ended choices and open ended results. This has been seen to give children a sense of independence, personal confidence and enthusiasm to engage in the child's own perspectives of meaningful play.

Throughout the first eight years of life *Movement in space* is directly related to balance, sensory integration, confidence and foundations for learning.

Research has shown that'...children who play in the forest tend to demonstrate better motor skills than children who play in a traditional playground.' (Moyles, Ed. 2007:183. Citing Fjortoft & Sagerie,2000.)

Natural environments usually offer: an infinite range of colours and shapes, temperature, textures, and patterns that relate to *visual discernment of growth (construction) and deterioration (destruction);* rich diversity of *sensory perception* in simple formats that encourage appreciation of appearance, contrasts and attention to the intricate details of *movement, differences* and *change* offer a wide choice of activity to suit different levels of confidence, adventure and physical ability.

Visual Perceptual Skills

Visual perceptual skills are strongly motivated within the world of nature, especially in relation to animals where detailed visual discrimination includes the skills of visual tracking and visual closure.

'children given opportunities to be in contact with animals display a deep curiosity and desire to know about the animals they encounter.'
(Moyles,2007:182)

Freedom to Move

Outdoor spaces offer more physical space, which supports greater freedoms of physical activity and therefore accidents may be less frequent and less serious than those encountered in the more crowded and intense indoor environments......

The children learn to take responsibility for their own awareness of what they can do safely. The natural outdoor environment addresses the output and input of sensory information from all the major sensory modalities and 'leads to the recognition that the entire brain is involved in movement.' (Callaway,2005:10)

Issues related to children's safety are integral to their ability to judge what level of activity can be accommodated safely on a moment by moment basis. The skills associated with safety are also interconnected with other areas of development such as those listed below:-

* *Secure balance* is inseparable from the development of ***postural* control**, which in turn is supported by information from: ***visual*, *proprioception*, and *motor systems*.'
* **Physical movement** and the development of visual eye movements and **associated visual perceptual competence are interdependent**.
* The **academic foundations of numeracy, reading and writing** are initially dependent upon the ability **to know one's 'position in space'** and associated **directional awareness**. (Goddard, 1988: 17-19.)

Physical Movement, Balance and Auditory Perceptual Skills

A growing body of evidence indicates that direct exposure to nature is essential for physical and emotional health. Early creativity and experimentation during free play can provide important foundations for future 'formal operations' and skills of creative performance.

The skills of balance, mobility and co-ordination, associated with physical movement have been shown to improve children's ability to negotiate challenges and explore related aspects of ability and safety. Natural environments can offer a wide choice of activity to suit different levels of confidence, adventure and physical ability. (Callaway,2005:10)

> 'Education cannot be effective unless it helps the child to open himself to life.........it is essential that a child's spontaneous movements should not be checked or that he be compelled to act according to the will of another.' (Montessori,1967:50)

Vestibular stimulation also influences specific physiological and biochemical changes in the body associated with emotional experiences.

'Immature vestibular functioning is frequently found amongst children who have specific learning difficulties and adults who suffer from anxiety and agoraphobia and panic disorders.' (Goddard,2004:17)

'Nature deficit disorder ...... diminished used of the senses, attention difficulties and higher rates of physical and emotional illness.' New studies suggest that the exposure to nature may reduce the symptoms of attention deficit hyperactivity disorder and that it can improve all children's cognitive abilities and resistance to negative stresses and depression.' (Louv,2006:34)

In contrast to the wealth of experiential sensory experiences presented in natural environments, some aspects of indoor learning environments may be seen to disrupt the child's sensory development e.g. manmade structures, buildings and machinery are thought to disturb the young child's developing auditory perception and integration of sounds.

> 'At birth, the human ear has the potential to detect frequencies from16hz low sounds up to 25000hz high sounds. Low frequencies sounds below 100hz are often felt as vibrations through the skin rather than heard.' and most adults have lost the range of hearing they were born with only retaining accurate hearing within the range of their spoken language of approximately 125-8000hz. The work of Johansen, using frequency specific music for improving hearing discrimination and speed and integration of auditory processing, has successfully helped children with learning difficulties such as dyslexia. In order to

locate the source of sound the brain interprets the small differences in time and intensity between how and when a sound is received in the two ears.'

'Nature finds expression through music - *From the whispering of the wind in the leaves, to the thundering of a stormy sea on the shore. Just as all living things share the characteristic of motion, all of life is sound....*' (Goddard, 2004:69,73,79,91)

The work of Rauscher & Shaw (1996) showed a clear 'link between music, and spatial intelligence – the accurate perceptual ability and mental imagery in pre-school children. (Cited in Goddard,2004:79)

Within any building sounds are distorted by reverberation and absorption.

Questions to consider:-

- At what point does auditory sound become 'obnoxious sensory stimulation...perceived as noise'? (Taylor p112)
- What influence might this have on the young child's auditory range of perception and development of discrimination?
- What auditory range might we suppose is perceived by children who have grown up in natural outdoor environments, living within nature's sounds and silences? (Ceppi,&Zini,1998:90&95)

Also one could consider how strong smells presented in manmade materials may disrupt the young child's natural range of ability to discern different subtleties of smell. Even when the natural sensory stimulus is very strong, nature appears to present a sense of balance and harmony that calms situations of potential frustration, fear or overwhelming stimulus with complementary contrast, a sense of predictability and natural elements of geographic control: gravity, density, force.

The world of nature illustrates a mastery of sciences. Within the natural world, children can feel and experience the material elements and physical forces that have been, and are yet to be, used within the construction of our technological world. Some educators might suggest that from the natural environment children can also discern 'what makes life possible.

Some religious and spiritual teachings have also related the qualities of different aspects of natural phenomena as inspiration to spiritual consciousness and personal aspirations. For example:-

Earth - 'The earth is always tolerant, patient and forgiving.'

Mountains - Mountains give us 'trees, herbs, and water.... We should learn from those mountains how to work for the benefit of others.' Mountains are very silent and favourable for spiritual development.

Trees - 'You should be as tolerant as a tree.'

Water – 'the qualities of water are purity, softness and refreshment.'

The honey bee – takes only a little from each flower, and teaches us not to take more than we need. (Narayana Maharaja,2005)

Similarly the native American Indians associate animals with different qualities of relationship with life, e.g:-

The ant represents patience and strategy, and teaches the positive results of team work.

The horse represents stamina, riches and power, and teaches loyalty to those you trust.

The deer represents deliberation, great awareness and speed, and teaches gentleness and peace.

The hawk represents observation and patience and teaches the importance of taking the right action at the right time.

The mole represents sensitivity to touch and vibration and an understanding of mother-earth energy, and teaches self-reliance and cheerfulness. (Palmer,2001:11,198-199,111,193,227.)

When given an opportunity to observe, day after day, parent birds feeding their young, children can perceive the adult birds' outstanding commitment and stamina within their parenting role.

Thus, the animal kingdom presents simple and clear aspects of relationship with life for a young child to perceive and appreciate. The child's inner awareness and external freedom to spontaneously associate with wild plants and animal life can support an active interest in gardening and the care of domestic animals. (Montessori,1967:71-74)

Outdoor play may help children develop a deeper and clearer understanding of the relationship between man's activities and the ecology of the earth. Watts proposes that young children educated within a natural outdoor environment can embrace 'the unity of nature' through their sensory–motor experiences, and their thinking evolves a 'naturalistic shape' and growing awareness of the 'various applications of nature's universal laws.....' (Cited in International Froebel's Society conference,2004:34). Many young children whose suburban life style does not include outdoor educational experiences may not understanding natures influence upon their everyday life style. For example, for some young children, milk is a white liquid called cows-milk or sometimes goats-milk, sold in a carton at the supermarket. One can only guess how the young child might comprehend the word cow or goat when s/he has only seen cows in picture books or *maybe* from a car driving past fields. Indeed anyone's comprehension of the word cows-milk might be rather obscure, without a direct experience of how mammals suckle their young or, better still, calves feed from their mother's milk and the human process of dairy farming or hand milking.

As adults, the young children of today will be facing new and important issues on the further developments in the use of genetic technology within both horticultural and animal farming, animal experimentation and the evolution of human genetic sciences.

> '...more importantly, there is an urgency to provide young children with wild environmental experiences and to let them know how beautiful the natural environment is to protect it for the future and for all the children of the earth.' (Moyles, 2007:183)

Conservation and growing levels of pollution within the inner cities and urban environments are also important issues that young children of today will be faced with as adults.

Within the world of nature, God's presence is tethered to a complexity of environmental issues related to survival.

When man works in harmony with nature, issues of ecology are related to man's endeavour and God's mercy, together this brings abundance.

When man works in harmony with nature, issues of survival are related to mans' ability to work in harmony with the divine life force; this brings sustainability.

> Learning to care through the growing and harvesting of vegetables.
> Learning to share through the growing and harvesting of fruit.
> Learning to love through the growing and sharing of flowers.

The research of Cobb in 1977 concluded that 'inventiveness and imagination' was *rooted* in 'early experiences in nature'. (Cited in Louv,2006:93) This supports the growing development of natural spaces, woodlands and green spaces, as beneficial projects for children and adults to share in city and urban environments. (O'Brian,2005:43)

Steiner described an essential feature of young children is that they give up their 'whole being to the environment....,' (Steiner, Rudolph 1988:28) and the essence of gratitude develops out of a 'bodily-religious relationship' with movement and the senses. Feelings of thankfulness, gratitude, joy may emerge 'out of *one's feeling life*' when 'beholding any of nature's phenomena..... This gratitude lives in the physical body and it must dwell in it, since otherwise it would not be anchored deeply enough to develop a natural mood of appreciation' (Steiner, Rudolf. 1988:128-129). The young child initially learns through his feelings rather than his mind or intellect and this is how he perceives beauty and experiences joy and formulates his expression of intelligence and child-like purity of thought.

Montessori suggested that unnatural possessiveness in children, seen as a desire to seize and often destroy, is resolved when children are supported with natural environments which help them aspire towards the best part of their nature, which 'tries to understand life, so as to protect and improve it', and through 'intelligent insight' help living things. (Montessori, M.1988:201) Montessori also suggests 'It is therefore easy to interest them in taking care of plants and especially animals'. She describes one morning when she observed the children 'all seated in a circle on the floor around a magnificent red rose that had opened up during the night. They were silent, peaceful, completely absorbed in contemplation.' (Montessori, M. 1967:71)

'For everything going on in nature is permeated by a hidden music, the earthly projection of the "music of the spheres." Every plant, every animal actually incorporates the tones of the music of the spheres.' (Steiner, Rudolph 1982:19)

Giving a discourse on the book Sri BhagavataArka Maricimala by Srila Bhaktivinoda Thakura Narayana Maharaja,2005 Bhaktivedanta Narayana at Badger California: June 18th, 2005.
Palmer, J.D. *Animal Wisdom*. London; Element, 2001:11,198-199,111,193,227
Montessori, M. *The Discovery of the Child*. New York; The Random House, 1967:71-74.
International Froebel's Society conference july2004:34, University of Surrey Roehampton.
Moyles, J. Ed. *Early Years Foundations* Maidenhead Open University Press, 2007: 183
Ouvry, M. *Exercising muscles and minds*. London; National Children's Bureau, 2003: 93.
O'Brian, L & Murray, R. *Forest School and its impacts on young children: Case studies in Britain. Elsevier/*Urban Forest &Urban Greening. No. 6, 2007.
Steiner, R. *Necessity and Freedom*. London; Anthroposophic Press, 1988:128-129
Montessori, M. *The Absorbent Mind*. Oxford; Clio Press, 1988:201.
Montessori, M. *The Discovery of the Child*. New York; The Random House, 1967: 71
Montessori, M. *The Discovery of the Child*. New York; The Random House, 1967.
Steiner, Rudolph. *Balance in teaching*. New York: Mercury Press, 1982: 1

Promoting A Multisensory Live, Love, Learn Approach – Self-Directed Discovery Learning

❖ Creativity is the gift of movement
Joy is the gift of love
Happiness is the gift of being present
Peace is the gift of calm contemplation
Gratitude is the gift of sharing
Devotion is the gift of life
Reverence is the gift of humility
Patience is the gift of time.

Only through the power of unconditional love can we hope to provide an abundance of creative opportunity for personal empowerment and self-directed learning.

Creativity and co-operative interaction are the foundations of multisensory learning. Multisensory integration creates depth and richness to our interaction with the world around us through the heart and soul-spirit. Thus, when multi-sensory information is framed within areas of creative freedom and passionate interaction, learning can be experienced as personal discovery within an infinite future potential for meaningful expansion into our fullest potential. What I have written is not presented as a curriculum as such. I have tried to illustrate how learning can be presented within a mind map that creates its own presentation of the human auspicious intelligence alongside a celebration of life experiences through aesthetic appreciation and natural enthusiasm.

As Robert Barron writes in his book *And Now I See*
'God is reliable in his love and delightfully unpredictable in the way that he demonstrates it.'

Creativity, multisensory learning, aesthetic appreciation and divergent thinking plus some heart magic, is born when ideas, feelings and experiences flow togerther like the water within a stream, where an infinite freedom is continaned within the boundaries of the geographical terrain and the earthly laws of physics.

The true master can successfully support others to discover for themselves: attention to small detail, authentic passion and genuine understanding. The apprentice thereby learns, over a period of time, to achieve what the master can already do with natural ease and uses these skills to develop his/her own natural field of excellence.

Multisensory scaffolding for *Self-Directed Discovery Learning* through:-

    i.   Creative activity

ii.   Authentic social and physical interaction,

iii.   Co-operative games

iv.   The organic development of experiential projects of enquiry.

Scaffolding learning from a multisensory perspective comes from the heart and soul-spirit connection. From this sweet place activities and interaction embraces a natural balancing of mental and physical activity. A harmonious combination of both musical and structural aspects of creativity, organically integrate imagination with a tangible expression of creative interaction. This organically supports desires to gain conscious awareness and understanding.

Multi-sensory activities embrace a wealth of sensory experience whereby motivation and focus are intrinsically directed by environmental scaffolding. An expansive relationship with an indefinable potential presents qualities of creative engagement and supports future development of awareness.

Multi-sensory activities do not necessarily have a predetermined goal or measure of achievement. Sensory integration may embrace a spectrum of intelligence that was previously unacknowledged by the participant and thus aspects of learning may not necessarily be attributed to specific interactive games or activities.

Knowledge and skills are secondary to the abstract qualities of enjoyment and pleasure of participation. Creative consequences extend like an over-flowing river into new domains beyond perceived normal boundaries. Each individual's unique human design is nurtured as a tender gift.

When multisensory materials are carefully designed they can intrinsically meet different styles of learning, different levels of skill, and sensory perceptual differences. The teaching benefits offered by multisensory didactic materials can be helpful to a wide age range, and a broad spectrum of ability and interest.

Creativity and co-operative interaction are the foundations of multisensory learning. Multisensory integration creates depth and richness to our interaction with the world around us through the heart and soul-spirit. Thus when multi-sensory information is framed within areas of creative freedom and passionate interaction, learning can be experienced as personal discovery within an infinite future of meaningful expansion and full potential. Multi-sensory Living and Learning is not a curriculum as such, it is presented on this website as pedagogy, illustrated through a compendium of games, creative activities and carefully designed learning materials. Learning can be presented within an auspicious mind map approach that facilitates its own presentation of our human intelligence alongside a celebration of life experiences through aesthetic appreciation and natural enthusiasm.

> The true art of teaching is to creatively present multisensory information through an integrated spectrum of accurate conceptual communication and cognitive intellectual understanding.

Helena Eastwood

<u>Areas of science and different areas of intellectual thinking</u> can nurture, encourage and inspire higher levels of awareness through supportive scaffolding within the practicalities of our everyday living.

<u>Simple structures of communication</u> can deeply nurture seeds of encouragement for meaningful experiences and the accompanying sweetness of personal empowerment. It is the very nature of this simple and successful scaffolding that wisely supports our evolution into higher realms of consciousness. Can we empower our children to develop their individuality and creativity beyond that of the limitations of ourselves and present day thinking and today's standards of media entertainment?

The following a-d describes the author's presentation of consecutive aspects of sensory experience within a constructive and meaningful learning experience.

a. *Sensory stimulus* - assimilation of sensory information presented by the environment to the physical sensory receptors.
b. *Concrete integration* *of sensory information - p*hysical multi-sensory enrichment. Experiential experiences, constructional sensory-motor activity. Memory and recall of information.
c. *Abstract* thinking activity i.e. feelings related through:- intuitive perception and extra sensory awareness, fantasy, mood, disposition, attitude, associated past memories and desires for repetitive sensory experiences and conceptual understanding.
d. *Creativity-* imaginative *integration of a and b (sensory experiences with concrete, and abstract thinking skills with* authentic and unique aspects of personal individuality. The initiation of *h*eart and soul connections and *spiritual experiences* of reverence, nurture, dreams, morals and beliefs, compassion, gratitude and appreciation.

A four day experience of play and learning on a natural beach environment is described below as an example of the above (a-d) in practise:-

<u>Day one (a)</u> Mobility - sensory exploration, assessment of environment, testing and establishing boundaries, knowledge of the environmental geography.

<u>Day two (b)</u>
<u>Increasing the sensory</u> experiences by physical efforts that initiate <u>gross motor interaction</u>.

For example running away from the waves; splashing, diving, sitting in the shallow waves; throwing sand, digging a hole, covering yourself or someone else, burying things in the sand; playing chase games on the sand, or in the water, stamping on shells and worm castings, collecting seaweed or driftwood for a fire, collecting other items from shore line old rope containers etc.. Sensory experiences upgraded to a maximum, <u>exploring environmental and social aspects of control</u> and testing boundaries. Excitement and enthusiasm, over enthusiastic, attention seeking /challenging behaviour seeking/engineering stronger sensory stimulus, a strong sense of action and reaction.

Day three (c)

Relating to the environment through creative activity. Collect objects for artistic and constructive projects. Building and decorating sand structures, sandcastles, waterways, three dimensional structures, village and road designs. Surfing a waves, learning to swim, playing catch on the beach and or in the sea; constructing a sun shade, tent, or wind break from sticks and stones and hotel building.

Day four (d) A day of relaxation, a heart-felt accommodation of the previous three days experience, recapping and remembering, recall and meditation. Embracing *Spiritual experiences* of reverence, compassion, gratitude and appreciation.

The author considers that successful learning is based on a series of experiences, framed, on several occasions, within the same environmental and sensory context. The above four day example can be transferred into other scenarios; whereby self-directed exploration and learning can be addressed on three different sessions. This may or may not be specified as different days or consecutive days but certainly there would ideally be one or more night's sleep between each session. A fourth session is an optional extra and it can be included after any time lapse after the third session.

Where are We Today

When multi-sensory information is framed within areas of creative freedom and passionate interaction, learning can be experienced as personal discovery. This opens the learner to an infinite potential for meaningful expansion into a love of life and learning.

Multi-sensory Enrichment:

- ✓ Presenting a wide spectrum of associated sensory information.
- ✓ Supporting comprehensive understanding
- ✓ Encouraging conceptual understanding
- ✓ Stimulating feelings of aesthetic appreciation.
- ✓ Participation is guided by personal choices and preferences.

> E.g. Finding a strawberry in a bowl of assorted different fruits.
> Feeling the strawberry shape and texture .
> Watching the development of a strawberry as it grows on a plant.
> Make some strawberry jelly or jam
> Smelling and eating a strawberry.
> Eating strawberry jelly and strawberry ice-cream.

VERSUS

Multi-sensory over-whelm

- One high level of sensory experience dominates over other sensory perceptions.
- Personal preferences have no influence;
- A concoction of different sensory experience; so diverse that the mind experiences a sense of chaos.
- Mental hyperactivity and/or hypersensitivity.

> E.g. someone is playing loud heavy metal music in a communal space.
>
> Boisterous young people having a party with loud music, dancing, shouting too each other because of the loud music, drinking, and eating.
>
> Intense perfumes and body smells.
>
> They have flashing lights on the disco dance floor.

The examples in the boxes above illustrate that multi-sensory experiences, may not necessarily be desirable for successful living and learning. Multi-sensory at its best presents opportunities for enrichment, diversity and expansion; at its worst it can present over stimulation and hyperactivity, wild chaotic activity and adrenaline based types of excitement, drama and addiction.

Thus multi-sensory presentation may range from a man-made concoction of intense stimulation; to a broad spectrum of meaningful sensory scaffolding, structured to support sensory integration and intellectual understanding.

Overwhelming levels of unrelated stimulus and focus on illogical abstract sensory experience can create a sense of over-stimulation and chaos. Similarly multi-sensory may have a strong overwhelming influence that either entertains or disturbs our sense of reality; and prevents new learning, foundations of understanding and development of appropriate skills.

Ideally multi-sensory scaffolding for learning incorporates subtle and primary sensory information. When sensory information is experienced within a conceptually sound presentation, it can offer a wide spectrum of expansion into further learning, related interests, enquiry and potential for diversity. An example of expansion and diversity are presented in the following list of activities that present a comprehensive approach to 'learning to Knit':-

1. Beating a repeated rhythm on a drum, [establishing a physical awareness of rhythm and repetition.]
2. Plaiting a thick cord,[acquiring a sense of tension and control of a length of cord.]
3. Finger knitting, [making a chain of loops with one thread and seeing how it can be pulled undone.]
4. French knitting, [using an implement to move the thread over each pin.]
5. Traditional knitting using thick wool and chunky needles. [Then using thinner and shorter needles]

Extensions into associated skills for the above consecutive stages of learning could be any of the following activities:-

Threading buttons and beads first at random then as a sequenced pattern.
Weaving
Carpet making with a tool.
Spinning to make wool thread.
Tying a bow with shoe lace or ribbon.
Learning rope knots.
Learning to make a net of thin rope.
Needle felting.
Sewing on Binca material.
Crochet.
Embroidery.

Multisensory Living and Learning

Celebrating the mind - body - spirit potential through natural play and learning, art and design, creative expression, poetry and prose, sharing and caring.

Our materially rich world of object-bound entertainment prevents ourselves and our children from natural creative occupation; no longer do we take time to spontaneously celebrate or authentically communicate or express genuine gratitude - these things cannot be bought as a prepack package of convenience. Our easy life of robots and machinery, our world of electric slaves and power struggles, distract us from playing with the flowers, listening to the birds and rolling on the grass. Without these freedoms and spontaneity, where does the inspirational flow of creativity find its source? When does the heart burst into songs of communication that overflows into a space of natural play and learning?

Through creative activity we can facilitate personal expression, social interaction, and spiritual growth. Creative games and activity, by their very nature, do not have a pre-determined measure of success.

Detailed and accurate sensory information is essential for learning through discovery and imitation. When sensory information illustrates detailed and associated structural information, within a conceptual context of communication, the learner can gain a broader and more detailed understanding.

Sensory information is paramount to all learning, but the depth of human potential goes far beyond integration within the physical sensory system. Human potential embraces feelings, imaginative thoughts, conceptual understanding and multi-levels of consciousness. This gives our learning the added potential to go beyond that of imitation or simple copying.

> 'In other words, you must see why everything that awakens intense interest in children also helps strengthen their memory. We must increase the power of memory through the feeling and will and not through simple intellectual memory exercises.' (The Foundations of Human experience, Steiner 1996:page137)

Interactive games and creative activities motivate learning through social interaction and multisensory aesthetic experience. Thus, individual and unique creative variations are held within the boundaries required for mastery of desired and required skills. Creative expression is directed as a unique moment by moment interaction. Many aspects of exploration, that might otherwise be defined as failure, become windows of learning and encouragement. The celebration is thus experienced in the doing and the sharing, rather than competitive levels of academic achievement. Through creativity we embrace the universal love that sanctifies faith and unites us within the grace of joy and peace.

Creativity is born from heart magic - when ideas, feelings and experiences flow together like the water in the stream; where an infinite freedom is contained within the boundaries of the geographical terrain and the earthly laws of physics.

Multisensory learning is fundamental to the integration of creativity, aesthetic appreciation and divergent thinking. The deeper the understanding through open ended learning, the more opportunity the learner has to transfer the learning appropriately into other situations.

Maria Montessori pioneered didactic (intending to teach) apparatus that promotes sensory-motor activities and develops skills of differentiation related to colour, 2D and 3D shape, sound and smell. Montessori methods place a particular emphasis upon the importance of training the child to isolate, refine, improve, and make sense of specified areas of sensory perception and discrimination.

Eastwood Education approaches learning through multi-sensory integration as a basis for discovery learning and conceptual understanding. Through our senses we recognise elements of our world that support inner assessment and judgement.

This approach to multi-sensory learning requires environmental scaffolding that inspires:-

- a broad spectrum of creativity and aesthetic appreciation,
- development and mastery of skills,
- self-correction,
- co-operative interaction and internal self-discipline.

'....thus you can now comprehend judging as a living bodily process that arises because your senses present you with a world analysed into parts.....Here the act of judgement becomes an expression of your entire human being.' (The Foundations of Human experience, Steiner 1996:page144-145)

When consciously looking at our reactions and interactions we can consider all aspects of our life as part of our way forward to higher levels of learning and consciousness. We can thereby acknowledge a sense of greater responsibility for what and how we experience what we bring towards ourselves, and what interaction we chose to follow.

Steiner considered that before the change of teeth the young child is 'essentially an ensouled sense organ entirely given over in a bodily religious way to what comes towards it from the surrounding world' and that sensory experience 'permeates the child's entire organism.' He suggests that whatever is happening in the child's environment is wholly and subconsciously received by his senses and thereby also affects his soul and spiritual development. [Steiner, R. The Child's Changing Consciousness, Anthroposophic Press; New York, 1988: pages 40&75)]

Helena Eastwood

Steiner presented that we have 12 senses incorporated within our inner sense of 'life':-

The sense of 'I'	The sense of hearing
The sense of balance	The sense of speech
The sense of movement	The sense of seeing
The sense of thought	The sense of colour
The sense of temperature	The sense of taste
The sense of touch	The sense of smell

These twelve senses are experienced within our capacity to integrate the three states of thinking, feeling and willing.

The nature of everything that constitutes a human being is partly cognitive (thinking), partly feeling and partly willing. These three things 'work together and are interwoven into a unity..... What is cognitive is mainly cognitive, but also has aspects of 'feeling' and 'willing' and this is the same with 'Feeling' and 'Willing'. (The Foundations of Human experience, Steiner 1996:page137)

Steiner described the twelve senses in three groups of four:-

a) The four lower physical senses of *life, touch*, movement and balance give us a sense of our physical being through the BODY. These senses are exercised through the *will* and subsequent movement of the limbs.

b) The four middle senses of *smell, taste, warmth and sight (colour, shape, form and movement)*. These senses are associated with our perception of the surrounding environment. These senses establish an organic sense of organisation and rhythm which relates to our inner feelings and emanates from the original nature of the soul.

c) The four higher senses of hearing, language, thought and Ego are experienced through our relationship and interactions with others; our cognitive and conceptual senses that emanate from the spiritual qualities of our being.

> *Clean Heart*
>
> *Clear Mind*
>
> *Compassionate Disposition*

The spiritual quality of our being is expressed through *authentic interaction*. The author presents that authenticity is an integration of the following three aspects of human interaction:-

Active Communication – An outward expression of our inner disposition; a reflective projection of inner thoughts, feelings and desires.

146

Compassionate Listening - perception of someone's (or something's) outward expression of communication.

Interactive Sharing – an intimate exchange that integrates external perceptions with compassionate listening and active communication.

'Only through the power of unconditional love can we hope to provide an abundance of creative opportunity for personal empowerment and self-directed learning.'

Helena Eastwood

<u>This is the Day</u>

This is the day that only I can live!
These are the steps that only I can take
This is the work that only I can do.
This is a moment I can share with you.

These are the visions that only I can see.
These are the sounds that only I can hear.
These are the hands that I use for play.
These are words that only I can say.

These are the thoughts that only I can think.
This is the moment only I can celebrate.
'If' is the only doubt that can deceive.
These are the blessings only I can receive.

This is the grief only I can forgive.
This is the art only I can create
This is the love that only I can feel.
God's blessings the only ones that heal.

Now is the life that only I can live.
Still is the time that I know as mine.
This is the gift only I can send.
This is the day that will never end.

Helena

Appendix 1

PART 2 – A LIVE LOVE LEARN APPROACH

Multisensory Learning as the Foundation of Natural Play and Learning and Child-directed Creativity

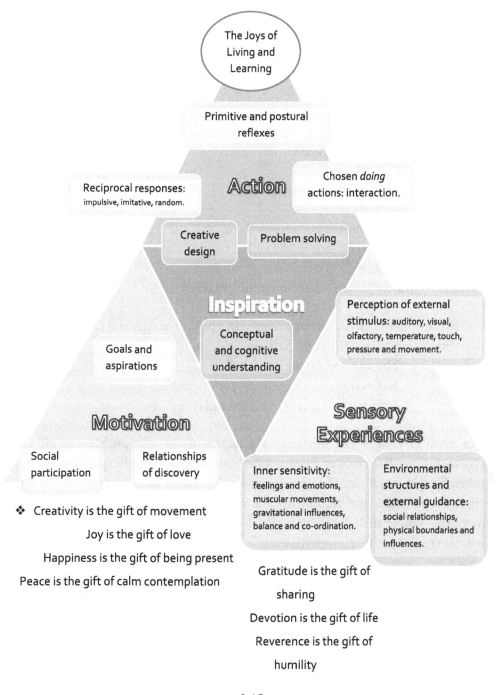

The Joys of Living and Learning

Primitive and postural reflexes

Action

Reciprocal responses: impulsive, imitative, random.

Chosen *doing* actions: interaction.

Creative design

Problem solving

Inspiration

Perception of external stimulus: auditory, visual, olfactory, temperature, touch, pressure and movement.

Goals and aspirations

Conceptual and cognitive understanding

Motivation

Sensory Experiences

Social participation

Relationships of discovery

Inner sensitivity: feelings and emotions, muscular movements, gravitational influences, balance and co-ordination.

Environmental structures and external guidance: social relationships, physical boundaries and influences.

❖ Creativity is the gift of movement

Joy is the gift of love

Happiness is the gift of being present

Peace is the gift of calm contemplation

Gratitude is the gift of sharing

Devotion is the gift of life

Reverence is the gift of humility

The 'Live Love Learn' approach presented by the author as Eastwood Education is a scaffolded multi-sensory approach to learning. Eastwood Education is not presented as a curriculum as such. It illustrates how learning can be presented within its own presentation of human intelligence through celebration of aesthetic appreciation and natural enthusiasm. Creativity and co-operative interaction are the foundations of multisensory learning. Multisensory integration can create depth and richness within our interaction with the world. Thus, when multi-sensory information is framed within self-directed learning, creative freedom and passionate interaction, learning can be experienced as personal discovery and infinite future potential for meaningful expansion.

Scaffolding learning from a multisensory perspective comes from the heart. From this sweet place activities and feelings embrace a natural balance of mental and physical activity. A harmonious combination of both musical and structural aspects of creativity that organically integrates imagination with a tangible expression of creative interaction. This supports our natural desire to gain conscious awareness and understanding.

Adults can provide a harmonizing balance of care and encouragement in the form of:-

    (a) Personal interaction: Compassion
                                 Boundaries
                                 Authenticity

    (b) A safe physical environment with freedom to:
                    Explore
                    Experiment
                    Creatively manipulate environmental resources

    (c) A socially interactive environment whereby free play, creativity and child-directed learning are positively supported through: -
                    Sharing and caring
                    Reflective and complimentary interaction
                    Independent and co-operative play.

Working on small easy steps and simple steady improvements can anchor our efforts to seed new growth within the harmony of *Highest Good* and our individual capacity to live, love and learn together. Simple structures of communication can deeply nurture seeds of encouragement for meaningful experiences and accompany the sweetness of personal empowerment. It is the very nature of this simple and successful scaffolding that wisely supports new levels of thinking that can encourage and nurture supportive scaffolding within the practicalities of our everyday living. Can we empower our children to develop their individuality and creativity beyond that of the limitations of our present day? Our children are the future; their lives could take them far beyond where we are now. Their thoughts may create a different future for mankind. Their thoughts can pioneer new dimensions, fulfilling the maturity of mankind's destiny into realms of expanded consciousness. These realms could leave the present knowledge and structures as an immature, infantile beginning, caught in the influence of sensory information. Hopefully our children will initiate steps towards new realms of thought and sincerity, and embrace positive energy powers far beyond infantile ignorance and childlike innocence. We do not need to teach our children anything, for all we know is possibly too limiting to be useful in their future. Their strength is in their ability to creatively go beyond our *today* and expand their thoughts across fields of enlightenment. They may powerfully support the establishment of true harmony within the earth planet's future ecology. What we can offer is simply: loving shelter in their early development; heartfelt celebration of their undaunted creativity; and reverence for their higher levels of consciousness. We are their carers not their keepers, our endeavours and God's mercy will guide them into their future.

As the carers of children of the future *golden age*, it is time to embrace a new form of education for all ages and all talents: Embracing a new approach based on natural play and multisensory learning.

<u>Together we can</u>

Aspire to go beyond what has been done before.
Make gratitude the most important part of your day.
Know that the natural world nurtures the secrets of life.
Embrace our soul-spirit as the source of wellbeing.

So Be It   Love and light, Helena

When I feel love I see beauty.
When I feel grace I hear comforting sounds.
When I feel gratitude I perceive mercy.
When I have faith I feel the compassion of unconditional love.

A famous composer once said, 'If I don't feel the music in my heart!   The listeners won't *hear* the music!'

Appendix 2

PART 2 – A LIVE LOVE LEARN APPROACH

Eastwood Education *Celebrating beyond the conventional into an abundance of potential.*

A Multisensory Approach to Learning Through Creative Expression, Multi-Sensory Interaction and *Self-Directed Discovery Learning*

Creative foundations for Literacy and Numeracy:-

- ✓ A rich resource of games, activities and creative incentives.
- ✓ Didactic resources designed to facilitate 'Discovery Learning'.
- ✓ Scaffolding for self-directed and self-correcting approaches to learning.

The rich sensory compendium of activities, games and interactive learning materials is designed to enhance: exploration and creative expression. The priority on creative expression encourages: reception and expression of aesthetic appreciation, self-directed focus and mastery of conceptual understanding. Eastwood Education uses creative activity, sensory integration and social interaction as natural catalysts to support authentic communication and enhanced participation.

Eastwood Education provides multi-sensory foundations for basic:-

Literacy skills: language enrichment, handwriting, spelling and creative writing.

Numeracy skills: number values, the base ten system and multiplication tables.

Geometry and algebra: expanding mathematical skills through investigation and conceptual understanding.

Art and design: basic 3d and 2D integration through a progressive curriculum of sensory exploration and spontaneous creative expression.

Creative writing Helena presents Creative Writing as a multisensory art of personal exploration and spiritual development. Her creative multi-sensory approach engages a wide range of age and ability with her own compendium of creative language activities enhance authentic communication and an enriched sense of living.

The resources are suitable for children [and adults] of all ages and ability (from seven years and over). Interactive participation can creatively accommodate spontaneous enthusiasm and erratic participation. Adult supervision can organically facilitate younger participants to join in appropriately at their own level of ability

PART THREE
A WAY THROUGH

Contents

The Order of Development

The young baby first learns to move its limbs. In the womb some babies learn how to put their thumb in their mouth in order to suckle on their thumb. This illustrates the primary importance of movement as key to our sense of wellbeing. Kinaesthetic and sensory experiences are thereby superior to abstract thinking processes especially during early development.

1. Movement
   In order to engage in personal and self-directed interaction with our environment we have to relate to our physical body and sensory perceptions through body movement.
2. Sensory Perceptions
   Our accommodation of perceptual skills with movement facilitates our ability to integrate sensory perceptual information.
3. Co-ordination.
   Movement and sensory perception combined as mental activity in the brain and thereby facilitate co-ordination skills and personal interaction.
4. Pre-determined actions
   Co-ordinated interaction with the environment facilitates co-ordination of thought and movement. This provides opportunity for exploration and experimentation and initiates social interaction.
5. Interaction
   Personally motivated interaction supports communication skills and social development.
6. Investigation
   Investigation supports inventive influences over the environment, discovery learning and self-directed learning.
7. All the above combine to develop cognitive intelligence, positive behaviour patterns, personal preferences, and authentic aspects of sharing and caring.

A brief look at Steiner's perception of child development

0-7 years. [Physical growth]
Steiner described the early years from birth to seven as predominantly a time of:-

- ○ Physical growth,
- ○ Co-ordination of movement,
- ○ Reception and accommodation of sensory perception.

The focus during these years is one of gratitude that can also initiate an innocent and natural love of God.

7-9 [Metamorphosis of Thinking]
He presents these years as *the metamorphosis of conceptual thinking*. The child's inner world of Imagination becomes a key influence to the development of conceptual thinking and a notably disposition of happiness, balance and harmony prevails

9-12 [Metamorphosis of Feeling]
Steiner presents that the child now becomes aware of aloneness and the growing awareness of inner feelings is generally kept within him/herself. The child may feel exposed and vulnerable within a strange and often socially over demanding world. However, the will to *love* others is awakened and blossoms within these early years of pleasure, positivity and purity.

12-14 [Metamorphosis of Will]

The child now addresses a personal quest to succeed and do well within their worldly surroundings. This is supported by their growing ability to think of a situation from another person's perspective. The developmental focus is on social interaction, social structures and an awakening of social responsibility. Creative endeavour and craft skills can now be developed from a personal inner sense of aesthetic appreciation.

13-15 [Synthesis of Thought]

The adolescent gains a sense of self-worth through a confrontational attitude and associated struggles. The focus is on gaining knowledge of *the self* as an individual learning to co-ordinate the inner self with the outside world.

15-17 [Synthesis of Feeling]

The focus is to find and establish a natural and authentic presentation of the true self. The lower nature is revealed outwardly while the higher nature develops within inner feelings of a maturing personality and a *love of life*.

17-21 [Synthesis of Will]

The adolescent matures into adulthood. These years initiate genuine consideration of the three questions: Who am I? Where have I come from? Where am I going?

12 Points of Simplification

Some of the best parenting and teaching skills are established through an ability to <u>simplify</u>

Creative Parenting, Creative Listening, and Special Time response and interaction are all founded on an approach that is designed to help the recipient to explore freely and with supporting witness. the witness conscious awareness of themselves and their relationship with the present environment.

1) Simplifying Communication, e.g. "sorry we cannot do that at the moment" pause, take a moment to relax, or a simple "Yes" or "No" response. To illustrate that you are listening a simple uh, uh, or hmm can be comforting and encourage the speaker to safely explore further thoughts and feelings.

Simple Communication and Authenticity

This gives time for comprehension and conceptualising what is being said by the listener. When we present too much language to children, they are so busy listening to the verbal presentation, that their comprehension and subsequent responses are inhibited. Simplification can be presented as:

- a single question related to the most important issue at any given time.
- simple 'yes' or 'no' or 'don't know' answers.

2) <u>Simple requests</u>: Children generally will relate to the last thing said, therefore for optimum understanding and positive responses present requests in a simple one at a time format.

3) <u>Simple environments</u> means - natural materials and colour schemes, opportunities to experience and explore natural surroundings, materials and events through all the bodies senses. Allocating a period of free-time to simply enjoy being in nature following natural rhythms.

The inverse ~ overstimulation; i.e.: TV, videos and computer games; and toys that make shocking and or repetitive noises; chaos & clutter in the home.

4) <u>Simple explanations and answers</u>

Adults need to answer according to the child's age, ability and interest. On many occasions <u>a simple Yes or No answer</u> is sufficient and helpful, and often empowering.

If the answer is too simple the child will feel encouraged to ask another question and thereby establish greater clarity from their own perspective.

If the answer is too adult or complicated the child will be overwhelmed and their own path of enquiry will be disrupted or blocked.

If the child is asked to meet adult levels of social and emotional communication..; the child learns that communication is related to adult drama and adult issues (e.g. the mortgage is not paid/ the partner is abusive/ unfaithful). This adult level of communication inhibits the natural space needed for the child to communicate and explore his/her own desires, emotions and social interactions.

5) <u>Simple Routines and Rhythms</u>. When these are associated with natural aspects such as morning / afternoon/ evening / night-time, e.g. When you have finished that game…. We will need to …….. We can discuss going to the park after lunch….
Children cannot embrace their own personal enthusiasms and rhythms when activities are contained within schedules structured on *clock time*, specific timetables and pre-fabricated structured curriculums. When free play perspectives and opportunities are held within ridged time restrictions child-directed learning, exploration and experimentation are also restricted.

6) <u>Simple Clothes</u> with the least possible restriction on physical movements and play activities, e.g. A specified wardrobe of every day play wear and another for really messy activities like playing in the mud or painting; velcro straps on shoes, light waterproof rainwear; hooded jumpers instead of hats. Thick woollen stocks and wellingtons etc. [Research identifies toggled strings on clothes especially on the waist and hoods of coats as the cause of a high percentage of children's accidents.]

7) <u>Simple and beautiful toys</u>: the more natural and the less the toy does the greater the opportunity for the child to self-direct play in a creative and inventive manner. Children enjoy discovery learning which will supports their intellectual development. Most toys present a predetermined play potential and specified structure/style of learning. Simple environments and simple toys made with natural materials encourage children to develop their own styles of learning, their own imaginative ideas, and their own passions of interest. [Rudolf Steiner promoted this aspect in children's learning environments.]

8) <u>Kindness</u>
Acknowledge the child's situation, communications and strengths and weaknesses, abilities and disabilities. Avoid bribes and rewards (e.g. "You can have a puppy when you stop sucking your thumb."), they inevitably cause the child stress and or unnecessary confusion about the real issue of concern. Provide positive responses - always create a yes; e.g. I'm sorry but I don't want to buy a puppy, but when you grow up and live in your own

house, then you can consider having a puppy of your own; or "we're not going to have a puppy, but you could ask to help look after .....(a friend or neighbour's dog)"

9) Choices: Instead of a no – give a positive choice. It is bath-time – would you like to have a few drops of lavender in the water or would you like some plastic cartons to play with.

Two choices or something else that we both agree on. For example, 'I now have time to take you to the woods or to the park or somewhere else that we both agree on' and 'I'm sorry, I cannot let you do that, but you could try and find another choice that we can both agree on.'

10) Share activities together in a way that each person's age and ability is positively and usefully accommodated and appreciated.

11) Children need to gain practical experience in order to understand information, instructions and Illustrations. They need information, instructions and Illustrations to be presented clearly and simply with accompanying good examples of behaviour to imitate.

Children need practical experience in order to understand boundaries, expectations and morality. They need related information, instructions and examples to be presented repeatedly, clearly and simply. It is important to present information without a judgemental or negative attitude.

12) 'Change the environment not the behaviour' this approach gives adults the opportunity to meet challenging behaviour with a creative solution that provides both the child and the adult with empowering options within any situation. Changing the environment liberates the child to freely engage in challenging behaviour within a safe and neutral environment. It is important the environment is neutral rather than actively encouraging.

For example children playing excitedly and noisily in the back of a car may become a dangerous distraction for the driver who will then wish to discipline the child/ren into quiet sensible behaviour. However, the children may be too young to control their excitement or too board to manage a long car journey. In these circumstances the adult would need to use a strong fear based discipline in order to override a child's natural boisterous behaviour. For this example using the 'Change the environment not the behaviour' approach may mean pulling up outside a field and taking timeout to run around and play for a while. Then, when the child and/or the adult feels the child can manage to sit quietly in the car, all can safely continue the journey. Alternative options could include Motorway service stops preferably with an outside children's play area. At worst the driver may stop the car and refuse to continue the journey until the passenger's behaviour was appropriately safe and sensible.

Another example of challenging behaviour is when a child takes to smashing up toys. The 'change the environment' may mean that the adult removes the best toys and leaves the child to destroy the rest. Alternatively a batch of old or car boot toys may be provided in an allotted time and place. It is important that challenging behaviour is not rewarded with adult lead dramas and equally challenging adult behaviours or adult disciplinary responses that can easily be over-ridden/out-manoeuvred or trashed by a wilful child.

For the most drastic cases of unacceptable behaviour the old fashioned response of removal into a different environment may be helpful. However, this removal should not present to the child feelings of isolation or exclusion, as so often seen with the naughty chair or stand in the corner approach. It is important the removal into a quieter or otherwise more supportive environment should include the adult carer e.g. the very young child can be placed on the adult's lap, or the adult and child may both leave and return home together. The author often presents the example of when she was out shopping and after filling a trolley with shopping the behaviour of the child accompanying her became unmanageable so she left the trolley in the shop and they walked home together. [note that this child was probably unable to manage the extended time and stimulus presented by the supermarket shopping environment.

This 'Change the environment not the behaviour' approach is key to the 'Creative Parenting' philosophy. The success of this approach is dependent upon how creatively the adult can organise a 'yes' solution that suits all concerned i.e. the wellbeing of all - adult/s, child/ren and the environment.

Older children and teenagers can appreciate that a 'yes' environmental solution might need so time to organise 'and that is life!' A 'No' boundary is much easier to accept if a 'Yes' situation is a foreseeable future solution. The Creative Parenting responses present that the request has been heard and that "I will let you know a soon as I can support what you want."

When the responsible adult creates a natural pause behaviour can be witnessed and positively processed by all those involved due to circumstantial restrictions rather than a disciplinary action or 'No' response. Without a suitable pause behaviour and reactions can become dramatic and impulsive. The levels of interaction can thereby be experienced as a hectic illustration of chaos with little opportunity to learn from experience. Our ability to self-discipline is directed by a conscious awareness of what we are doing and how it is going to affect our present environment and long term achievements. The learning of any skill is founded upon practice and perseverance which require self-discipline and a conscious perspective on desirable results.

Interaction within an environment supports personal levels of understanding, inner motivation and positive endeavour through and self-discipline.

Special Time

- Moments of heart-full soul spirit sharing
- Trusting and appreciating the other persons chosen actions and interactions.
- Gentle moment by moment responses of genuine care and authenticity.
- Taking time out to *explore, feel, reflect and listen* without any judgement and free from any preconceived agenda.
- Nurturing our emotional disposition rather than goals or levels of achievement.
- Resting our physical body from worldly demands and practical work.

> Now the door is open
> Heaven is here to stay.
> No more thinking – worrying
> Plenty of space to play.
> Laughing, crying, being,
> Dancing, eating, singing.
> Our dreams are unfolding
> Our peace ever deepening
> Hearts warmly opening.
> I celebrate your journey
> and the love that brings us together
>
> (From *The Tides of Time* by Helena Eastwood)

✓ Adults need to authentically acknowledge when their own issues have disrupted communication and listening skills. E.g. Be honest about your ability to listen properly. "I'm sorry I can't listen properly right now, I will come and listen to you - as soon as I can".

✓ In situations where the responsible adult cannot allow the person/child to do what s/he wants to do, firm boundaries can be presented from a compassionate place of listening and communication. For example, the adult can simply say, "I'm sorry I can't let you do that." This illustrates that the adult has thought about what the person/child wants to do and having acknowledged their wishes communicates the responsible adult's perspective as regrettable but necessary. Hasty and/or intense attempts to control adverse behaviour are often seen as a lack of understanding. Then the person/child may become frustrated because s/he believes they have not been *heard*.

✓ Avoid all forms of praise because this style of positive feedback is a personal judgement and the recipient will feel vulnerable to the issue of being judged. Even when they have pleased you they are working with how you are feeling about their behaviour and when the praise stops the person/child will consider the risk that you may be displeased. Even positive judgements illustrate that you are projecting your feelings onto their behaviour and this emphasises the risk of negative judgements and feelings and the risk of social emotional entanglement. The aim of giving Special Time is to allow the other person a space to express their feelings and engage in behaviour without risk of judgements and disciplines so that the person can safely and fully engage in a therapeutic process for their own healing and empowerment.

The *Special Time* adult may illustrate their companionship and attention with:-

- <u>Passive Listening</u> including appropriate eye contact and reassuring physical contact/holding
- <u>Active participation</u> through parallel or co-operative modes of interactive play.
- <u>Active Listening</u>

This level of listening requires that the verbal responses, tone of voice, facial expression, gestures and body language directly relate to the activity and harmoniously flow alongside the activity and chosen modes of personal expression.

Giving total attention, consciously 'switching off' one's own views, thoughts, desires and opinions, allows the special time adult to present full attention and to be singularly focus on all aspects of listening.

- <u>Reflective participation</u>
  Auditory reflection may encourage the learner to engage in an on-going process of spontaneous <u>recall and review</u> initiated by reflective verbal feedback.

> Vygotsky proposes that 'specifically human forms of psychological communication are possible because man's reflection of reality is carried out in generalized concepts' (Vygotsky,1986:8.) Vygotsky also describes how, when faced with a task that challenges them, children will often engage in a verbal conversation with themselves. (Cited in Hartland,1991:27; Vygotsky,1986:30)

- <u>Enriching Language Content</u>
  Reflective language may also present to the learner vocabulary and descriptive language that is beyond what may have been present within a solo activity and accompanying verbal interpretation or spoken monologue.

- <u>Extending</u> Observing the child's play and supporting with the provision and organisation of environmental materials and subsequent enriching follow-up activities. <u>Focused Attention</u> on another person's/child's activity and communications. When we share play and learning activities together social interaction and creative expression unite to expand the experience beyond anything

> Children clearly direct how they wish the adult to participate within their games....... This approach recognises the importance of the egocentric perspective within child initiated play and the potential for the adult to support the child extending into what Vygotsky describes as the child's *Zone of Proximal Development*. (Vygotsky, 1986)

- <u>Occasional activity related questions</u> This can expand the learners thought processes and encourage exploration, experimentation, consequential analysis and discovery learning.

<u>A special relationship......</u>

The foundations are made of love and respect.
The walls are made of trust.
The rooms are filled with blissful harmony
And furniture of truth.
The roof is of enlightenment
And the sunlight shines straight through.
The garden is one of peaceful growth
And rainbow colours of every hue.

(From *The Tides of Time* by Helena Eastwood)

Special Time

Unconditional love is present when we feel completely positive within the process of giving, such that anyone's negative responses of resistance are perceived from a positive loving perspective. This is the essence of the success in *Special Time*. *Special Time* is a loving willingness to be with someone without any personal agenda of any kind. Only under these circumstances can another person have a positive healing influence on someone else's negative energy patterns.

Every adversity is initiated by the belief that 'I cannot feel safe loving you because you don't really love me! or 'You don't love me enough!' This negative formula is self-fulfilling and will remain unresolved whilst one or both parties are unable to create a positive alternative for giving and receiving love. In many cases the only positive is to separate and be alone again. This action releases the tensions of negative forms of co-dependence and encourages both parties to note the good things that are missed and turn to a more spiritual path for inner happiness. Alone we are encouraged to find a way of relating positively within ourselves, and warmly embrace what life offers from a simple and positive perspective

Thus: Negative plus negative equals disturbance and disruption.
Positive plus negative equals a positive direction towards neutralisation of negatives.
Negative plus positive (love) equals positive
Positive plus positive equals Divine harmony and peace.

All unhappiness comes from negative origins that hold a dominant position somewhere in our conscious or subconscious state of being. If we want to clear the negative energy we have to find what positive influences are blocked by a negative energy and subsequent negative thoughts. Finding what gives the negative energy the ability to suppress our naturally positive disposition is often an essential part of this process. This form of self-enquiry can initiate an important area of learning that would otherwise have been missed. Again being with children and remembering our own positive childhood memories can help us to reconnect with our original positive disposition - created when the soul-spirit connects with the heart and brings life to our conception.

Clearing negative energy blocks may involve a connection with a healing energy that our conscious mind believes can and will clear the negative energy block. One way or another we inevitably initiate a request, with complete faith, that a divine energy from source transforms the negative energy into its natural positive form. The work of Dr. Bach who created the Bach Flower essences clearly describes how a person's inborn disposition can be expressed in a negative or a positive form. Each Bach flower remedy is noted for the negative aspects that it can transform into positive a disposition. For example: Chestnut is noted as a remedy for failure to learn from past mistakes and when taken it is noted for bringing about a positive ability to gain knowledge and positive learning experience. [Dictionary of the Bach Flower Remedies –Positive and negative aspects by T.W.Hyne Jones]

If everyone had Dr Bach's understanding we all may accept our faults without judgement, in the knowledge that they are only the prickly outer casing that over protectively withholds our best qualities. As confident is gained a safer place is found in which we can flourish and find our true potential.

Adults can provide a harmonizing balance of care and encouragement in the form of:-

(a) Personal interaction: Compassion
                        Boundaries
                        Authenticity
(b) A safe physical environment with freedom to: Explore
                                Experiment
                                Creatively manipulate environmental resources
(c) A socially interactive environment whereby free play, creativity and child-directed learning are positively supported through: -
                                Sharing and caring
                                Reflective and complimentary interaction
                                Independence and co-operative play.

(d) <u>The Keys to Empowerment</u>
    ○   Each individual's learning potential is acknowledged and encouraged.
    ○   All knowledge is subject to *Personal Experience.*

- *Choice* is fundamental to every individual.
  - *Authentic creativity* is essential to natural play and learning.
  - *Compassionate understanding* comes from co-operative sharing.

Trust, gratitude and appreciation are embraced within a positive attitude <u>A special relationship......</u>

The foundations are made of love and respect

- <u>Occasional activity related questions</u> can expand the learners thought processes and encourage exploration, experimentation, consequential analysis and discovery learning.

To ask a question gives the person who presents the question an opportunity to address what they need to help them manage a situation constructively rather than reactively. A question and answer exchange gives both parties an opportunity to share and explore; hopefully this provides those involved with a better understanding of themselves and the other person's perspective.

Asking a simple empathetic question related to the immediate circumstances can help those involved to relate to the practicalities of the present and thereby avoid abstract fears related to past and future situations. Appropriate and gently presented open-ended questions can illustrate that the question is offering a supportive listening space rather than a judgemental or reactive response. For example: *'How can I help you?'*; *'What would you like me to do?'*; *'Would you like me to.........?'* *'Is there anything that would be good for me to know about?'*, *'Is there anything that you have not told me?'*; *'How are you feeling?'* *'What do you feel most uncomfortable about right now/at the moment?'*

Most people would want to talk to a person about their lack of appropriate social interaction or antisocial behaviour. However, in most situations lack of appropriate social interaction occurs when the person feels unable to accommodate a situation comfortably or express unresolved inner confusion and conflicts of interest. Therefore questioning a person about the reason for their behaviour would usually cause additional stress and anxiety within a situation that is already beyond manageable. The person asking a question needs to consider carefully the value of *any* form of verbal interaction. Then if a question is desirable the person needs to consider what <u>*Open Question*</u> might be helpful to the situation.

If the words: when *what, when, who, where, which, and how*, are followed by 'are', 'did', or 'can' they encourage personal responses and enquiry.

E.g. What are your favourite animals? Who did you see at the park? What can you see?

Open Questions

Shared learning experiences through open ended interactive questions:-

How are you feeling? Can I help you? What would you like me to do? Would you like to tell me about........?

Open questions are those that <u>do not</u> have a specified answer, they are notable for encouraging a personal response and review choices. They may invite and initiate personal and social responses, sharing of choices and ideas, the integration of past, present and future, spontaneous communication from genuine interest and/or social interaction.

Open questions support and encourage:-

- Consideration of environmental choices.
- Creative thinking and imagination
- Related social and environmental opportunities
- Personal and social responses sharing choices, ideas and the integration of past, present and future.
- Spontaneous communication from genuine interest and desire to share social interaction.
- Additional levels of consciousness.

When what, when, who, where, which, and how are followed by 'are', 'did', or 'can' they encourage personal responses and enquiry:

What are your favourite animals? Who did you see at the park? What can you see?

Closed Questions

Closed questions are often loaded with judgment, e.g. 'What's the matter with you!!? 'That was a stupid thing to do wasn't it!!?' 'Your screaming is making me angry'. It is important that a child or person *is not* blamed for the other person's emotional upset. Sharing in a simple and honest way about our feelings can be helpful for everyone concerned; e.g. 'I'm feeling angry and right now I need to find/have a quiet space.' This honest straight forward style of communication can help others to recognise and empathise. Thus the emotions one person senses in the other person can be acknowledged without an overwhelming sense of personal responsibility

Closed Questions often require the description of factual knowledge and/or adult initiated ideas and social directives. They normally relate to specified knowledge and experience

E.g. What is your dog's name? Which is the biggest? What is the time? Etc.

Closed Questions relate to specified knowledge and experience. For example: Is your dog called Tom? Do you want extra peas? Did you put your own shoes on today? etc. Closed questions can encourage logical thinking and memory skills; however they usually generate Yes or No answers.

<u>Yes answers</u> can be more easily expanded into personalised and/or imaginative responses; e.g. ***Is that*** .....your blue hat? Yes, it's my blue school hat.

My mum said it had to be blue but I wanted a pink one, I don't like the dark colour it is a sad colour......

Who gave you that lovely hat? My Granny gave me this hat she knitted it for my birthday and it is really warm. It has a soft cosy lining.......

Does your dog like to play? Would you like anything extra? Are those shoes difficult to get on?

Even the more open style of *what, when, which, where, who, why,* questions can be very limited when followed by the word 'is' i.e. what is ......when is ....etc..

<u>No answers</u> to closed questions do not generally encourage interactive social behaviour. Also, negative answers may disempower personal confidence and individuality. No answers tend to discourage personalised and/or imaginative responses and emphasis negative feelings. No answers tend to discourage personalised and/or imaginative responses. They can also generate 'I don't know' responses and feelings of anxiety and inferiority.

Questions that initiate No (negative) answers can be motivated by:-

I.   A need to control,
II. A negative judgement,
III. A resistance to social interaction and communication,
IV. Unnecessary interference or unwanted interference.

Even the more open style of what, when, which, where, who, why, questions can be very directive when followed by the word 'is'.

When is your ....Where is the ....etc.

Holding Meaningful Boundaries

Boundaries need to be _**Authentic and Meaningful**_ - related to aspects of living

Boundaries coming from – _**Genuine Involvement**_ - an illustration of doing your best

Boundaries create a way for you to _**Come to a New Place Within Yourself**_ - an example of the art of being.

*Abstract –involuntary –intuitive, spontaneous, imaginative, responding to feelings and sixth senses.

*Concrete –voluntary – exploration, creativity, planning, problem solving, doing-actions, responding to external stimulus, constructional activity.

> "Life itself is tender," she said. "just as our own hearts are tender. Life is full of beauty, just as our world is full of beauty. Life is intelligent, just as our minds are intelligent. To deny yourself love means that you deny yourself tenderness, beauty, and intelligence.
>
> [Quoted from 'Daughters of Joy' by Deepak Chopra page 203]

TWELVE Effective ways to strengthen self-directed behaviour and thereby weaken abstract mind dominance and primal survival responses within everyday situations and social interaction.

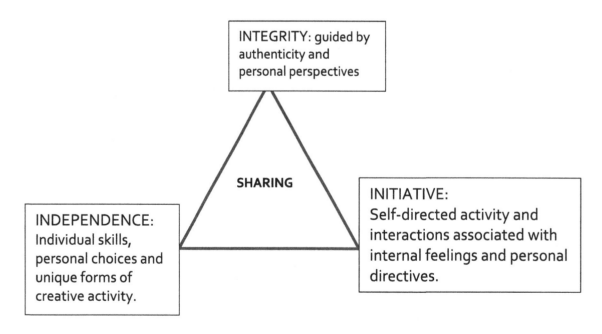

1. <u>Positive social experiences</u>. One to one social interaction based on authentic motives and genuine appreciation. Avoid drama responses related to past and future experiences and issues. Stay in <u>the present</u> with integrity acknowledge genuine feeling and responses without presenting them or justifying them as positive or negative responses, just be your best in every situation

2. <u>Choices</u> Within the context of personal preferences choices are essential to self-directed behaviour.

3. <u>Questions</u> Simple questions with Yes or No answers, a one word answers or single phrase answers.

4. <u>Scaffolding small steps of independence</u> If a carer sets up a set plan then it is helpful to either follow it through or apologise for changing the plan…….. without judging oneself or anyone else. Scaffolding is stronger if plans are followed through and when plans are disturbed it is important to keep to the simplest path on a moment by moment practical adaption to the present reality. Scaffolding for any present situation, can only be strong if it is based on the present reality. Scaffolding needs to be created to accommodate the present reality rather than past dramas or future expectations.

5. <u>Occupational games and activities</u> e.g. cooking, card games, crosswords, darts, gymnastics. If an activity does not involve some form of social interaction then the social isolation may encourage obsessional and exclusive forms of repetitive activity.

6. <u>Outdoor adventures</u> meditational quietness, play or physical activity in natural areas of land e.g. woodlands, beaches, meadows, springs and rivers.

7. <u>Outdoor hobbies</u> e.g. creative play, golf, photography, orienteering, horse riding, plant and animal identification, tennis, fishing, boating.

8. <u>Music, Singing and Dance</u> e.g. playing an instrument, dance classes and social gatherings for music and dance, improvised music making etc.

9. <u>Craft activities</u> e.g. <u>pottery</u>, weaving, <u>spinning</u>, embroidery, <u>knitting</u>, drawing and painting, etc.

10. <u>Spiritual activities</u> e.g. sharing of spiritual and religious ceremonies, personal exploration of meditation, faith, prayer, gratitude and celebration.

11. <u>Participation in community events</u> e.g. Shows, barn dances, bowling, regular church meetings, auctions, clubs etc.

12. <u>Projects</u> e.g. tree planting, recycling, gardening, caring for farm animals or pets, conservation endeavours, etc.

The above list presents ways that we can encourage constructive self-directed behaviour. The following chart illustrates what can be done to discourage anti-social behaviour and encourage constructive and positive self-directed behaviour. The approach is centred upon changing the environment in order to encourage positive social interaction and self-directed endeavour. Obviously boundaries and consequences are a natural aspect of all social and environmental interaction. However, when a child presents unsuitable behaviour in a specific situation the adult carer can avoid issues related to boundaries and discipline by changing the environment in order to encourage more suitable behaviour, more positive social interaction and self-directed [rather that copied or repetitive] interaction with people, places and things. An example of this approach would be if a child is shouting and screaming in a restaurant or in a travelling car, the adult may leave the restaurant or park the car and go into a field or a play park.

This strategic approach can deter negative behaviour and survival issues and enhance a positive attitude and constructive self-directed activity. The aim of this approach is to use the environmental situation to enhance personal empowerment through self-directed activity and minimize stress and anxiety caused by personal survival issues such as safety and comfort.

Change The Environment Not The Behaviour

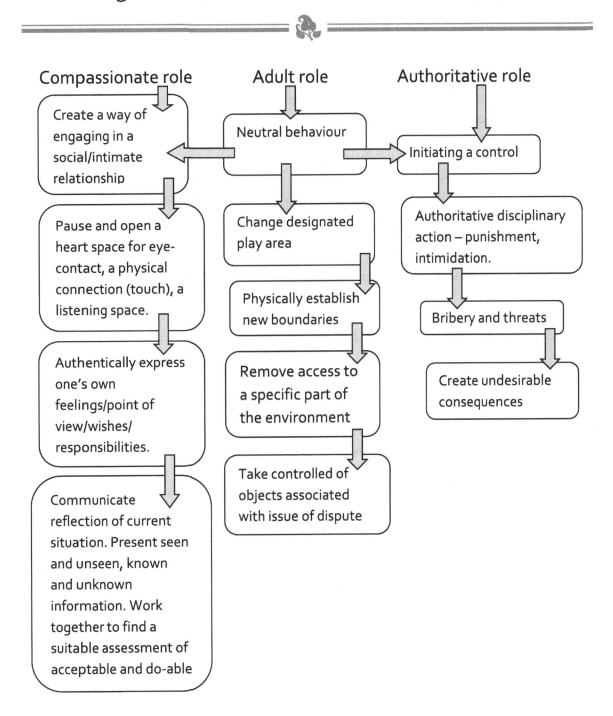

Compassionate role

Create a way of engaging in a social/intimate relationship

Pause and open a heart space for eye-contact, a physical connection (touch), a listening space.

Authentically express one's own feelings/point of view/wishes/responsibilities.

Communicate reflection of current situation. Present seen and unseen, known and unknown information. Work together to find a suitable assessment of acceptable and do-able

Adult role

Neutral behaviour

Change designated play area

Physically establish new boundaries

Remove access to a specific part of the environment

Take controlled of objects associated with issue of dispute

Authoritative role

Initiating a control

Authoritative disciplinary action – punishment, intimidation.

Bribery and threats

Create undesirable consequences

It is easier to use the environment, e.g. social example, gentle guidance, positive associated experiences, to avoid or dissolve bad habits and/or anti-social behaviour in young children (3-7). To organise disciplines and more positive environments can get progressively more challenging in later years, when it is difficult to ensure improvements and hard work to correct already established negative behaviours.

When adults do not support the young children in the early years, the child's own growing conscious discernment is likely to be overwhelmed by established behaviour patterns. The weight of associated experiences, feelings, fears, and anxieties can then consequently exaggerate an initial negative attitude and corresponding behaviour.

For example a little girl would slap or hit people when she felt unsafe with their mood or behaviour. This action did not appear to involve genuine aggression or any specific desire to hurt or provoke retaliation. However, she often got defencive and aggressive responses, which exceeded the intensity of her own behaviour. Thus, her own Antisocial Behaviour was creating stress through others whose negative responses and mildly aggressive social interaction encouraged the young child to feel she needed to be able to develop levels of aggression and defence that would protect her from feeling vulnerable in the future. Her level of cognitive development was not able to consider all the related elements of her situation at this young age her responses were limited to a simple survival level.

A child rarely consciously pre-meditates negative attitudes or behaviour. However, anti-social behaviour may become a learned attention seeking activity. It is important to the child is given help to find the desire to behave more socially, then the adult and child can work towards organizing strategies that will help the child establish positive social interaction.

For example a child wanted to operates a tailgate on a removal lorry and he repeatedly pushes the button when the adults are unloading.

The adults could say to the child "if I say 'Stop' can you stop? The child answers "yes" Together they do a test run of STOP and GO using the button that operates the tailgate. The child is then given permission to operate the tailgate her under the adults stop and go instructions. This focused occupation of the child's participation may minimise the risk of accidents. If the child fails to do this task correctly he is given a different environment where he can play more safely. A further chance to operate the tailgate can be given when an adult can give one to one supervision and facilitate that the child takes a step away for the switch on the STOP command and then steps forward again on the GO command. This stepping away helps the child not to 'play' with the button and unwittingly cause an accident.

Anti-Social Behaviour

Most adults instinctively know that disruptive behaviour needs to be neutralised in order to avoid habitual anti-social behaviour and minimised adverse consequences.

There are two opposite and equally extreme forms of interruption

1 _Rewards as a comforter._

Eg. Giving a treat such as sweets, cakes, video or a new toy. This may work well at the time but it teaches the child that disruptive behaviour brings rewards and thus the child is motivated to instigate disruptive behaviour in order to gain a reward. From the adults perspective the reward is a way of helping the child to 'feel loved'. However, from the child's perspective the reward is 'the way to get love'. This is obviously not true as no one can ever get love from material objects.

2 _Domination/intimidation_ - Whereby the person/s who wishes to stop/interrupt the disruptive behaviour creates an even stronger more dominantly influential behaviour in order to win or regain control. This approach involves the adult presenting a stronger illustration of the child's disruptive behaviour, i.e. screaming, shouting, violent and/or threatening behaviour.

This usually works _at the time,_ however, the child is motivated to develop higher levels of disruptive behaviour in the hope of winning in a future round. This highly effective method of domination over disruptive behaviour also motivates the disruptive child to _learn (from example)_ effective skills of influence and increasing confidence in the powers of anti-social behaviour.

The passive response is to ignore the attention seeking anti-social behaviour. Yes it is important not to reward or adversely react to anti-social behaviour. However, there are some situations where this option is not acceptable in terms of the care and safety of the child, the environment and other people present. Ignoring the behaviour may also encourage the child to try harder and up the anti-social performance to even higher levels of disturbance. Also, one must consider why the child is unable to engage in positive social interaction. So we come to the question of how to interrupt the negative behaviour without ignoring, rewarding or winning through domination.

Seek to identify and alleviate the cause

Why is this child unsettled, why is this child unable to engage in socially suitable activity - natural play and learning. It could be said that all disruptive behaviour is a call for some form of attention or help, or the expression of stress and anxiety. We must address the child's underlying needs and identify- what survival issue is feeding this disruptive behaviour.

A list of possible reasons might be:-

I need to get back into my body, I need to be actively doing something meaningful to me.

My mind is going too fast I need everything to slow it down

I feel anxious, I need to get ready to protect myself.

I need to raise my adrenalin flow.

I need to be with someone I trust.

I do not feel safe in this situation.

This situation scares me because.....

This is not a safe and suitable play environment for me right now.

I need to run around and be boisterous

I need to get warm

I need *you* express the bad feeling I can feel inside *you*, NOW, so that I can feel prepared for the challenge, then I won't be so hurt by you having an outburst of unpredictable and probably unreasonable behaviour.

I need you/everything to slow down.

I need you to, leave me alone/stop helping me.

I need rest, I'm tired

I can't manage any more of this situation/experience.

I can't manage what you are asking of me.

Something is happening inside me:- which does not feel good; that I can't control; that I can't understand; *that I can't explain to you!*

I need some food, I'm hungry/ my blood-sugar level has dropped too low.

My body needs help I feel unwell/pain/discomfort.

Positive ways to interrupt disruptive behaviour The following list is set out in consecutive order.

- º   Ask a question:-
- º   Holding- (see separate section for more detail)
- º   Change the environment (chart)
- º   Blocking i.e. using your physical body to create a block between the disruptive person and the aspect of the environment most adversely affected.

Take firm hold of any object instrumental to the disruptive behaviour.

Create a physical boundary e.g. a door or blanket or pillow between disruption and surrounding environment and/or persons.

Gently and firmly hold one (or two) wrists and with a warm hearted disposition give information using the very minimum of words and gentle, clear body language.

- º   Give two choices

Would you like to a or b?

A third choice is to present anything else that might be suitable to both of us.

Disruptive behaviour can be

- Unsuitable to the situation-eg wiping sticky fingers on new clothes for sale in shock
- Unsuitable to others present -Unsociable
- Potentially or actually causing physical harm to the environment to a person's or events
- Potentially or actually likely to cause physical mental emotional damage.

Common causes for antisocial behaviour

1. Overwhelmed -unable to shut out unwanted stimulus.
   Too much unfamiliar or a overbearing social interaction
   In close proximity with people I don't know or l feel uncomfortable with

2. In Transition:-
   Unable to meet the change/s in circumstances.
   Loss of supporting companionship- mother, father, sibling, teacher, friend, familiar companions (child, adult or pet!) and /or environment.
   Unable to accommodate invading stimulus-
   'Oh what a wonderful castle do you see how that drawbridge is going up.'
   'Johnny is coming to paint with you.'
   'Is time to tidy up for lunch now.'
   'No you can't have a piece of this cake until Aunty comes to tea tomorrow.'
   Unable to keep appropriate body temperature.
   Ie. Too hot or too cold or to changeable.

3. Boredom -
   Unable to motivate self-directed activity
   Unable to engage naturally in a way that feels right
   Unable to relate to what is being requested of me.

4. Frustration
5. Anger

ANGER

Anger is associated with left brain dominance that creates a dramatic view of the situation. It is commonly caused by excessive language simulation and/or separation from related feelings and heart and soul-spirit energies.

Anger is caused by hormones (e.g. adrenalin and testorone) that trigger chemical reactions in the brain and associated behaviour:-

control - primitive male dominance, desire to control another person's actions, punish, intimidate or get revenge.

fear related primal/primitive issues of survival, needs, comforts and desires.

Low self esteem lack of confidence, emotional disturbance, vulnerability, not feeling good enough to meet what is perceived as required, requested or demanded - overwhelmed by external demands.

In order to overcome anger one needs to instigate integration between left and right hemispheric brain activity. This can be done by using techniques such as such as tapping.

The following list of activities encourage right hemisphere brain activity and encourage hemispheric integration:-.

thoughts of gratitude,
appreciation,
natural aesthetic beauty,
movement and physical exercise,
creative activity,
low stimulus environments,
singing,
dancing,
prayer,
chanting,
meditation,
going inside to find the feelings that are being suppressed,
acknowledging inner feelings and emotions
authentically,
expressing feelings through some form of communication i.e. language, pictures, expressive sounds,
exercises that uses co-ordination, gentle strength, stamina and focus or endurance.

Managing Disruptive Behaviour

Most parents instinctively know that disruptive behaviour needs to be neutralised if the adverse results are to be minimised. However, there are two opposite and equally extreme forms of interruption that adults may use in an attempt to control the behaviour of a disruptive child:-

1 *Rewards as a comforter:*

Eg. Giving a treat such as Sweets, cakes, video or a new toy. This may work well at the time but it also teaches the child that disruptive behaviour brings rewards. This association may motivate the child to present disruptive behaviour in order to gain a reward. For some children the reward is receiving special attention from an adult carer who may otherwise remain busy and distracted by an activity that exclusive or unsuitable for sharing with a child.

2 **_Domination/intimidation_**: Whereby an adult, who wishes to stop or interrupt a strong illustration of disruptive behaviour creates an even stronger more dominantly influential behaviour in order to win or regain control. This type of adult response can be seen as an adult response to screaming, shouting, violent and/or threatening behaviour.

This may work *at the time*, however, the child is motivated to develop higher levels of disruptive behaviour in the hope of winning in a future round. This method of highly affective domination over disruptive behaviour also motivates the disruptive child to *learn to copy* more effective skills of influence and an increasing confidence in the powers of anti-social behaviour.

The question of how to interrupt negative behaviour without rewarding and without winning through domination remains one of further consideration:-

- Seek to identify and alleviate the cause of the disruptive behaviour, why is the child unsettled, why is the child unable to engage in socially suitable activity and 'natural play and learning'. It could be said that all disruptive behaviour is either 'a call' for some form of attention or help, or the expression of stress and anxiety. It is helpful if the adult carer can assess the child's underlying needs and identify what survival issue is feeding this particular presentation of disruptive or controlling behaviour.

The following is a list of ways in which we can actively address disruptive behaviour - they are set out in consecutive order.

o Ask a question:-

How can I help you?; what would you like me to do?; Would you like me to.........? Is there anything that would be good for me to know about? Is there anything that you have not told me? How are you feeling? What do you feel most uncomfortable about right now/at the moment?

- o Holding- (see separate section for more detail)
- o Change the environment (see chart)
- o Blocking; i.e. using your physical body to create a block between the disruptive person and the aspect of the environment most adversely affected. Alternatively blocking can involve taking a firm hold of any object instrumental to the disruptive behaviour such as a stick, the hand used for hitting or hair pilling.
- o Create a physical boundary e.g. a door or screen or blanket between disruption and surrounding environment and/or persons.
- o Gently and firmly hold one or more wrists and with a warm hearted disposition give information using the very minimum of words and gentle, firm body language.
- o Gives two choices

Would you like to a or b?

In some situations it may be helpful to empower the child with a third choice:- You can....a or b or create a third choice i.e. 'present anything else that might be suitable to both of us.'

Disruptive Behaviour

Disruptive behaviour can be:-

- Unsuitable to the situation-eg wiping sticky fingers on new clothes for sale in shock
- Unsuitable to others present -Unsociable
- Potentially or actually causing physical harm to the environment to a person's or events
- Potentially or actually likely to cause physical mental emotional damage the

Common causes

(a) Unable to shut out unwanted stimulus.
Too much unfamiliar or a overbearing social interaction
In close proximity with people I don't know or l feel uncomfortable with

(b) Transition:-
Unable to meet the change/s in circumstances.
Loss of supporting companionship- mother, father, sibling, teacher, friend, familiar companions (child, adult or pet!) and /or environment.
Unable to accommodate invading stimulus-
'Oh what a wonderful castle do you see how that drawbridge is going up.'
'Johnny is coming to paint with you.'
'Is time to tidy up for lunch now.'
'No you can't have a piece of this cake until Aunty comes to tea tomorrow.'
Unable to keep appropriate body temperature.
Ie. Too hot or too cold or to changeable.

(c) Boredom -
Unable to motivate engagement in activity
Unable to respond naturally
Unable to relate to the environment in a way that feels right or is being requested of me.

Anger

Anger is associated with left-brain dominance which can create a dramatic, abstract or imaginatively fearful, view of the situation. Predominant abstract thinking may be caused by:-

> Excessive language simulation;
> Environmental over stimulation;
> Lack of physical safety; fears related to primal/primitive issues of survival;
> Oppressive environments that restrict freedom of movement and creative expression; and/or needs, comforts and desires;
> Low self-esteem, lack of confidence, emotional disturbance, vulnerability, not feeling good enough to meet what is perceived as required, requested or demanded - overwhelmed by external demands.
> Distress caused by separation from feelings related to a sense of wellbeing;
> Issues of control fuelled by primitive defences, male dominance;
> Emotional disturbance and desire to control another person's actions, to punish, to intimidate or get revenge.

High levels of hormones (e.g. adrenalin and testorone) that trigger chemical reactions in the brain and associated angry, aggressive and over reactive behaviour:-

In order to overcome anger one needs to instigate brain activity that integrates both left and right hemispheric brain activity. This can be done by using gentle, aesthetically beautiful or low stimulus environments that support chanting, singing, dancing, prayer, meditation, movement and physical exercise, creative activity based on art or design, pictures or symbol and colour. Focused physical activity that uses:- co-ordination, strength, stamina, endurance. The 'Tapping'(E.F.T) technique helps to clear feelings that are being suppressed. All these activities instigate right hemisphere brain activity and encourage hemispheric integration.

The following is a list of ways in which we can interrupt disruptive behaviour. The order of presentation is not specific as different circumstances will require a different style and order of response.

Ask a question:-

How can I help you? What would you like me to do?; Would you like me to.........? Is there anything that would be good for me to know about? Is there anything that you have not told me? How are you feeling? What do you feel most uncomfortable about right now/at the moment?

Holding- (see separate section for more detail)

<u>Change the environment</u> (chart on page)

Blocking i.e. using your physical body to create a block between the disruptive person and the aspect of the environment most adversely affected.

Take firm hold of any object instrumental to the disruptive behaviour.

Create a physical boundary e.g. a door or screen or blanket between disruption and surrounding environment and/or persons.

Gently and firmly hold one or more wrists and with a warm hearted disposition give information using the very minimum of words and gentle, firm body language.

<u>Give two choices</u>

Would you like to a or b?
You can....a or b or present something else that might be suitable to both of us. This option allows the option to create a third choice that has not been previously presented. However, the third choice is only considered if all those involved are willing to include the third choice as a real option.

Emotional Disturbance

Michael Gazzaniga writes "the left brain weaves its stories in order to convince itself that you are in complete control." (Cited in the Introduction of '*Loving What Is*' by Louise Hay.)

Square One by Dr. Joseph Maroon - Cortisol the Flight and Fight hormone.

In this book Dr Maroon presents the following:-

> <u>Fear</u> is related to primal/primitive issues of survival and safety.

> <u>Control</u> - primitive dominance initiated by male energy through a desire to control another person's actions, punish, intimidate or get revenge.

> <u>Low self esteem</u> lack of confidence, disempowerment, emotional disturbance, vulnerability, not feeling good enough to meet what is perceived as *required* or *requested* or *demanded*, i.e. overwhelmed by external demands and unable to establish a personal appreciation and purposeful engagement with one's life.

Creative Listening and Special Time.

Based on the work and teaching of the late Rachael Pinney who pioneered work on If you want to listen to a child or you want a child to listen to you firstly make sure you are at the same eye level as the child so that natural eye contact can be established. This also avoids an intimidating *standing over* position that may disturb the child's confidence and thereby create a non-communicative disposition.

1. Be honest about your ability to listen properly. 'I'm sorry I can't listen properly right now I will come and listen to you as soon as I can.'

2. When offering a listening space try to be still make eye contact and an authentic commitment of time, body and feelings.

3. When a child presents auditory communication the listener needs to pause and take time to evaluate the degree of listening required for the response that is needed. Sometimes a simple momentary mmmmmm.or aha or the single word response is sufficient. Yet, there are also times when a relaxed openness is required of the listener, whereby, only with an open-ended period of listening-time, together with an open minded commitment to the listening process are essential to a possible outcome of positive communication and desired levels of witnessing and the best possible level of mutual understanding.

4. Sometimes a moment of eye contact for a brief moment of caring physical contact is more important than verbal responses and reassurance.

5. Reflect back to the child what you think they have said. This gives the child the opportunity to be confidently interpret what you have heard, qualify any misunderstandings. This reflective response to listening also gives the child time to consider what he had said from his own perspective of personal reasons, requests and responses.

6. Reflector and recap in a non judgmental way when one or more children have come to present their own views on a disagreement.

7. Never underestimate the depth of the child's feelings or the amount of courage and effort associated with their communications. When this dialogue of Reflective Listening is successfully presented inevitably the children solve the problems themselves. reflection gives children time to assess their situation and their feelings more clearly.

8. Listening is hard work they in question how you are feeling yourself and what uncomfortable issues the Childs communication is bringing are within yourself at that time.

9. Similarly adults can reflect on their own behaviour and apologise when their own emotional issues have dominated communication and listening skills.

10. In situations where the adult cannot allow the child to do what he wants to do, firm boundaries can be presented from a compassionate place of listening and communication. For example the adult can simply say I'm sorry I can't let you do that.' This illustrates that the adult has thought about what the child wants to do and having acknowledged the child's wishes communicates the adult perspective as regrettable but necessary. Hasty and/or intense attempts to control the child's behaviour are seen by the child has a lack of understanding the consideration for the child's level of desire, and the child becomes frustrated because he believes he has not been *heard*. It is important the adults

187

communicate at the child that his desires are not able to be accommodated in the present situation.

11. Negative and disruptive feelings' within the adult are generally more frightening for the child when they are not openly acknowledged, than when they are openly communicated. For example, I feel very angry that you scribbled on your bedroom wall or I feel very angry that you did not listen when I told you not to do it. These honest comments can help the child realise that your anger is to do with their own or another person's behaviour rather than rather than their personal existence, they themselves.

Exploring how we feel

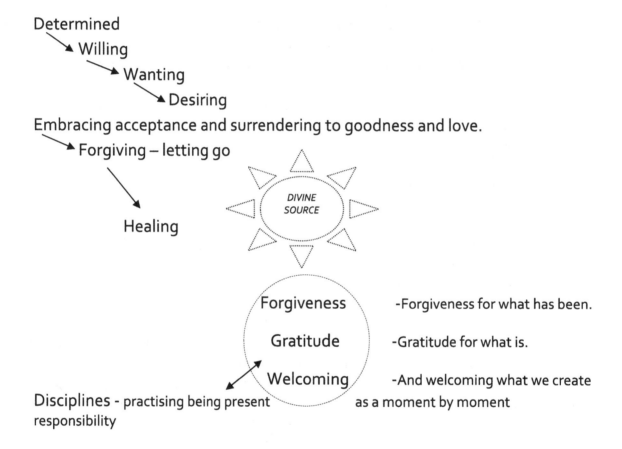

Determined
    Willing
        Wanting
           Desiring
Embracing acceptance and surrendering to goodness and love.
    Forgiving – letting go

DIVINE SOURCE

    Healing

Forgiveness   -Forgiveness for what has been.

Gratitude   -Gratitude for what is.

Welcoming   -And welcoming what we create

Disciplines - practising being present   as a moment by moment
responsibility

Techniques of Reflective Interaction within High/ Scope Nursery Education

High/Scope evolved as a *practice* based on the following three areas of study: practical interpretation of Piaget, observations of children, and traditional nursery school practices.

The adult's role is predominantly informal with an emphasis on listening to the speech of the child, respectfully participating in the child's pretend and role playing activities, and creatively

{}

supporting language development, which includes a special emphasis on verbal reflection of the child's activities and disposition. The High/Scope approach presents that:-

- 'learning comes from within'
- 'personal initiative' directs the child's active learning
- Control needs to be shared between the adults and children
  'The adult's role is to support and guide young children through their active learning adventures and experiences.' (Hohmann, 2002:3)
- The adults do not dominate, direct or overpower the child's choices of activity and emergent style of learning.
  In agreement with this approach the work of Rachel Pinney presented that 'the power to learn resides in the child' (Pinney,1992:3-5) and that:- 'In Learner-Directed-Learning the learner decides what, when, how much and in what manner he wants to learn.......He is learning at his own pace at his own selection and in his own way.....' (Pinney,1992:12&13)

Within the High/Scope approach to early year's education, there appears to be a strong emphasis on passive reflection of the child's egocentric perceptual and social disposition. Having acknowledged the child's present level of engagement, the supporting adult's reflective language is thought to facilitate the child's further development of socialised language and thinking. In this way, the adult reflects the child's level of mental development at that particular time and this style of adult assistance is thought to encourage the child's intellectual progress.

The High Scope approach to conflict resolution

The six stages presented by High Scope for addressing conflict resolution are listed below. This approach embraces the Creative Listening approach originally presented by Rachel Pinney as shown in brackets.

1. *Approach quickly and calmly*
2. *Acknowledge the children's situation*   (Reflecting)
3. *Gather information*   (Listening & Reflecting)
4. *Restate the problem*   (Recapping)
5. *Ask for ideas for solutions*   (Open ended Question, Listening & Reflecting)
6. *Be prepared to give follow-up support*.   (Listen, reflect, recap, question)

The Reggio approach to children's early year's education presents children as competent learners, personally responsible for their own actions and their own educational development, in charge of developing their own abilities, embracing their own goals and their own thinking within a holistic integration of information and understanding. Teachers in the Reggio schools organically organise their own approach to situations which integrates of all the above considerations related to creative and reflective listening, special time and conflict resolution.

Anchoring abstract mental activity in to reality through self-directed activity

Helena Eastwood

The young child learns to explore and experiment with their ability to influence the physical environment within the context of social interaction and self-directed 'play and learning'. During play, focused attention and interactive manipulative behaviour is supported by the integration of multisensory information. The very nature of play demands that the body's sensory nervous systems acknowledge sensory information. Self-directed activity involves a meaningful relationship with the whole spectrum of sensory perception within the context of intelligent and conceptual understanding. The author proposes that consciously directed thinking and self-directed learning are dependent upon:-

- The use of <u>willpower</u> to motivate physical activity.
- The <u>perception</u> and <u>integration</u> of sensory information
- <u>Consciously directed thinking</u>
- Directed use and application of <u>Memory skills</u>
- <u>Hemispheric integration</u> i.e. co-ordination and integration of left and right brain activity.

The earliest example of hemispheric interaction normally occurs when the young infant relates to auditory sounds. The sounds heard by the right ear are processed in the left hemisphere and the sounds heard by the left ear are processed in the right hemisphere. In this simple example, integrated auditory information from both hemispheres is essential for the accurate location, identification, and comprehension of auditory information. The young child's development of language skills (speech, comprehension and verbal expression) can be severely affected if the auditory information gathered in each respective hemisphere is not integrated appropriately. Auditory integration difficulties are now known to cause poor and delayed language development.

Similarly multi-sensory information is located in different areas of both the left and the right brain hemispheres. Meaningful play and learning is dependent upon multi-sensory integration e.g. sights, sounds, movement, touch, auditory and visual information.

Self-directed play and learning uses the will to focus and prioritize different areas of sensory information to support and motivate self-directed activity within a real environment.

The author proposes that any difficulty with hemispheric sensory integration is the first and most important consciously organisation of thinking. Indeed one could say that conscious organisation of left and right hemispheric information is fundamental to a self-directed activity and thinking. However, if hemispheric sensory integration fails to develop normally consciously directed play and learning will be greatly disrupted. The resulting limitations on consciously organised thinking then inhibit self-directed learning.

**Our abstract mental activity has little or no connection with a genuine awareness and knowledge of practical and moral consequences. The ideal way to work with abstract mental activity is to anchor it into meaningful and practical forms of constructive activity and production. Activity that can anchor the abstract thinking into practical aspects of reality might include:- hiking, climbing, gymnastics, dancing, playing a musical instrument, compositing music, photography, digital media projects such as videos and documentaries, sculpture or DIY; home improvements or house building; or gardening, farming or animal husbandry. Profitable projects might include the creation or production of media entertainment and computer based jobs and programming careers. When the abstract mind is <u>not anchored</u> into forms of real interaction, then it is likely to direct obsessional abstract activity as fictional forms of entertainment. These can include computer games and other digital forms of screen entertainment. Recreational drugs, adrenalin based competitive and or dangerous entertainment, excessive and perverted sexual activity and 'hunting in its basic survival format as in hunting animals or other forms of primal hunting activity e.g. big business operations, fighting in the forces or specialist response teams, or the development of advanced technology especially that of weapons and energy or other potentially wealth producing products or campaigns e.g. 5G. for the promotion of 'faster' internet entertainment, Facebook etc. In some situations a highly intelligent person with a dominance of abstract mental activity can become involved with sophisticated crimes, especially frauds or scams. Intelligent crime based projects are ideal for those with dominant abstract mental activity because abstract thinking rarely considers moral regulations. Thus dominant abstract thinking can shelter the person from conscience and realistic views on possible consequences. Dominant abstract thinking may result in primal survival tactics as a way of addressing everyday needs. Without the use of constructive self-directed activity a person may fail to apply themselves to operative work; paid employment or resourceful approaches to requirements for daily needs and wellbeing, such as healthy food, appropriate clothing, adequate sleep, etc. This level of predominantly survival based primal activity can lead to high levels of begging activity along with psychological issues of blame, resentment and jealousy. The author classifies begging as an activity that every person may take up in some point of their life. Begging could be classified under four headings:-

• Asking parents and other family members for financial help, food, shelter, use of a vehicle etc.
• Circumstantial misfortune and financial difficulties can take anyone into the state benefit systems. In these situations venerable victims to adversity and poverty are directed away from their own constructive self-directed efforts and closed into a support system that does not accommodate personal enterprise with any acceptance of a self-directed source of income. If state benefits included a flexible option to earn extra income of a stated amount then those receiving benefits would be encouraged to explore self-directed activity that could enhance their income and wellbeing. However, our present income support systems do not encourage self-directed activity and indeed the level of dependence is increased by the lack of flexibility and limited support for creative and self-directed responsibilities. These systems are most rewarding to those who take on the financial support from a professional begging perspective. Professional begging, and fraud are by their nature more successful if directed by abstract survival thinking and thereby remain free from

conscience and conscious constructive responsibility. The abstract thinking processes do not identify lying or cheating as an adverse of anti-social form of interaction.

• Another form of begging that can be successfully directed by abstract thinking is the optimists approach to circumstantial opportunity. This approach is very much a part of the scam activities of the present day. Scams are based on an interactive project that functions like traditional gambling and betting but without any socially accepted formatting. Thus conscience has no place in these get rich quick, optomistic responses to circumstantial opportunity perceived and orchestrated through abstract thinking skills and subconsciously organised abstract dreams.

Abstract thinking may be very imaginative and resourceful but it will also lack the ability to consider another person's perspective on adverse experiences and situations.

Without an anchor into ones practical reality excessive domination of abstract mental activity, in the long term, may cause depression which could lead to medication and even suicide.

Depression is often rooted in mental disturbance compounded by issues founded upon a lack of:-

1. self-directed activity
2. Authentic creative expression
3. Authentic and unique interaction with people, places and things.
4. Authentic and original social interaction.

   Depression and mental disorders are often accompanied by high levels of intelligence. Intelligence can organise ways of disguising or even justifying a person's lack of self-directed activity and obsessional needs justify and motivate control strategies, external competitive entertainment, adrenaline based activity and Obsessional Compulsive Behaviour.

Sadly main stream medications do not necessarily help correct these types of mental disorder and medications are designed to cover up the true level of depression. Ultimately for many the use of drugs (either medical or recreational) exaggerate the person's abstract mental activity, lack of self-directed interaction and absence of authentic social relationships. Sadly medication can also adversely influence a person's consciously organised mental activity and therefore distort their perception of reality. When abstract mental dispositions are all encompassing the person will have less self-directed activity to act as a safety net that reinstates a genuine sense of reality. In these circumstances an early death through suicide or misadventure can be contrived as a way of obtaining relief from the abstract fears dominating the person's mind.

The author proposes that abstract mental activity has no specified connection with conscious awareness and knowledge of consequences. Between the age 11 and 14 the growing level of conscious thinking would normally encourage the young person to consider

(a) Their own circumstances and the likely consequences of their action.

(b) Their own situation and personal perspectives of what, where, when and 'if' propositions related to chosen interactive activity.

(c) Their own assessment of another person's situation and personal perspective on interaction and feelings.

When normal social development is compromised during this 11 to 14 period optimum development of self-directed behaviour and social aspects of compassion may be unnaturally restricted. Abstract thinking may then become a compensatory response for a lack of confidence in self-directed interactions from a personal and unique perspective. A compensatory dominance of abstract mental activity may distort perceptions and interpretations of reality and instigate that imagination, dreams and survival perspectives are allowed to direct interactions without any conscience or conscious perception of social protocol and genuine personal interaction from natural sharing and caring perspectives.

Abstract thinking generally relates to primal survival issues —needs and greed and imagination —fears and fantasy. When the interaction between two people is dominated by abstract thinking the resulting behaviour is predominantly primal and narcissi.

The present day digital world of communication has opened a new impersonal passive form of communication for everyone. Digital communication systems do not require real person to person interaction. The lack of personal interaction also excludes logical and conscious observations that would facilitate one's ability to:-

* witness one's own actions and
* be witnessed by others who are observing.

This abstract system of communication as an opportunity to hide from real feelings and create a fantasy of illusion. This illusion can be used to create an 'in-love' euphoria or a false system of monetary manipulation. This new form of professional begging/fraud is far advanced in its sophistication where by the vulnerable and victims of adversity are given false hopes for future happiness.

The abstract nature of media communication and entertainment create:-

* a dominance of subconscious instinctive survival responses.
* motivate complex strategies of control
* encourage the abstract thinking mind which automatically excludes emotions of guilt
* exaggerate motives that feed desires for power, fame and fortune.
* present an extensive repertoire of examples illustrating the human capacity to manipulate people, places and things from an impersonal system of responses.

Helena Eastwood

Concluding Summary

Abstract mental activity

Abstract mental activity is by its very nature linked with subconscious primal survival issues. Conscience and God-consciousness have no part in the abstract fantasies, dreams and imaginary fears and dramas. Media and internet based communication stimulates abstract thinking in the brain. When brain activity is dominated by abstract thinking the persons behaviour can be focused on external control and manipulation; e.g. Nasserist perspectives, bullying and other forms of intimidation, telephone scams, internet scams and siba bulling.

Conscious logical, conceptual and integrative thinking

Conscious logical, conceptual and integrative thinking supports:-

- Co-ordination of left and right hemispheric brain activity
- Integration of sensory information
- Conceptual understanding
- Practical interaction with the environment
- Self-Directed Learning
- Self-correction
- Pre-determined assessment of consequences
- Structural practical activity
- Practical forms of art and craft activity.
- Authentic social interactions.
- Positive participation
- Compassionate understanding
- A moral conscience

['Happiness is the way' by Dr. wayne Dyer]

An ABC for Sharing, Caring and Creative Parenting

Foundations for the nurturing of empowerment as individual thinkers and independent personalities, successfully sharing happiness and co-operative social communion with each other, our planet earth and the source of all creation.

An adult apprenticeship into authentic attitudes of acceptance and appreciation.

Boredom brings the breaking of basic boundaries with boisterous behaviour.

Control cannot change challenging behaviour or stop others from creating challenging circumstances.

Challenges create the courage to co-operatively construct creative choices.

Compassion for children's curiosity and creativity comes with calm communication and coordinated cooperation.

Discovering different dynamics for daily development.

Doing dynamic dancing.

Distraction disturbs and disrupts daily development.

Enthusiasm establishes easy enterprises of enjoyment.

Exploration, experimentation and enthusiasm are essential for everyday empowerment.

Excessive equality erodes the expression of our individual existence.

Freedom flows from flexibility and favourable feelings.

Family and friends facilitate feelings of friendship.

Gratitude grows in gardens of genuine goodness.

Hope and happiness help us to honour open-heartedness and honestly.

Happiness harmonises the brain hemispheres.

❖ An understanding of the divine and the spiritual,
does not grow within the constraints of institutional religion
but is rooted in love, peace and compassion.

Innocence includes integrity, and inspires interest in individual ideas and ice-cream!

Joyously juggling jobs on the journey.

Kindness is the key to coping comfortably.

Listening and laughing, living and loving.

No is not negative when it is negotiable, nevertheless the nothingness of neglect creates a negative nature.

Patience to persevere, promotes productive processes.

Provide pleasing places for the promotion of play and playful propositions.

Providing positive responses pleases people.

Planning for perfection petrifies the present process.

Postponement punctures the passion of the present.

Playfulness precipitates pleasures and passions.

Pickled patience preserves the properties of the present.

Personal participation promotes perception, perseverance and playful perspectives.

Question the question to qualify and quantify the quest

'Rong' responses are a *right* part of learning.

Rigorous repetition requires rest and rejuvenation periods.

Rhythmic repetition builds reservoirs of remembrance.

Regular routines require respect for repetition and recognition of rhythms and religious feelings.

> ❖ Time is a circle in eternity
> Patience is an appointment with flexibility
> And now is the creation of opportunity.

Situations supporting self-direct stimulate success and satisfaction.

Sweet spontaneous singing sooths the sleepy child and satisfies the soul.

Simple small steps sow the seeds of success.

Today's taunting and teasing turns into tomorrow's temper tantrums.

Treasures of time and togetherness are in today and tomorrow.

Understanding unhappy moments and underlying upsets.

Understanding is the ultimate uniqueness of unconditional love.

Wishes work well with wisdom - wishes are winning what we want with the wisdom to wait.

Watching what is wonderful.

EXtending into extra exercise and extra effort extends the extra into excellence.

EXciting experiences are exhausting and expensive.

EXamine excuses extensively to expose the exact explanation.

Yesterday's yes is yet to be yours.

Zebras at the zoo zip through the zigzag zone!?.

> ❖ Through windows of enlightenment
> We see ourselves in natural play and learning.
> As each universe opens to our star guided journey away and back again.

Book List for Caring, Sharing and Creative Parenting.

Hawthorne Press have produced an outstanding selection of books that support Natural Play and Learning and Creative Parenting

The Seven Spiritual Laws of Success for Parents by Deepak Chopra; Harmony Books, 1997.

Helena Eastwood

Spiritual Midwifery by Ina May Gaskin

Guide to Childbirth by Sarah Buckley

Promoting Normal Childbirth: Research, Reflections and Guidelines, Editor; Sylvie Donna

Gentle Birth, Gentle Mothering by

Anger by Thich Nhat Hanh

The Gentle Art of Blessing by Peirre Pradervand; Cygnus Books (www.cygnus –books.co.uk.)

How to Talk so Kids will Listen and listen so Kids will Talk by Adele Faber & Elaine Mazlish

Loving What Is and A Thousand Names For Joy and I Need Your Love are three books written by Byron Katie; Rider Books, 2002, 2007, & 2005.

The Ringing Cedars Series, Books 1 - 8 (Book 1 Anastasia Book 3 - Creative Parenting and Book 6 - Education) Viadimir Megre; Ringing Cedars Press. www.ringingcedars.com

With God in Mind by Bert Hellinger; Hellinger Publications, 2007
The Deepest Desire is always fulfilled. Its object can only be something we already have. Just as a thirst for life is actually a drinking from the cup of life, a continuous quenching of this thirst. To live is the deep desire to be fully present. The drive to live is the urge to receive what is given to us in its fullness. The thirst and the drinking have become one and therefore we do not need to desire something new, search for a different experience, some kind of supplement to our life. The deepest desire is simply the unfolding of what is already here.' Page 156

Doran by Linda Scotson

Son Rise by Barry Neil Kaulfman

Nordic Childhoods and Early Education Ed. By Johanna Einarsdottir and Judith T Wagner; Information Age Pub. USA 2006

Nordic childhood settings present the success of 'Nordic societies that function largely through consensus.' Democracy, egalitarianism, freedom, emancipation, CORPORATION and solidarity collectively create the good childhood at both individual and group levels In Nordic early childhood setting.'....' Democracy ensures that children have a voice; egalitarianism ensures that children's voices have influence; freedom expands therefore horizons and the sphere of their influence; and emancipation gives them room to explore their options, energised by youthful inquisitiveness and passion for learning, largely uncompromised by adult authority and supervision. '.....' 'The ideal of co-operation requires compromise and shared responsibility and therefore speaks more to the *individual in relation to the group*.'...... 'solidarity instils a sense for belonging to a society with a shared history, tradition, language and cultural practices and is considered an essential aspect of *good childhood*.' 'Perhaps the freedom Nordic children experience from their earliest days, coupled with other elements of the good childhood, namely corporation, consideration for the group and the social conventions passed along as a function of the solidarity principal, promote acceptable behaviour even in the absence of strict adult supervision and control.'((Nordic Childhoods Page 293-294) 'in toddlers all under the years Of age, milling about on an underground PLATFORM in the snow suits, waiting for a train headed for the forest where their outdoor preschool is located. Then the care teachers are nearby, but they do not order the children to stay away from the edge...' of the Platform. (Nordic Childhoods Page 189)

'I have photographs of preschoolers cutting apples with paring knives....... As well as pictures of four year Olds hanging by their knees from a tree branch high above my head, while their classmates use a real saw and a power drill to construct a fort.' (Nordic Childhoods Page 290)

How to Really Love Your Child by Dr. Ross Campbell; Scripture Press,1977

Dr Campbell details three vital things to help your child find love and emotional wholeness:

- The necessity of physical touch
- Eye to eye contact
- Focused attention.

"Unconditional love is an ideal and impossible to attain completely, but the closer I can come to it....... the more I will be satisfied...." page 33

Models of Love the Parent Child Journey by Joyce Vissell and Barry Vissell; Ramira Pub 1986. "Every day we are models for our children. How can we demand that they become loving unless we model that for them." Page 33

PART FOUR
HEALTH, HEALING AND HAPPINESS

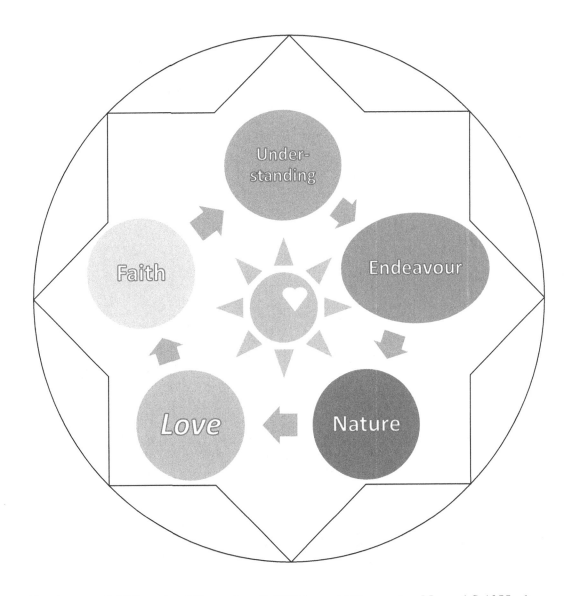

Facilitating Self-Enquiry, Discerning Self-Help and Discovering Natural Self-Healing.

Contents

Good Health

Dietary Basics for Health and Healing

- ➢ Eat to live, not live to eat.
- ➢ Eat for need, not for greed. [Adults and many children of today eat when they want to eat, rather than eating when they are genuinely hungry.]
- ➢ Unsuitable eating creates illness and dis-ease
- ➢ Excessive eating excludes healthy exercise and encourages unhealthy entertainments.
- ➢ Fasting is a great healer.
- ➢ Water brings the gift of life. [Tap water is purified with added fluoride which is a natural chemical *bleach*. This is not helpful inside the delicate balance within our body cells. Drinking a large mug of pure warm water first thing in the morning is recommended as a cure for all our health issues. This flushes out any build of uric acid in the kidneys and supports effective kidney function throughout the day. Our kidneys flush toxins out of the body which helps the body to manage the free-radical contamination and any build-up of adverse plaque deposits; e.g. in the eyes causing cataracts and in the arteries restricting blood flow. The author collects nature untreated water from a community spring at the village church. The are many other options available e.g. SWS smart Water Systems 01558 668064
- ➢ Sunlight is a great source of health and happiness and it is always free!
- ➢ One man's food is another man's poison

An Optimum Healthy Diet

Omega oils, found in unheated krill oil (Nutrigold), fish oil (salmon), olive oil, flax and hemp oil, borage (starflower seed)oil and black cumin seed oil. (www.biopurus.co.uk)

Amino acids, found in protein foods - meat, dairy, soya, nuts and seeds, beans and pulses, and liquid amino seasonings.

Vitamins - found most profoundly in fresh organic raw fruit and vegetables.

Minerals e.g. iodine, potassium, magnesium, calcium, selenium - found most profoundly in fresh organic raw fruit and vegetables and organic molasses.

Every Day Health Foods

Organic fruit and vegetables preferably raw or juiced - otherwise baked or steamed

Raw salad and green vegetables and parsley

Avocados, sweet potatoes

Bicarbonate of soda (baking powder)

Sprouted seeds and beans e.g. mung beans, sunflower seeds.

Soaked Chie seeds

Red grape juice, pear juice, grape fruit juice (not from concentrate or pasteurised and organic if possible)

Papaya fruit and seeds

Fresh spring water

Kombucha

Om Creations activated raw foods cereal

Organic Quinoa

Organic buckwheat

Organic Stevia Syrup

Barley drink (coffee alternative)

Organic cold pressed Coconut oil

Raw organic chocolate (preferably dark)

Organic nuts, mixed or just skinned almonds

Cold pressed Flax oil

Liquid amino seasoning (use instead of table-salt by adding to food after cooking according to individual taste and needs)

Sea-salt instead of table salt for use in cooking and sprinkled on food according to individual taste

Foods to Avoid

- All artificial additives – flavourings, colourings and preservatives.
- Yeast risen breads and added yeast in savoury foods etc.; hard cheeses; standard salt and black pepper; pork and red meat; GMO foods especially corn and wheat; foods with added wheat protein-gluten.
- Meat and eggs from caged birds, chicken etc. Processed non-organic dairy products.
- Coffee and alcohol and tap water and water in plastic bottles.
- Paleo hacks describe 9 easy ways to make your coffee healthier. Avoid artificial sweeteners and cane sugar, only use organic coffee beans, and organic full fat cream, eat a snack before or during your coffee drinking, add organic cacao powder and a little cinnamon, and organic butter or coconut oil. Avoid drinking coffee after 2pm.

Advances in Agriculture and Food Processing Techniques

The ever growing forces of technology have refined foods further and further within each decade. Dr. D'Adamo describes two examples of the results of this in terms of the removal of foods from their natural state:-

'For example, the refining of rice with new milling techniques in 20th century Asia caused a scourge of beriberi, a thiamine deficiency disease, which resulted in millions of deaths.

A more current example is the change from breastfeeding to bottle feeding in developing third world countries. This change to a highly refined, processed infant formula has been responsible for a great deal of malnutrition, diarrhoea, and a lowering of the natural immune factors passed on through the mother's milk.'

The author would also like to relate the adverse effects of <u>hybrid wheat and corn crops</u>. The new hybrid strains of wheat used over the last few decades have been developed in order to meet the bread and cake industry which thrives on the gluten content in the wheat. The higher gluten content (now up to 12%) enables bread and cakes to be light and aerated (more expanded and greater in size for weight) without becoming crumbly. The higher and the more elastic or rubbery the gluten is in the wheat, the more the bread expands and the commercial food industry thereby gains greater financially profit.

<u>GMO</u>

The gluten in the wheat flour is a form of protein and the stronger bonding qualities are gained by the additional complexity of the gluten protein molecules. This disrupts nature's original balance of carbohydrates, simple protein and accompanying nutritional support required for successful digestion. The unnatural DNA structure in modern day hybrid crops cause unnatural levels of acidity in the human body and ecological disruption. GMO crops produce infertile seeds that cannot be used to grow another crop. The seed producers thereby gain a financial leverage and control on the production of cereal crops because the farmers have to buy in special fertile seeds for each successive crop.

Helena Eastwood

The modern day hybrid crops of wheat and corn are for many people causing digestive difficulties and mounting residues of undigested waste. By-products accumulate in the colon and/or stored in the body's fatty tissue. Also the GMO crops have been specifically developed to be resistant to chemical pesticides such as Round-up etc. which are now known to adversely affect the health of animals and people. Also growing GMO crops can adversely affect organic crops grown nearby. There is much concern for the additional adverse effects to health that will be experienced by the growth and use of Genetically Modified-G.M.O wheat and other crops in future food production. [Wheat Belly by Dr. William Davis]

Protein Foods

Protein – complex proteins, meats, eggs and meat substitutes
<u>Eggs</u> Eggs are a whole food that offers a full spectrum of nutrition for good health. However, every egg is a small replication of the biological wellbeing of the chicken that laid it. Thus eggs from intensive commercial production may include the same nutritional deficiencies, infections e.g. (Salmonella), antibiotics etc. that are present in the hens that have laid the eggs. Intensive commercial production of eggs would normally involve feeding the hens on GMO grains (i.e. corn and wheat) and waste foods not certified for human consumption.
<u>Fish</u> Fish is generally one of the healthiest meat sources, also white meat is generally easier to digest than pork and red meats. However, the pollution in the sea and commercial fish production can adversely affect fish because of where they live and what they eat. Commercially reared fish at fish farms such as salmon may be fed on GMO food and foods containing artificial additives. Commercial fish farms may also use antibiotic drugs and artificial hormones etc. to increase their health and size. Some prepared fish meat such as kippers are treated with artificial colourings and flavourings.
<u>Pork</u> The structure of pig meat is very difficult for the human digestive system to break down into a digestible format. This is why pork is traditionally cured in natural salt. However, the salt level is then also adverse to our maintenance of good health and pork today also contains many unnatural chemical salts such as the glutamates.
<u>Commercially reared caged birds, chicken and rabbit.</u> Cage reared animals like pork and other non-organic meats would normally be subject to GMO foods; antibiotic drugs and hormones and other artificial additives to increase resistance to ill-health and promotion of growth.
Beef <u>organic</u> beef is generally best because it avoids the use of GMO foods, antibiotics, and growth hormones.
Welsh Lamb is probably the most naturally reared non-organic meat.
Wild caught rabbit and game may also be a good naturally source of non-organic meat.
Soya foods offer a good meat free protein food. However, it is important to note that the soya plant demands a lot of minerals from the soil to support production of the high protein beans. Therefore non-organic soya is not recommended because it is likely to have received a notable amount of artificial fertilizers. The chemical fertilizers are then absorbed into the soya plant and used to produce the crop of beans. The soya plant has a reputation for absorbing all manner of minerals including aluminium in order to gain high levels of soil nutrition. Intensive Commercial soya bean production may have led to research reports against soya bean products due to the adverse levels of intensive farming and associated unhealthy methods of attaining high yields.
Quorn Quorn is a Mycoprotein and as such it provides a simple protein food easier to digest than fresh meats.
Collagen protein is used in the body to support production, maintenance and repair of connective tissue found in the skin and joins. The author uses the Perfect Keto Collagen powder or Higher Nature Aeterna Gold Collegen powder drink to supplement a deficit of collagen peptides and enhance the body's ability to heal joint and skin problems

Gluten Grains

Grains containing Gluten are:-	Gluten free alternatives to wheat include:-
Wheat, including spelt, cous cous, semolina, Kamut; Barley Rye The author associates gluten intolerance with co-ordination difficulties and gross motor problems often labelled 'butter fingers' or 'clumsiness'.	Quinoa, Amaranth, Millet Tapioca Buckwheat Chickpea Gram flour Rice Maize and corn [Avoid non organic corn is usually sourced from GMO crops which are grown using strong pesticides (RoundUp and others that are known to cause adverse health issues to ourselves and our pets.]

Oats contain a protein called Avenin, which closely resembles the Gluten protein in wheat. This protein in oats can also cause adverse reactions in some people and especially young children. Also, for those on a strict gluten free diet, it should be noted that most oats, either when growing in the fields or milled into flour, will be contaminated to a small degree with other grains.

Beans

Natural seeding of new plants every year ensures any plants ongoing existence. Beans are an easy and nutritious food source for ourselves and animals. In order to prevent animals eating the whole crop of beans nature has put a toxin into the bean which animals know should be avoided or at least only eaten occasionally in small quantities. Fortunately we can address this issue by soaking and cooking beans before we eat them:-

1) Soak beans overnight then tip away the water and wash them thoroughly before cooking.
2) Boil the beans vigorously until they are completely soft, or better still, pressure cook the beans.
3) Mung beans are excellent; they have the lowest levels of toxin, and they are easy to cook and especially easy to sprout. Sprouted mung beans provide an excellent raw source of bean nutrition. The sprouting process neutralises the phytic acid which is a natural preservative that also makes seeds and beans less suitable as a general food source. Adduki, butter beans and broad beans are all good but they still need soaking and high temperature cooking. Runner beans are best when they are still young and thin. When the runner bean pods contain well grown beans the beans can be removed from the pod and well-cooked separately. Kidney beans are the most difficult beans to cook to the optimum neutralisation of toxicity and generally not advised as a regular food source.

The Ten Key transporters for healing and cellular health
(Promoting health within the body cells and organs)

The author's personal approach to healing has been focused upon the work of a medical researcher who studied the body's use of certain dietary substances essential to the transportation of materials into and out of the cells as a foundation to everyday repair and urgent healing.

The author now focuses on seven key supplements that are supportive to different aspects of the body's potential for optimum health and fitness. These ten supplements are listed below with a brief description of what and where they may support healing and a recommended source of supplier.

1. Inulin

Inulin is a simple sugar found in many plants but in notable quantities in dahlia, chicory, onion and garlic bulbs. It is used in the food industry to make foods hard, such as sticky lollies and other similar types of confectionary and noted as a health supplement. Some countries have added inulin to foods to promote colon health. This simple healing sugar is able to support the movement of good things in to a cell and waste materials out of each cell. 100% pure organic inulin is recommended as an aid to *improving* the correct balance of bacteria in the intestines. This is why in some countries inulin is added to foods to help promote good colon health.

'There is little folk law attached to its history, but in medicine the dahlia comes into its own. The tubers contain a kind of inulin known as dahlia, which, in the form of diabetic sugar, is prescribed for diabetic and consumptive patients. It was used in World War ll for the army. It was not until 1929 that it was discovered in America that dahlia tubers had been used medicinally for centuries in Mexico.' ('*The Language of Flowers*' by Lesley Gordon; Web&Bower,1984)

Inulin is normally produced within the body and it can be used for intercellular transportation by every cell in the body. It is one of the 'healing sugars' called saccharides which are normally made in the body for ongoing use to promote cell–to–cell communication and optimal immune responses. The eight simple mono-saccharides [mannose, glucose, galactose, fructose, xylose, N-acetlglucosamine, N-acetylgalactosamine and N-acetylneuraminic acid] are used in the body for transportation of beneficial materials to specific organs and cells and the transport of waste materials out of the body cells through the kidneys. In some cases, as with the Chinese runners, glyconutriant food sources that provide some or all of the eight essential saccharides may increase endurance and vitality beyond our expectations. Glyconutrients help the immune system, whether it is overactive or underactive, and support the repair and maintenance of cellular tissue. Humans have the capacity to transform sugars from one saccharide form to another, but unlike the plants, we cannot normally make even simple forms of sugar from just sun, water and air (carbon-dioxide). Inulin is a polysaccharide that can be broken down into smaller molecules called oligofructose. ('*Sugars That Heal*' by Emil I. Mondoa and Mindy Kitei; Ballantine Books, 2001 pages 17,23,35,51)

Inulin is a simple sugar and is in no way related to the Complex Sugars (polysaccharides) that are detrimental to our health, causing the adverse effects of acidity and other health problems. Dr. Cleave presents in his book 'The Saccharine Disease' all manner of diseases as the result of eating a diet high in complex sugar (refined cane sugar) and refined carbohydrates (starches, grains). (Cited in *Food Combining for Health* by Doris Grant and Jean Joyce; Thorsons, 1984.)

In the lungs saccharides and Lecithin keep the respiratory system healthy and prevent adverse effects from dust, congestion and infection. Recovery from any lung condition is directly related to the amount of oligofructose the body can make to meet the demands required for healing. By supplementing with extra inulin the body can make more oligofructose and thereby improve efficiency of healing and good health can be greatly improved

In the kidneys oligofructose is used to facilitate dialysis. The author found that kidney conditions can be supported through a healing crisis with the external supplementation of inulin in regular doses as required each day.

Inulin can support the movement of substances from the blood into and out of the cells and for this reason this simple sugar is supportive to the control of diabetes and all healing processes throughout the body even in areas where it is not normally of critical importance.

> The author used inulin to supplement a special diet overseen by her local doctor to support her through Diabetes. She used inulin instead of going on to Insulin under hospital care and supervision. The local GP gave her four weeks to prove that her then critical diabetic condition could be managed without insulin injections. The author also used inulin to help her son stay healthy during his long recovery from a congenital liver condition.

Inulin is essential to the normal functioning of the kidneys and the elimination of excessive uric acid. The author used this sugar to support the absorption of simple sugar from the blood and into the body cells. It was an essential part of her management and ultimate recovery from diabetes. *Insulin* is used in the body to regulate the sugar levels in the blood and *Inulin* is used to transport the sugar from the blood into the individual body cells which promotes the health and healing of damaged cells. The author has found 'Now' organic INULIN has presented the best results for improving health issues.

2. Vitamin C This vitamin has a major job as transported for other supplements that the body needs. It is important to note that absorption of calcium into the body cells requires both vitamin C and magnesium. Nutrigold sell Bioactive Mixed Ascorbates –a combination of calcium, magnesium and potassium already linked with vitamin C for easy absorption into the body cells. The Mixed Ascorbates supplement is 'worth its weight in gold' for its support to health and healing. Calcium supplement in a bio-absorbable form can aid recovery from heart conditions and bone repair and degeneration. This supplement can also help ease nervous conditions if it is also combined with a calcium pantothenate (B5). Nutrigold have qualified nutritional advisors available to help customers attain what programme of supplements may best suit their personal needs. An additional vitamin C supplement can also be taken as well as the Mixed Ascorbates if more vitamin C is required. Vitamin C is also essential to the absorption and cellular maintenance that uses collagens such as skin firmness and joint movement and repair.

3. Lecithin

Lecithin emulsifies fats thereby preparing them for appropriate absorption and utilisation within the body. Lecithin and vitamin C are both important for the conversion of cholesterol into valuable bile acids, an essential for the successful digestion of food in the stomach. When lecithin levels are not appropriate for the biological processing of cholesterol, high levels of cholesterol accumulate in the blood and are later deposited as gallstones or around the inside of the arteries. Lecithin also contains nutritional and supporting substances that help in the maintenance and repair of nerve cells within the brain and nervous system, the lungs and many other areas of the body. Lecithin is very important for daily maintenance and repair of the respiratory system. Unbleached lecithin liquid is the purest form, and in this simple liquid state it can be absorbed directly into the body without needing the complex digestive process required for absorption of the lecithin granules. Lecithin supplement, in the author's experience, has aided rapid recovery from nervous conditions and been very helpful to smokers in the process of giving up smoking. It has also helped students under the stress of exams and other forms of academic pressure.

The **Quest** unbleached-Lecithin capsules are made of gelatine which is difficult to digest and may be considered unsuitable for those following a vegetarian diet. The author recommends that (after softening the capsule with warm water) one uses a sharp knife to split the capsule open so that the contents can be scraped out and added to a spoonful of desirable food. The lecithin content is thick and sticky and therefore clings to the inside of the capsule. **Nitrigold**.co.uk market an outstanding Non-GMO soya lecithin powder Superlec Plus. This powder includes additional nutritional support which helps the body maximise the use of the lecithin to help the body to heal the nervous system and aid the reception of oxygen into the body cells by supporting good healthy lungs. The Nutigold Super Lec Plus is a powder that combines Lecithin with other areas of nutritional support to help the body maximise the use of the lecithin to help in the maintenance and repair of nerve cells within the brain and nervous system and aid the reception of oxygen into the body cells by supporting good healthy lungs.

Lecithin is also used generally to promote repair, health and healing. Together with coco nut oil this fat can promote rapid and outstanding nerve cell healing and maintenance.

Lecithin is essential to the health of our lungs because it supports the regulation and maintenance of the lubrication fluid that allows the lungs to move smoothly with each inhalation and exhalation. Any chest disorder can be helped with a high quality lecithin supplement.

Lecithin and vitamin C are both important for the conversion of cholesterol into valuable bile acids, an essential for the successful digestion of food in the stomach. When lecithin levels are not appropriate for the biological processing of cholesterol, adverse levels of cholesterol accumulate in the blood and can be deposited as gallstones or around the inside of the arteries.

NOW and IVOVITAL Organic make a liquid sunflower lecithin liquid lecithin is the easiest form of lecithin for the body to absorb.

Nutrigold CBD oil, Organic Black Cumin seed oil ; Biopurus and fish oil (cod liver oil or salmon oil) are all good for the brain and are also recommended for those with ADHD

Higher Nature 'Relax and Unwind@ a powder drink suitable for children and the whole family.

'Smart Focus' omega 3 & 6 (no fishy taste) jelly chewable rounds suitable for children over three years.

Higher Nature Complete Omegas 3:6:7:9 for children and all the family.

4. Black Cumin Seed Oil

This oil is renowned for its healing qualities in relation to most forms of injury and illness. Black cumin Seed oil has been used as part of the natural Ayurvedic healing methods used for many centuries particularly in the Eastern countries. (Ayurvedic Healing by David Frawley,2000:100) This oil contains a substance that is used in the body to absorb and utilize omega nutrition. For this reason it is noted for exceptional wide range of healing and health promoting qualities.

It appears to help in the provision and absorption of the essential range of omega oils, (supplied in omnivorous diets as fish oils). This oil appears to be especially helpful to all vegetarians and vegans, and especially those who are of the blood '0' type. It is recommended that the cumin seed oil is 100% cold pressed organic *Black Seed Oil.*

For those with a sensitive stomach it may be better to take the oil with an equal amount of olive oil or hemp oil mixed together with food or a little good quality natural honey. When taken before or with a meal this mixture is much better tasting, easier to digest and gentler to the stomach. However, as a dietary supplement it is important that the oil is not heated. Indeed all oils with the exception of coconut oil, are adversely changed when heated.

Also we can now buy Algae Derived DHA (Docosahexaenoic acid) omega-3 fatty acid derived from a natural extraction process. Natural sources:- certain Algae offer a Vegetarian source, and DHA enriched eggs and Oily fish. 'Biopurus' suppliers www.biopurus.co.uk tel. 01233 501098. Now double Strength DHA-500; Nordic Naturals do a range of DHA products.

5. Curcumin

This substance is the core component in Turmeric which has been used for healing for thousands of years in the Ayurvedic approach to health and healing. Any imbalance, damage or faulty condition in the body can initially cause inflammation. Inflammation is the body's first form of defence which is designed to encourage focused healing and minimise further secondary damage. Unfortunately long term inflammation and prolonged or overactive defence mechanisms in the body also create adverse conditions of tissue blockages, cellular stress, deformities and degenerative dispositions. Modern research has illustrated that curcumin can help promote healing and natural balance to any area of the body where adverse health conditions are present.

Turmeric 3D produced by 'Organixx' – ORGANIXX.COM/TURMERIC-3D

Curcumin Gold this product provides an exceptional absorption potential. This product has a unique bioavailable formatted curcumin together with Algae derived DHA and Ginger oil extract. A homemade dietary supplement can be made as a paste made with turmeric, black pepper and coconut oil

6. Magnesium

Magnesium is now recognised for its importance to cellular function, and transportation of nutrition into the cells. For example calcium-magnesium is recommended for heart deterioration, magnesium is also considered essential for the repair and maintenance of healthy nerve cells, neurological development and healing.

Magnesium is the wonder healer for all the systems in the body that use trace elements and mineral salts for intercellular health and healing. This aid to healing includes an element of balancing of mineral levels - and the alkalisation of the blood. Magnesium is essential for the absorption and utilisation of calcium which is essential for a healthy heart and all the body's muscular strength and fitness. Magnesium is found in nuts and seeds, black strap molasses, whole grains, soya and sea foods. It can also be purchased in a pure salt crystal form which is water soluble. In a tablet form, Higher Nature do a 'True Food Magnesium' supplement (www. highernature.co.uk) that can aid the restoration of depleted magnesium levels. Magnesium citrate is the form of magnesium most commonly found in fruit and vegetables and a mother's breast milk, and it has the least interference with the regulation of hydrochloric acid levels in the stomach. Nutrigold (www.nutrigold.co.uk) produce a magnesium supplement called Citrizorb, this citrate form of magnesium is presented as the most easily absorbed form of magnesium supplement. Nutrigold also do a Magnesium Supper Plus complex of Magnesium Citrate and other important supplements which can greatly increase the benefits of a bioavailable (i.e. easily absorbed) magnesium supplement.

7. Nitric oxide

Nitric oxide is found in beetroot, spinach (remember the Popeye cartoon), hawthorn berries (the hawthorn tree is no longer common to the English countryside, be very careful not to eat poisonous berries from of other trees and shrubs) The aminos l-arginine and l-citruline CO_2 supports the body's own production of Nitric Oxide. [Advanced Bionutritionals sell a Nitric Oxide Supplement called Circ02 together with free test strips to find out about nitric oxide levels in the body.] Dr. Mark Stengler promotes the importance of Nitric Oxide and the Nobel Prize winning research that has identified how Nitric oxide supports everyday health and outstanding healing within the body cells, tissues and organs.

8. Nascent Iodine

Iodine is essential to the health of the thyroid. Iodine deficiency is hard to detect and may easily be over looked especially in the elderly and those with mental illnesses. As a supplement it is important to be cautious about how much iodine is taken and that supporting nutrition is also addressed so that the iodine can be used appropriately within the thyroid. The natural source of iodine is found in seaweed and kelp tablets provide a balanced nutritional source. Nutrigold Kelp and Nettle

Liquid iodine needs to come from an organic source and supplemented with balanced nutrition to help absorption and productive use within the thyroid. For example the author also eats brazil nuts for additional selenium as well as a full spectrum of nutritional supplements and organic foods. Guggul – the sap from the Myrrh tree is also recommended as a support for the utilisation of any Iodine supplement.

Best Health Nutritionals produce a supplement called THYROID Performance Plus and Higher Nature sell a Thyroid Support formula 'Organixx' – ORGANIXX.COM/Nascent Iodine BioCare, Nutrisorb Liquid Iodine [as a tasteless alternative form of Potassium Iodide]

Dr. Steven Gundry: Biog.paleohacks.com/3-ways –to-heal-your-thyroid-naturally

9. Glutathione (gsh) This is produced in the body using vitamin 'B's and other nutrition. Glutathione is essential to the immune system and brain functions (including memory). Glen Rothfield describes it as the MASTER anti-oxidant. Our production of Glutathione is essential to the health of our neurological system and mental functions and maintenance of mental health. The body produces Glutathione to protect the body cells from free-radicle damage and to maintain cellular health. Sadly oral Glutathione is damaged in the stomach and pesticides demolish natural Glutathione in food crops. Grsultra.com 'Scientists Plan to "Cure" aging'.

L-Glutamine, l-Cyctine, selenium, zinc and alpha lipoic acid help the body produce Glutathione. 'GRS Ultra' is a supplement designed to help the body produce Glutathione and maintain cell defence. ['NOW' sell a Glutathione (gsh) supplement powder; 'Power Health' sell L-Glutamine powder this amino acid can support healthy blood and muscles]

10. Collagen Perfect Keto Collagen powder or Higher Nature Aeterna Gold Hydrolysed Active Marine Collagen drink to supplement a deficit of collagen peptides and hyaluronic acid in the everyday diet and thereby enhance the body's ability to address every day wear on joints and skin problems and damage.

Collagen drink with hyaluronic acid and vitamin C produced by Higher Nature

Further recommendations for the promotion of good health and natural healing:-

Organic Liquid Stevia Extract produced by 'NOW' This is an amazing healthy sweetener that has no sugar contentment and so it is not averse to the healthy maintenance of the bacteria in the guts and it has no adverse effect upon blood sugar levels.

Wheat free Paleo Italian Facaccia Bread

Dave on Paleo Hacks describes how to make this high protein, low carbohydrate, healthy fats recipe.

Bicarbonate of Soda

This is an alkaline substance that helps the body to neutralise acidity. An abnormally high level of acidity is present with illnesses and when stress, disruption and damage are present within the body's cells. Creating an alkaline balance is essential to all areas of health and healing. The author recommends a daily alkalizing drink as follows: -

One teaspoon of backing powder or Bicarbonate of Soda added to a glass of water with organic lemon juice. (Lemon juice is the only acid food that has an alkalizing effect in the body.) Stir and leave until the fizzing has subsided. (This will minimize naturally occurring burping and/or rectal wind) This drink is also an internal cleanser for the whole length of the digestive system.

Another alkalising remedy is the water drained from slow cooked pearl barley grain. However, the grain itself is the same as all grains an acid forming food when eaten.

Baking powder is also a good natural and safe cleanser for internal and external use.

Baking powder or bicarbonate of soda powder alkalises the blood and it is also an internal cleanser for the whole length of the digestive system that can easily be added to regular meals.

Slippery Elm Powder

This herb is made from the bark of the slippery or red elm. The powder is mucilaginous which means it creates a protective coating over mucous membranes that soothes and facilitates healing. It contains easily absorbed nutrients that aids digestion and convalescence. When a small amount of powder is added to food it can aid recovery from any problem within the digestive system (e.g. stomach, bowels) and has a cleansing effect both internally and externally when applied to burns and wounds.

This powder has outstanding alkaline quality that helps cleanse the intestinal system. The organic powder is best and most effective. Slippery Elm powder will support all aspects of health and healing throughout the intestines and digestive system, from the stomach through the intestines (gut) and on into the bowels. A little powder sprinkled on food or made up as a liquid paste before or after eating can help recovery from vomiting, diarrhoea and colon disorders. The paste can be made up with any liquid food according to taste. The author uses the Oatly Cream plus a little alternative sweetener if required.

Organic Slippery Elm powder can be bought from www.iherb.com and www.organicherbtrading.com

Xylitol is a simple sugar made from naturally occurring Birch tree extract, is now sold in the health food shops as a sugar alternative that promotes health and healing, however, it is also a good laxative, so small amounts are recommended for general use in a daily diet.

James White organic Ginger Zinger and Organic Turmeric shot www.zingershots.com

Fasting
We all fast overnight and this is essential for our health because this is the time when the body cells are regenerated, repaired and cleaned of toxins and waste materials. Present day Research suggests that the body can repair itself during period of fasting with an intensive use of stem cells. This phenomena illustrates that fasting can induce the body to use its inner healing techniques more effectively using stem cells. Fasting gives the body an opportunity to focus on tissue and organ maintenance and repair. It is recommended that we do not eat immediately (during the preceding three hours) before going to bed and ideally evening meals should be small and light. Some recommend not eating any solid foods after dark. Any type of fasting directive may be usefully extended on a regular weekly or monthly basis.

Extending the length of a fasting period can be related to any of the following:-

1. Restricting food intake as a whole.
2. Simplification of the foods/drinks.
3. Optimising nutritional intake.
4. Restriction to a pre-specified category or range of foods.

1-4 and other specialised diets all help minimising the digestive work and cellular level of disruption caused by the food eaten.

Copper
In remote areas of the world there are reports of those who live to 100 years and possibly decades beyond. Much speculation has gone into how they reach their incredible old age. Indeed they do live close to nature with good water, sunlight, exercise and fresh natural foods. However, there are those who believe that they also benefit from a high content of copper in their soil, which supports the plants good health and strong growth because it is essential to the reception of sunlight through the process of photosynthesis. Foods high in copper e.g. avocados, could possibly help us all to keep young, fit and healthy.

However, copper supplements are not specifically recommended because they can be detrimental if taken when copper levels in the body are already at the required level or higher. Also copper supplements may not provide the copper in a natural and absorbable form; then the copper remains a heavy metal element adversely stranded within the body cells. Thus, the bioavailability of metal elements is critical. For example when the body is struggling to absorb an iron supplement, headaches and constipation can be caused. The True Food Easy Iron (Higher Nature) can help the body to absorb the iron more efficiently also advised is to drink plenty of water and <u>coconut water with lemon juice</u>. **Hyaluronic** <u>acid</u> is used in the body to balance optimum water maintenance within the individual body cells.

There are also health recommendations for drinking from a copper mug (curejoy). However, one needs to be careful about copper as a metal because it is often mixed with other metals to give it added strength. Copper bracelets are also recommended for health reasons and the ones that have only the copper against the skin and stainless steel as extra strengthening within the design are likely to be best. Wearing a copper bracelet against the skin gives the body the option to absorb the copper through the skin according to need and each individual's ability to utilise the metal element successfully within the body.

<u>Groundology</u> The author has known several children with mental and emotional challenges who have refused to wear shoes and chosen to walk everywhere barefoot every day for several years as a natural way to establish successful healing and personal empowerment. Doctor Koniver describes clearly how and why these children have been able to help themselves to recover from personal adversity.

> Some people put copper inner soles in their shoes to help neutralise electro-magnetic interference within the body. Others have a ring of copper wire around the bed frame that is attached to a copper 'earthing' rod set in the ground. The natural 'earthing' quality of copper is thus used to neutralise any electrical disturbance and this helps the body to sleep and heal during the night while we are at rest. You-tube 'The science of grounding' – Laura Koniver MD. Presents 'Earthing' as a practical way of receiving health supporting earth electrons and neutralising adverse environmental static electricity. [Earthing and grounding mats and sheets www.groundology.co.uk]

The WaveRider
This devise provides scientifically proven technology that effectively neutralises the harmful effects of radiation on living cells. The world of today demands that every living thing is stressed by the onslaught of EMR (ElectroMagnetic Radiation) given off by electronic devises. The use of computers and mobile phones has been seen to disrupt the delicate electrical pulses used during intercellular communications within the human body. Today the present promotion of 5G frequency for mobile internet connections is causing serious concerns about the wellbeing of all life on our planet such that some countries are the

The Advanced Tachyon products
These products emit an energy that has been scientifically shown to neutralise sub-molecular stress and help cells return to their natural optimum performance and correct structural nature. The author has used these products to protect her health and promote healing with outstanding results.

ElectroCleanse - Elimination of Parasites

The presence of harmful unseen and often undetectable parasites within our body tissues was identified by the late Dr. Hilda Clark. She used precise electronic frequencies to eliminate the harmful parasitic micro biotic life forms from the human body tissues. Today the Dr. Clark Research Association presents an up-to-date ElectroCleanse tool for the elimination of parasitic invasion of body cells seen as a disruptive influence to both health and healing. Conditions of adversity caused by parasitic invasion within the body's disrupt both repair and maintenance of cellular tissue.

The liquid **grapefruit seed extract** (Higher Nature **Citricidal**) Papaya seeds can also support the elimination of parasites from the body.

Rebounder Exercise mini trampoline

This form of exercise is quick and easy and only needs a meter square for the duration of the actual time of exercise. Also the tight trampoline membrane makes this exercise particularly good for stimulating the Lymphatic system and blood flow and the sprung surface does not stress the joints.

Electronic Laser Acupuncture pen

Sono-Photo Dynamic Therapy

Stem cell Therapy e.g. EmCell-Ukraine

The Light Stream Wand David Sereda

Oxygen therapy

Oxygen therapy is now considered a successful way to approach all areas of healing in the body, and particularly noted for facilitating outstanding recovery from brain damage.

[Nutrigold do a supplement called Oxycel which is designed to enhance the bodies absorption of oxygen in to the cells. Hyperbaric Oxygen Therapy (HBOT) – Primal force supplements by Al Sears MD use Rhodiolarosea –A Herb supportive to improving oxygen in the blood

Aerobic Oxygen – is a liquid supplement that stabilises negative ions of oxygen-Oxygen molecules in purified ionized salt water]

The Blue Room Light Therapy that specifically provides safe and healing levels of **Ultra-Violet Light.** This aspect of light therapy is also used in the Photo laser therapy that is now available as an alternative to chemo-therapy for successful treatment of cancer and brain tumours.

A Healthy Gut and Essential Nutrition

For those on the autism spectrum concerns about dietary health are focused upon the absorption of essential nutrition and the establishment and maintenance of a healthy gut biotic-flora.

Muscle testing is probably the easiest way to attain a simple at home guide to foods that are helpful and those foods that may be adverse to an individual's health and wellbeing. The Hay Diet is probably one of the simplest guides to improve day to day meal planning. This approach presents a simple food combining structure based on avoiding combinations of complex proteins and carbohydrates within the same meal. The author considers that many autistic children address this issue successfully with their unusually restrictive issues related to food. To establish a healthy diet that is structured to meet a specific individual's health and nutritional needs, the author has found the following Hay Food Combining Dietary guidelines worth considering:-

- Organic foods may contain the best nutrition, especially organic home grown organic vegetables.
- Raw juice of fruit and vegetables offers an exceptionally high nutritional content of sportive enzymes, vitamins and minerals. (Note: only naturally ripened fruits contain the health giving fruit enzymes and supportive probiotic sugars.
- Fermented foods such as Tofu, Kefir, Sauerkraut, dairy free yoghurts, Sourdough breads, Kombucha, fermented ginseng are considered helpful to the gut probiotic balance.
- Exclusion of processed cane sugar is recommended using of alternative sweeteners e.g. Stevia, or raw cold pressed organic honey or date syrup or agave syrup.
- Wheat and other Gluten grains are avoided.
- Food intolerances and irritable bowel reactions may be caused by artificial additives, gluten grains, and cow milk products, (Note that butter fat need not be excluded when following a dairy free diet).
- Non organic wheat and corn products may be produced using GMO crops.
- Breads made with yeast and savoury yeast based foods, e.g. Marmite may damage the balance of healthy bacteria in the gut.
- Include plenty of cold pressed organic oils i.e. avocado, olive oil, Black Cumin seed oil (www.biopurus.co.uk), raw coconut oil, hemp oil and CBD oil (Nutrigold) (note: Turmeric and black Pepper supports the body's ability to absorb and utilise CBD oil.

Natural support for health, healing and happiness is now available from established companies with specialised knowledge and experience in this important area of progress based on natural healing and optimum health.

The author recommends <u>supplements from three outstanding English companies</u> Nutrigold and Higher Nature-True Food and Quest Foods:

The following Nutrigold and Higher Nature-True food supplements are especially related to <u>brain health and repair</u> of the nervous system.

- ✓ <u>Nutrigold;</u>: CBD oil [this organic raw oil does not cause addictive side effects], Oxycel, <u>Mixed Ascorbates</u>, Superlec Plus-Lecithin powder, Sublingual Vitamin B12 and organic Ashwaganda, Multi 'B' vitamin complex, Vitamin B12 Sublingual, Super Mag Plus magnesium citrate plus 'b' vitamins, Vitamin C Complex Powder with citrus bioflavonoids.
- ✓ <u>Higher Nature</u>: Theanine, Advanced Brain Nutrients, Astaxanthin and blackcurrant, Omega 3:6:9 Balance, Bio Minerals a plant based multimineral complex. True food 'B' complex and Bio-transformed vitamin C with citrus bioflavonoids or calcium ascorbate vitamin C powder.
- ✓ organic Inulin Now can also help nutrition and hydration of individual brain cells and the removal of toxins out of individual cells.
- ✓ Essential oils that can help improve mental brain functions and stress or anxiety related issues are sage, peppermint and lavender.
- ✓ D3 and B12 Cobalamin(/Folate the natural food format of folic acid;
- ✓ Boswallia extract (Indian Frankincense) This ayervadic supplement is made from the sap of the Boswellia Serrata tree. Produced by <u>Now</u>; Solgar; IHerbThorn; Health essentials Direct High strength powder.
- ✓ NAC (n-acetylcysteine) (Green Valley Natural Solutions offer a supplement that contains a recommended dose of NAC plus other supporting nutrients) NAC supplements can restore Glutathione levels within the body and support outstanding healing for Brain cells and the nervous system; aiding recovery from degenerative diseases such as Parkinson's and dementia and other causes of damage to the brain and nervous system.
- ✓ Quest Vitamin Ltd: Enzyme Digest with peppermint oil; Amino Complex – Quest Vitamins Ltd Uk
- ✓ Matcha – finely ground green tea from Japan.

Appendix 1

COMPANIES AND RECOMMENDED SUPPLEMENTS

Biopurus
Black Cumin seed oil; Organic Hemp oil with a high (3,4%) CBD content; Argan kernel oil
An extensive range of Naturally grown, cold pressed (raw) oils (www.biopurus.co.uk) Tel 01233 501098 Ashford, England

NOW Foods
Organic Inulin Non GMO (This organic inulin has been notably more effective than other non-organic formats.)
Better Stevia Organic Liquid Stevia Extract
Glutathione NOW sell a Glutathione (gsh) supplement powder. If taken without food, on an empty stomach with a large glass or two of water, before going to bed at night, the body may be able to absorb the Glutathione. Cyctine and selenium help the body produce Glutathione. 'GRS Ultra' is a supplement designed to help the body produce Glutathione and maintain cell defence.
Organic Sunflower Lecithin Liquid

Nutrigold –
Raw CBD oil
Organic Ashwagandha
5-HTP Complex
Curcumin
Mixed Ascorbates;
Supamag plus;
Multi B Complex;
Superlec Plus (Lecithin powder);
Mega Strength Probiotics (25 billion blend of gut probiotic bacteria)
Oxycell (antioxidant)
Colex (Natural botanicals, L-glutamine and Bifidobacteria)
Kelp and Nettle (A natural source of iodine)

Higher Nature, Truefood supplements:-
CollaFlex Gold Pure marine collagen for joints and skin with hyaluronic acid and vitamin C
PRO-EASY Live Bacteria Powder for adults and children
Thyroid Support
Truefood Easy Iron;
Colloidal Silver and free booklet about the research on the outstanding health giving qualities of Colloidal silver.
Citricidal liquid grapefruit seed extract

223

Truefood Calcium magnesium;
Truefood Pet vitamins and probiotic powder

Quest,
Super Once A Day (time released multi-nutrients);
Unbleached Lecithin capsules (the gelatine capsule can be discarded if one meticulously scrapes the thick lecithin gel from the inside of the capsule shell.
Amino complex

Alpha Femme
G FACTOR with Garcinia and KETO GENIX weight management complex and VITAL DETOX Internal Cleanse Formula UK

Wholesale Health Ancient Minerals Magnesium Salt Crystals. This is a cheaper but less absorbable from of magnesium often used in the bath for absorption through the skin. Wholesale Health Ltd 01606889905.

Advanced Bionutritionals Nitric Oxide Supplement together with free test strips to find out about nitric oxide levels in the body.

Perfect Keto Collagen powder to supplement a deficit of collagen peptides in the everyday diet and enhance the body's ability to address skin problems and high levels of skin damage.

Outstanding Research and Multi-vitamin, mineral and Probiotic supplements (Note: Imported goods may involve additional tax duty to be paid on delivery.)

The Psychobiotic *Revolution* *the book by C. Anderson presents that today's epidemics of depression, anxiety, obesity – even autism, Alzheimer's, and Parkinson's disease – may be treated by adjusting digestive bacteria. (Sited on National Geographic: Your Brain)*

Primal Force - Curcumin (Turmeric); Piperine (from papaya seeds); ginger root and galangal root Al. Sear, M.D. - The beta-amyloid plaque destroying discovery that won the Nobal Prize twice......

Science Natural Supplements Turmeric with BioPerine – Science Natural Supplements

Dr. Max Wolf - Heal-n-sooth Proteolytic enzymes e.g. Bromaline for healing and health.: **Living Well Nutraceutical** - proteolytic enzymes, flavonoids and ascorbic acid to address degenerative diseases and associated inflammatory conditions in the body.

Advanced Bionutritionals Dr. Shallenberger –

Gundry MD Dr. Steven Gundry

Rothfield Dr.Glen Rothfield MD
WELL of LIFE Jonathan Otto USA
Organixx, ORGANIXX.COM

Collagens anti-aging blend of bioavailable collagens + vitamin C
Turmeric 3D
E-plexx Organixx Supporting the body to maintain good Oestrogen hormonal balance

Quest Super Once A Day Time released Multi-nutrients (vegetarian, gluten and dairy free)

Higher Nature True food - Wise Woman; Well Man; and Supenutrition Plus

SUPERDOG all round pet True Food nutrition from Higher Nature

Pet Friend Ainsworth essences – Anti-Stress & De-stress Formula of the original Bach Flower remedies.

Herbactive Health – herbal tinctures made by Alan Hopking Herbal Practitioner www.herbactive. co.uk

Frequensea - Ionic Whole Food Tonic that contains Marine Photoplankton. Frequensea is an advanced liquid supplement for good health that is suitable and successful with even the most severe health issues. – thetruthaboutfoodandhealth.com Dr. Terry Tenant. To order www. onehundredpercenthealth.com or tel.01803 665529/0800 6950450

Cascading Revenol – probably the most advanced and unique bioavailable antioxidant formula that increases exponentially to neutralise multiple free radical molecules within the body.

Intra Max Completely organic advanced clinically proven nutritional supplement that includes health promoting superfoods and photo nutrients. Created by Natural Health Dr. Richard Drucker.

Salus Liquid Tonics The Salus herbal and fruit juices tonics Eprasat, Kindervital, and Saludynam are especially useful as a general daily supplement for healthy growing children. These liquid supplements can be added to water or juice to make a pleasant fruit drink. These formulas can help all ages from growing children, pregnant women to senior citizens.

Vital Detox Internal Cleansing complex – Alpha Titan Products Ltd.UK.

Fulvic Minerals ancient purity; Trace minerals/Amino acids/Detox

Colloidal Minerals and Trace Elements are noted as beneficial as an aid to the body's absorption of minerals and trace elements. The E*therium Gold* and Etherium Pink is presented as a natural source of minerals and trace elements, from deep sea-beds, that can promote healing and good health.(www.resonance-health.co.uk)

Sun Warrior Liquid vitamin and mineral Rush.
The Missing Link
Proteolytic Enzymes to clear Fibrin build up and associated adverse health conditions without Pharmaceutical drugs.

Anti-oxidants and Amino acids.

Anti-oxidants protect the body cells from degenerative illness and age related cellular deterioration. Anti-oxidants address the cellular breakdown caused by Free-radicals, i.e. adverse substances (toxins) which get stuck in the body. Vitamin supplements that help the body to protect itself from free radicals include Multi-B vitamins including B6 and B12, vitamin E, Beta-carotene, Lutein, vitamin D and Shrimp and Krill oil'. However Dr. Rothfield describes Astaxanthin as '200 times more effective than other more common anti-oxidants.

Citrus Maximu a powerful supplement of citrus bioflavanoids to combat inflammation that provides an exceptionally high level of antioxidants –

- ✓ Nutrigold: Oxycell antioxidant
- ✓ Higher Nature: Astaxanthin & Blackcurrant
- ✓ Astaxanthin Dr. Glen Rothfield recommends Astaxanthin as a 4-6mg daily supplement.
- ✓ Ashwagandha - This powerful herb has been shown to have powerful healing qualities; lowers stress hormones, fights cancer, improves blood sugar and more from Nutrigold
- ✓ Antioxidants in nature – Astaxanthin, and Pure Zanthin ULTRA Dr. Antony Holland O8oo 432 0419 Attitude booklet 'Walking on Sunshine'
- ✓ Quest Amino Complex
- ✓ Bragg Liquid Amino seasoning
- ✓ VITAL DETOX Internal Cleanse Formula - ALPHA Femme products UK
- ✓ PerfectAmino – Dr. Minkoff
- ✓ Quercetin and Green Tea combination as a high quality supplement. Quercetin is found in fruit and vegetables….such as apple, red grapes and berries including the skin, onions, salad greens as well as Quinoa and buckwheat.

A recipe of supplements to keep you young

- ✓ Ashwaganadha (Nutrigold)
- ✓ Nitric Oxide (organic beetroot juice; Nitrinol; Circ02 AdvancedBionutritionals
- ✓ L-Arginin
- ✓ Mixed Ascorbates –a combination of calcium, magnesium and potassium already linked with vitamin C to aid absorption.
- ✓ Grape seed extract
- ✓ Inulin (Now organic)
- ✓ MSM

- ✓ Magnesium (Nutrigold-Super mag plus)
- ✓ Cu cumin
- ✓ Collagen (Perfect KETO collagen; Higher Nature Aeterna Gold Collegen powder drink offers better absorption of collagen due to the addition of vitamin C and is)
  Lecithin (organic sunflower of Nutrigold soya based SuperLec Plus)
- ✓ Boswalia
- ✓ L-Glutamine powder (Power Health do vegetarian and vegan powder)
- ✓ Longevity Healthcare Secrets from the healthies 100 year olds by Kevin richardson

Appendix 2

TARGETING SPECIFIC AREAS OF DISRUPTED HEALTH AND HEALING

Stomach and digestion

- ✓ Organic Slippery Elm Powder
- ✓ ZYM-OTIC – vegan broad spectrum of plant sourced Digestive Enzymes – Nutrigold
- ✓ Enzyme Digest with peppermint oil – Quest Vitamins Ltd UK
- ✓ ACTIVE-PK Promotes the bodies process of converting nutrients into unusable energy. LCR Health CA
- ✓ Licorice root extract – Deglyrrhised Licorice root extract – Solgar
- ✓ Enzyme Digest with peppermint oil – Quest Vitamins Ltd UK

Colon and probiotic health

Gut Health

There is plenty of evidence today illustrating the relationship between gut probiotic health and general issues of dis-ease, illness and mental health. The most comprehensive and up to date information on pioneering gut health issues are presented in 'The Gut Solution presented by Sarah Otto. This is the most profound illustration of how our gut health i.e. a positive balance of good gut bacteria' is directly related to our physical health and mental wellbeing.

'The Gut Solution' Sarah Otto
Nutrigold sell a 'Mega Strength <u>PRO-OTIC</u>' high potency probiotic capsule supplement. Nutrigold– 'Colex' natural botanicals, L-glutamine and Bifidobacteria

Slippery Elm powder this organic herb powder can cleanse and alkalise the gut and help to neutralise both excessive and low acidity in stomach.

Collagen supplements can help repair the gut lining however, collagen needs vitamin 'C' and hyaluronic acid to help the body to absorb and utilise collagen

- ✓ Aeterna Gold Active Collagen Drink with Hyaluronic acid and vitamin C by Higher Nature is a powder food supplement suitable for adding to cold drinks and smoothies.
- ✓ Now Certified Organic Inulin a natural Probiotic Powder
- ✓ Colex Natural Biotanicals, L-glutamine and Bifidobacteria - Nutrigold
- ✓ Mega Strength Probiotics (25 billion gut probiotics) - Nutrigold

- ✓ Total Restore –a supplement designed to promote a healthy gut lining - Gundry MD
- ✓ PRO-EASY Live Bacteria Powder for adults and children Higher Nature
- ✓ Natural Cleanse Made by NIVING WELL Nutraceuticals
- ✓ 'The Psychobiotic *Revolution*' *written by C. Anderson*
- ✓ Probiotic for pets –Higher nature
- ✓ USA Dr. Marty Pro Powder Plus: digestive and probiotic support for dogs

Sleep and Stress

- ✓ Higher Nature Theanine with green tea
- ✓ Avena Sativa – liquid drops derived from oats.
- ✓ Primal Force 'Native Rest' a Natural sleep inducer
- ✓ Bach Flower Night remedy –
- ✓ Homeopathic Camomile 30x
- ✓ Nutrigold 5HTP complex contains L-5- Hydroxyptophan plus other supporting ingredients magnesium citrate, L-theanine and camomile to support relaxation and better sleep.
- ✓ Mark Hyman - Skin Cream with Melatonin – TeloRevive
- ✓ The 4-7-8 Yoga breathing technique and the Bamboo Kuning – Yellow Bamboo Breathing Technique.
- ✓ HERBAL MOOD SUPPORT Gundry MD
- ✓ Pure Sleep supplement by Advanced Bionutrtionals
- ✓ G FACTOR with Garcinia and KETO GENIX weight management complex.

Brain, Mental activity and Memory

- ✓ Heal your Drained Brain by Dr. Mike dow.
- ✓ NDR Protocol for Alzheimer's and Dementia a nutrition based protocol proved as to be a successful cure and ongoing preventative.
- ✓ The Coconut Oil and Low-Carb Solution for Alzheimer's, Parkinson's, and Other Diseases by Dr. Mary T Newport.
- ✓ The drinking of organic coconut water and organic red grape juice can also be effective as a way of hydrating the body cells and supporting detoxification. Alzheimer's and other types of degenerative disease have been shown to be linked with dehydration issues which inhibit detoxification within the body and specific biological processes within the body cells.
- ✓ Nitric Oxide CircO2 as a dissolvable tablet produced by Advanced Bionutrutionals
- ✓ Cerefolin NAC - This is an effective natural treatment only available by prescription on the national health.
- ✓ MemoryHack - www.NaturalNutrition.com Hacks Barbados
- ✓ Brain Support Plus GOLD LEAF Nutritionals Dr. Scott Olson USA

- ✓ RediMind contains acetylcholine and other ingredients to help mental functions and ongoing cellular brain health.[Review by Russell Wilton 6.12.2007]
- ✓ Primal Force Neuroproectin D1 a DHA-omega 3 fatty acid that protects the brain and cerebal cortex, optic nerves and skin. (NPD1) brings back lost memory: see Dr.Al Sears M.D. and details of the Primal Force Supplement for improved mental and memory functions.
- ✓ Primal Force Krill oil and Calamari (Squid oil) – Neuroprotectin D1 brings back memory
- ✓ Book 'How to SLEEP WELL' by Neil Stanley.Wiley
- ✓ Meditation in a bottle Zenith Labs Dr. Rhyn Shelton - Alpha Brainwaves for relaxation, positivity, mental health, good sleep.
- ✓ Neuroscience and the brain- Julia Lundstrom
- ✓ Julia Lindstrom ; 5 solutions for Adult ADHD
- ✓ Bergamot essential oil for recovery from a panic attack.
- ✓ Dr. David Jockers '12 nutrients that target and destroy cancer cells' and 'Super Charge Your Brain'
- ✓ Canna LS –The Green Gardener– High potency Phytacannabinoid from Hemp CogniGold Brain power
- ✓ The complete guide to reversing Alzheimer's by Glen Rothfield
- ✓ NDR nutrition based protocol for healing Alzheimer's and Dementia.
- ✓ Terminalia Schebula also known as Haritaki is an Ayurvadic herb and
- ✓ Astragalus is a Chinese Herb used to promote the body's production of NAC (N-acetylcysteine) Astragalus root powder or extract is a botanical supplement.
- ✓ V.E.N. Therapy relates sound and music vibration to inner healing through:- V-Vagus stimulation; E-Enhanced Dopamine; N-Natural Relaxation
- ✓ ADHD Research has recently presented that ADHD and similar mental disturbances can be reduced with additional supplementation of omega 3, found in fish oil and CBD oil and the benefits from these supplements can be greatly enhanced by also taking a turmeric (cu cumin) and black pepper supplement i.e.:

Cancer

- ✓ Fruit acid cures cancer called 'Corbisin' a natural tropical fruit extract that has been researched and proved as a natural cure to cancer that leaves your normal cells healthy and without any side effects. Dr.
- ✓ The Truth about Cancer.com - Ty Bollinger
- ✓ The Truth about Cancer/Eastern Medicine: Journey through Asia - Ty Bollinger
- ✓ RIGVIR – Natural Human Virus Therapy
- ✓ Cancer Survive – Chris Wark-Healing Cancer Coaching Programme-The Square One \The truth about DETOX
- ✓ Prevent and Beat prostate cancer with this powerful and proven - plant pigment by Glen S. Rothfield, MD (Quercetin combined with green tea or soy flavone genistein) Real Advantage Products – Ultimate PRO Support
- ✓ Eating Your Way to a cancer free life. Dr. Mark Stengler's Health Revelations.

Tinnitus

- ✓ www. tinitus 911.com - Jesse Cannone
- ✓ Supplement for Tinitus – Cordyceps Sinerisis mushroom 1gram twice daily.
- ✓ RingEase USA
- ✓ Astaxanthin as '200 times more effective than other more common anti-oxidants.
- ✓ Citrus Maximu a powerful supplement of citrus bioflavanoids to combat inflammation that provides an exceptionally high level of antioxidants.
  (Anti-oxidants are considered very helpful as a cure for this condition which is associated with inflammation within the Cochlea Nerve.)

Slimming

- ✓ Kokuto Mint Patch provides a concentrated Chinese herbal remedy that is absorbed into the body through the skin.
- ✓ Forza Garcinia, 3000mg plus UK
- ✓ Alph Titan UK Keto GeniX all natural ingredients weight management complex
- ✓ Slimming Ultra Keto-Lipovwn Utra Keto !00% natural organic ingredients. Slim Weight Loss Formula. Dr. Robert Nobeck
- ✓ Body Fokus active vitality Symbiotics pre and pro-biotics
- ✓ Slimming ThinMist – Livingwell 100% natural support for the pituitary gland to produce weight control hormones
- ✓ Dr Heinric program www. Leanbellybreakthrough
- ✓ Dr.Ran Maclaine – 'Vital Stem' deep fat solution, ACTIVE-PK- LCR Health
- ✓ ADITHINX3 Solaire Nutraceuticals USA

Eyes & Vision

- ✓ Good vision and healthy eyes are supported by the ayurvedic herb Saffron also known as red gold. Figs are also considered a good food for healthy eyes. It has been suggested that even a very small amount of good quality dried Saffron can improve a person's eyesight within a few hours.
- ✓ VISUALEYES Super potency of lutein and zeaxanthin plus by Higher Nature
- ✓ Astaxanthin and Blackcurrant by Higher Nature
- ✓ OcuFix 20/20 - GOLDLEAF USA
- ✓ Preserve MacForte Advanced by Dr.Ringold. Supplement for maintenance of the eyes and healthy vision.
- ✓ Ultra Vital Gold produced by Dr. Glen Rothfield contains Astaxanthin 4mg plus other supporting anti-oxidants.
- ✓ The Macular Degeneration Handbook, Simple Solutions for Saving Your Sight by Chet Cunningham

Pain

- ✓ Back Pain; Dr.Steven Baumhauer MindInSole
- ✓ Arctic Blast by Biostar Nutrition Pte.Ltd. This spray offers effective pain relief that supports and promotes the body's natural healing.

Heart and circulation

- ✓ HCY can be a sign of risk to heart attack. Your doctor can test your HCY levels in the body.
- ✓ Circu-defence Dr. Richard Gerhauser.
- ✓ HEART DEFENSE Dr. Gundry
- ✓ Circ02 AdvancedBionutritionals
- ✓ Nitrinol
- ✓ L-Arginin This also helps the body to produce nitric oxide.

Note: Dr. Nelson Brunton associates cane sugar as a cause of strokes because of the way it causes unhealthy coagulation in the blood. For this reason he also recommends that those who are going to be passengers on a long flight should avoid cane sugar both before and during any airplane journeys.

Arthritis

- ✓ Proteolytic enzymes 'The 5 Worse Foods to eat If You Have Arthritis' The Healthy Back Institute.
- ✓ Nutrigold Joint Support Supplement
- ✓ Higher Nature Aeterna Gold Collegen powder drink or Perfect Keto Collagen powder to supplement a deficit of collagen peptides in the everyday diet or enhance the body's ability to address wear and damage in the joints and skin problems or high levels of skin damage.
- ✓ Joint Fuel 360
- ✓ Peak Mobility Dr. Gundry
- ✓ Joint N-1
- ✓ Collagen Plus – Arthro Vite Ltd.
- ✓ Collagen Complex – golden greens Expert range
- ✓ Extend JOINT CARE Nutritional supplement for dogs
- ✓ Boswellia extract (Indian Frankincense) This ayervadic supplement is made from the sap of the Boswellia Serrata tree. NaturVet S.O.D.&Boswellia-extra joint support for dogs; Boswellia can also be given to pets as a powder.

Diabetes

- ✓ Inulin
- ✓ Barbery Leaf
- ✓ Stevia organic syrup
- ✓ Gluco Defend

Lungs

- ✓ Nutrigold Super Lec Plus - bioavailable Lecithin powder. Stirred into Oatly cream it makes a desirable desert that can be sweetened to taste and enjoyed by children and adults. This approach allows the supplement powder to be taken as needed as an occasional, regular nutritional support. [In critical conditions the author has known this supplement to support rapid and miraculous improvements]
  NOW organic Inulin

Teeth

- ✓ Cal Fluor x30 This homeopathic remedy is great for teeth problems (take three times a day when not drinking or eating for at least 20minutes, do not put the pill on or in anything metal i.e. do not use a metal spoon.
- ✓ Calcium magnesium supplement – Higher Nature True Food
- ✓ Eat organic free range eggs – maximum of one per day.

Appendix 3

BOOK LIST FOR ALTERNATIVE
AND NATURAL HEALING

DMSO – **Di**methyl **s**ulfoxide: a New Paradigm in Healthcare Natural Remedies by Dr. Hartmur Latest research based Documentaries '**The Micozzi Files**' 55 Natural cures for cancer, diabetes, Alzheimer's, dementia, and heart conditions. Fake Medicine Exposed and Insiders' Cures a monthly report by Dr. Micozzi

'**The Gut Solution**' Sarah Otto

'**Natural Medicine Secrets**' Jonathan Otto

'**Health Revelations**' Dr. Mark Stengler

'**Natural |Cures,** they don't want you to know' **by Kevin Trudeau**

Dr. Mary Newport author of 'The Complete Book of Ketones' Ted Talks

Groundology Earthing and grounding mats and sheets www.groundology.co.uk

'**Regain Your Brain**' Powerful New Scientific Discoveries That Can Help Regain A Youthful Brain - Awakening from Alzheimer's and other types of brain dysfunction.

'**Gupta Programme' online brain training and Holistic Health Programme that has supported those with chronic illnesses all over the world. Free trial**

Mito-Essence Dr. Al Sears nutritional powder supplement to give vital nutrients our cells need to stay in optimum health and overcome adverse health and age related decline.

www.the sacredsciences.com

The Endorphin Effect A breakthrough strategy for holistic health and spiritual wellbeing by William Bloom [page 130 There is a circuit of energy in the human body which magnetically attracts and absorbs the benevolent vitality of nature and the universe. page 285 A conclusion to the wild strawberry story. 'He switched on his Inner Smile to comfort any part of him disturbed by the nightmare. The whole dream was now understandable. It did reflect the previous day. First there was pressure and then there was pleasure. There was constraint and then freedom. The wild strawberry made perfect sense.'

The Donovan Sound Solution, the brain humming technique.(an ancient rhythmic technique said to stimulate production of Nitric Oxide using Toik sound healing rituals based on the 'brain humming' Om technique

The Art and Science of Vibrational Medicine
Love is medicine Project – Razi Berry
'**ithrive** Docu-Series' 9-Episode Documentary featuring 60 World Renown Doctors and Healers – Jon McMahon

The secret to Living Your Best Possible Life DVD series by Donald Walsh
Antidaote to old Age NT3 Dr. Marc Micozzi Insiders Ultimate Guide to Outsmarting "Old Age"

Smith Wigglesworth on Healing
Coconut oil Miracle by bruce Fife
The Miracle of Regenerative Medicine by Elisa Lottor
303 Naturral Healing Miracles by Dr. Fred Pescatore also The Natural Healing "Master List" by Dr. Fred Pescatore
Secrets of Underground Mediciner by Dr. Richard Gerhauser
The End of All Diseases – Simple and little known and proven cures for 7 of the most Dangerous Diseases by Jesse Cannone
Tachyon Energy **a New Paradigm in Holistic Healing** by Gabriel Cousens M.D. and David Wagner - Advanced Tachyon Technologies
Healthy with Tachyon a complete Handbook including Basic Principles and application of products for health and wellness by Andreas Jell
Own Yourself by Kelly Brogan M.D.-Treating anxiety, fatigue, fear and depression. Aloe Vera
The Natural Healing Choice by Lee faber, Abbeydale Press.2008
Alternative Health Homeopathy by Dr. Nelson Brunton, Macdonald Optima 1989
Homoepathic Treatment of Children's Ailments Remedies for Common Complaints by Dr. E, A, Maury ;Thorsons Pub Ltd. 1978.
Homoeopathy for the family pub: Homoeopathic Development Foundation Ltd.
Clinical Homeopathy by Anton Jayasuiya pub: Medicina Alternativa International, No 28, International Buddhist Center Road, Colombo 6, Shri Lanka.
Bach Flower Remedies by Julian Barnard
Biochemic tissue Salts by Dr. Peter Gilbert
Ayurvedic Healing A comprehensive Guide by David Frawley; Motilal Banarsidass Pub, 2000
Natural Medicine for Children by Julian Scott; Unwin Paperbacks London, 1990
The Vitamin Bible for Your Children by Earl Mindell; Arlington Books, 1983.
The Complete HOMEOPATHIC HANDBOOK Miranda Castro; Macmillan London 1990
100 Great Natural Remedies by Penelope Ody; Kyle Cathie Ltd, 1997.
Alternative Cures The Most Effective Natural Home Remedies for 160 Health Problems by Bill Gottlieb; Rodale, 2000.
The Herbal Drugstore The Best Natural Alternatives to Over the Counter and Prescription Medicines by Linda B. White and Steven Foster Rodale, 2000.
Cancer is not a Disease, Its a Suvival Mechanism by Andreas Moritz; Cygnus Books, 2009.
Wild Drugs a forager's guide to healing plants by Zoe Hawes; Octopus Pub, 2010.
The Herb Book by John Lust; A Bantam Book pub by Benedict Lust, 1974.
The New Guide To Remedies Parragon, 2002.
Acupressure Techniques A Self-Help Guide by Julian Kenyon (Thorsons 1987)
The energy That Heals by Jacques Steahle
VIRTUAL Medicine by Dr. Keith Scott-Mumby; Thorsons, 1999)
The Miracle of Colour Healing Aura Soma Therapy as the Mirror of the Soul by Vicky Walls; Thorsons, 1990.

Bach Flower Remedies by Non Shaw; Element Books, 1998.

The 38 Flower Remedies formally the work of dr. Edward Bach; Wigmore Pub, 1995.

Dictionary of the Bach Flower Remedies –Positive and negative aspects by T.W.Hyne Jones;The C.W.Daniel Company Ltd

Food Combining for Health by Doris Grant and Jean Joice; Thorsons, 1984.

The Hay Diet Made Easy, a practical guide to food combining by Jackie Habgood]

Improve Your Sight without Glasses by Science of Life Books, 1975.

The Magic of Magnesium by Dr. Eric Trimmer; Thorsons, 1987.

Organic Consumer Guide Thorsons,1990Ed. D Mabey and A & J Gear;.

Natural Medicine for children by Julian Scott Unwin Paperbacks London 1990

The Complete HOMEOPATHIC HANDBOOK by Miranda Castro;. Macmillan, 1990

Heal Your Body by Louise L. Hay; Eden Grove Editions, 1988.

The Healing Code by Alexander Loyd and Ben Johnson; Hodder &Stoughton, 2011

Theta Healing by Vianna Stibal.

Biochemic Tissue Salts by Dr. Peter Gilbert; Thorsons,1984.

The Saccharine Disease by Dr. T. L. Cleave; John Wright & Sons, 1974.

Before the Vet Calls by Francis Hunter MRCVS; Thorsons, 1984

The Treatment of Dogs by Homeopathy by K. Sheppard; C.W. Daniel Co. Ltd.1972.

The Treatment of Cats by Homeopathy by K. Sheppard; C.W. Daniel Co. Ltd.1972.

Homeopathic Medicine For Dogs A Handbook for Vets and Pet Owners by H.G.Wolff; Thorsons Pub Ltd. 1984.

Appendix 4

GOOD HEALTH

<u>Further information and support</u>

- ✓ <u>Arnica</u> Uk Parent Support Network – promoting Natural Immunity ARNICA.ORG.UK
- ✓ Square One by Dr. Joseph Maroon - Cortisol the Flight and Fight hormone.
- ✓ The Baking Soda Secret
- ✓ Live Foods For Winning Energy without Drugs by Charlotte Gerson –daughter of Dr. Max Gerson founder of the Gerson Diet for Healing
- ✓ Health Secrets for men by Dr. Rothfield
- ✓ The complete guide to reversing Alzheimers by Glen Rothfield
- ✓ Ty Bollinger Opting Out of Compulsory approaches to Vaccinations.
- ✓ Dr. Steven Gundry: Biog.paleohacks.com/3-ways –to-heal-your-thyroid-naturally
- ✓ Baking Soda – Mike Geary
- ✓ Dawn of Time nutrient -Primal force –
- ✓ GRS ULTRA supplement supporting production of Glutathione in the body. Dr. Oz Bioavailable Selenium and Sulphur.
- ✓ 12 Secrets to boost your testosterone naturally Mike Geary and Catherine Ebeling
- ✓ Unlock the Genetic Secret of Aging by Al Sears
- ✓ Fermented Soya 'natto'
- ✓ 'The Dark side of Wheat' and '21st Century Solutions to Depression' Green Med info
- ✓ Om Creations Activated Raw Foods Cereal www.omcreations432.com
- ✓ Organic WELLBEING BLEND a green powder – a harmonious blend of organic grasses, greens and algaes Marvelloussuperfoo.co.uk –
- ✓ The Herb known as Horse Tail is considered effective for improving poor bladder control.
- ✓ The Lemon Juice Diet by Therasa Cheung
- ✓ Grandma's Remedies by Cherry Chappell
- ✓ The Miracle of Olive Oil by Dr. Penny Stanway
- ✓ The Miracle of Bicarbonate of Soda by Dr. Penny Stanway
- ✓ Turmeric The Ayurvedic Spice of Life by Prashanti De Jagar
- ✓ Tibetan Secrets of Youth and Vitality How to look and feel younger using five ancient rites for stimulating your energy centres. By Peter Kelder, The Aquarian Press, Thorsons 1988
- ✓ The Complete Yoga Book The Yoga of Breathing, Posture, and Meditation by James Hewitt; Loepard Books 1995.
- ✓ 37 Steps to Happiness **t'ai chi** by Peter Chin Kean Choy; Ted Smart Pub,2001
- ✓ Master Level Psychocalisthenics by Oscar Ichazo
- ✓ The Endorphin Effect by William Bloom; Judy Piatkus, 2001.

✓ The A-Z of Vital Vitamins and Minerals; The Health Issues comprehensive guide to nutritional supplements.

✓ Square One by Dr. Joseph Maroon - Cortisol the Flight and Fight hormone.

✓ Eat and Heal How to Make Your Body Invulnerable to Disease by Dr. Andrei Dracea

✓ The Hay Diet Made Easy, a practical guide to food combining by Jackie Habgood]

✓ The Miracle of Fasting Proven throughout History For Physical, Mental and Spiritual Rejuvenation by Paul Bragg and his daughter Patricia Bragg; Health Science. {Research now suggests that water fasting encourages the body to uses 'stem cells' to repair and rejuvenate cells damaged by injury or disease. It may therefore be natural for all humans and animals to avoid food during illness and recovery from serious injury.

✓ Tachyon Energy A New Paradigm in Holistic Healing by David Wagner and Gabriel Cousens; North Atlantic Books, 1999.

✓ The Metamorphic Technique principles and practice by Gaston Saint-pierre and Debbie Shapiro; Element Books, 2003 (

✓ Becoming Who We Are Metamorphosis and People with Learning Difficulties. A Practical Guide for teachers, Practitioners and Care Professions by Dave Singer; Syntheses Pub,1993

✓ Blue Heron Health News www.blueheronhealth news.com

DVD

'Brain Humming' Jim Donovan and 'Sound Healing'
Dr. Stanley Jacob M.D. DMSO-Dimethylsulfoxide
Sacred Knowledge of Vibration and the Power of Human Emotions
GMO Film-Natural News.com and GMO OMG

Personal Empowerment

William Bloom
Matt Kahn
Deepak Chopra
Dr. Wayne W Dyer
Patricial Cota-Robies
Living Well Dr. Scott Olson
Mary Morrissey
Gregg Braden
Humanity's Team
Susan Bratton

Printed in the United States
by Baker & Taylor Publisher Services